The Abiding Companion

Michael B. McElroy

First edition copyright © 2010 by Michael B. McElroy
All rights reserved.

ISBN: 0-9830-6550-0
ISBN: 978-0-9830655-0-0

Dedication

This book is for Suzanne, who's been my companion for so long. Thank you for abiding with me, standing by me and believing in me. Your love has taught me more about God's love and grace than any book or preacher ever did.

"If you abide in my word, you truly are my disciples."
(Jesus, John 8:31)

Introduction

The coffee in his mug is steaming hot; the hardwood floor is early-morning cool to his bare feet. He sits at the little table in the kitchen of the farmhouse, surrounded by acres of corn. He opens his worn Bible to the place he marked yesterday. Before his family wakes up, before the day's work demands his time and energy, he sips the strong coffee, reads a chapter and ponders the ancient words in the still quiet.

She glances at her watch as the long call from the demanding client finally ends. She's climbing the corporate ladder, doing her best to balance her roles in the glass and steel tower downtown and in her modest suburban home. Her next meeting begins in fifteen minutes. It's time for a break. So she closes her office door, sends the phone to voicemail and takes a deep, cleansing breath. She slips the New Testament and a small journal from her purse and reads the chapter listed on the calendar she picked up at church. She records her reflections, just two or three sentences, in the journal. She exchanges the small books for a compact, checks her reflection in the mirror. She winks at herself to boost her confidence and walks out the door and down the hall to the meeting.

His roommate is already snoring when he returns to the dorm room after the study session. He is quiet as he climbs into bed and sets the alarm. He opens the Bible on his e-book reader and reads along as he listens to the chapter for the day through his headphones. Lying in his single bed, far from home, the words remind him of who he is and what he believes. He takes off the headphones, turns off his book light and prays before drifting off to sleep.

These people have different lives, but they have much in common. They're all busy, but they're all abiding in the Word. They're not living in a secluded setting, and they don't have hours each day to spend in contemplation. But they have found a way to incorporate time with the book they believe to be God's Word into their daily lives.

Another thing they have in common with many of us is that they are alone as they read. Maybe you have a spouse or a friend with whom you read and pray every day. But Bible reading is a solitary experience for most of us. We call it time with God, and it is. But maybe we also long for someone who can share and reflect with us.

I got the idea for this book while writing in my daily journal in January, 2007. I wanted to read, think about and write about a chapter of the New Testament every day. So I started with Matthew 1 on February 1. God blessed me to write a chapter each day for 260 consecutive days, finishing Revelation 22 and the first draft of this book on October 18.

This book was designed to be a companion reader to the New Testament. I urge you to read it as I wrote it—a chapter a day, every day. It will take a little less than nine months, or a year if you only read Monday through Friday. From the first day when I sketched the idea for this book in my journal, I've dreamed about you—seeing you read each day, first a chapter from the New Testament, and then the corresponding chapter from this book.

Jesus said, "If you abide in my word, you truly are my disciples." Abiding is more than just reading every day; it's taking time to think about what you've read and allowing it to change your life. Like a companion with whom you reflect on the daily portion, I hope these essays will stimulate your thinking and enhance your understanding of the text. Give God the glory for any help you receive from these essays, and forgive me for the errors and mistakes you find. I'm honored to be your companion as we abide in the Lord's word in the days ahead.

Matthew

Day 1, Matthew 1

Who's your great-great-grandfather? Maybe your family has some of those five generation photos, but few people in our time and place can trace their ancestry back through more than two or three generations.

I remember my great-grandparents. We took a trip to St. Augustine, Florida when I was a small child. I knew my grandparents. My son has some silver dollars they gave me long ago. But my mother is the only grandparent my son ever really knew.

I know a little more about my ancestry than I can personally remember because one of my mother's brothers was very interested in genealogy. He went to courthouses and cemeteries, linking our family's past to the present by studying musty old public records and weather-beaten grave stones.

Genealogy is a hobby to some people, a passion to others. Most of us long for some sense of connection to past generations as we wrestle with identity and mortality.

But to ancient Jews, genealogy was more than a hobby or a quest for identity. Knowing their place in Abraham's family was crucial to their economic, social and spiritual lives. When the Romans destroyed the Jerusalem temple in 70 A.D., more than a building was lost. The genealogical records upon which Jewish people had based their identity for centuries were lost as well, a devastating blow to a people who defined themselves as "children of Abraham."

What does the genealogy of Jesus in Matthew 1 mean to us as modern Gentile (or even modern Jewish) readers? I believe we should get a sense of the timeless faithfulness of God's promises and purposes. Generations were born and died, nations rose and fell through about two thousand years spanned by the brief record of who was the father of whom. God's announcement to Abraham about a descendent through whom all nations would be blessed looked far into the future. His plan would be realized even though some human agents in the story would be faithless and all would be flawed.

Through old prophecies and older promises, God assured his people that one was coming who would redeem and restore. After all those generations lived and died, Mary and Joseph trusted what the angel told them and accepted God's plan. The carpenter was willing to share the shame of Mary's premarital pregnancy in a culture that was all about clearly defined lineage. The angel said the baby in Mary's womb would be named Jesus because he would be the savior of his people. The prophet said his name would be Immanuel, because he would be God with us. And from the opening chapter of the New Testament, we are challenged to believe and embrace those trustworthy promises—to know him as Savior and live with the reality of God with us.

Day 2, Matthew 2

We usually don't enjoy hearing the words, "I told you so." That's because so often we hear them after failing to heed a warning, or choosing to ignore advice that might have saved us some expense or suffering. But sometimes we hear it in a good context, too. After a good meal, we tell a friend he was right about a certain restaurant, and he nods and says, "I told you so." When it's a confirmation of something good instead of a rebuke, we don't mind being told that we've already been told.

Matthew's habit of referring to prophecies that were fulfilled in Jesus reminds me of the good kind of "told you so." God had been telling Israel for centuries that Messiah was coming, and giving the covenant people glimpses of what it would be like when he came. And each time Matthew writes, "This took place to fulfill what the Lord had spoken by the prophet," it's like God saying, "I told you so."

Matthew was written by a Jew. His original audience was Jewish. They knew the Scriptures. When Matthew cited the prophetic reference for Jesus' name, the flight to Egypt, Herod's ruthless violence against the innocents and Jesus living in Nazareth, he was telling Israelites, "Look, it's him. Just like God said. Jesus of Nazareth is the promised Messiah." To the rest of us who may not be intimately familiar with the prophets, Matthew seems to say, "Look, this is no coincidence. All these facts and circumstances were predicted hundreds of years before the actual events occurred."

The references to fulfilled prophecy are interwoven with the narrative about the decisions made and actions taken by people in the story. It's a thing of mystery and wonder that God knew before what would happen, but the things that happened are the result of humans acting on their own will. In ways beyond our ability to explain, God uses the willing obedience of his people as well as the wicked rebellion of his enemies to accomplish his purpose. God spoke through angels, dreams, stars and Scripture to guide and lead Mary, Joseph and the Magi. They understood God was directing them, and they obeyed, fulfilling God's purpose. But when wicked Herod had the opportunity to get guidance from God, he responded with fear, anger and violence. In a futile attempt at self-preservation, he ordered the deaths of all the little boys who by virtue of their age and birthplace might be the new-born king the Magi had sought.

Do you respond to God's revelation with humble obedience or with angry rebellion? Herod soon died in infamy, but God's plan rolled on, precisely on track, right on time. Doesn't it make more sense to cooperate with him?

Day 3, Matthew 3

Matthew segued from a picture of Joseph, Mary and the young boy Jesus living in Nazareth to the adult Jesus coming to John for baptism. Jesus wasn't alone in going out to the wilderness to be baptized by John. The people from Jerusalem and all around the Jordan were flocking to hear the preacher who dressed like a prophet from the old times and preached the old prophets' dominant theme to Israel: "Repent!"

John identified himself as the one Isaiah foresaw when he described himself as a voice from the wilderness preparing the way for Messiah. He mixed no words when he rebuked the religious elite and called them to genuine change to be fit for the coming kingdom. He told them it would do no good to claim kinship with Abraham and warned of fiery judgment for those who rejected the message.

John's baptism was associated with repentance, turning away from sin and to God. When Jesus (who was sinless) came to the Jordan to be baptized, it was not about repentance, but a public identification with God's messenger and purpose. As Jesus validated John's ministry, the audible voice of God and the visible presence of the Holy Spirit attested to Jesus' own identity.

The baptism of Jesus marked the beginning of his public life of preaching and calling disciples and working miracles to show he was who he claimed to be. When you and I submit to baptism in the name of Jesus, we are publicly identified with him and with his people. The New Testament connects baptism with faith and repentance, and with a confession of faith that Jesus is the Son of God. It is associated with the promises of the gospel—forgiveness of sins and the gift of God's Holy Spirit. The letters in the New Testament written to young Christians describe their baptism as being buried and raised to walk in a new life. That new life is in Christ. Baptism was commanded by Jesus and his apostles after Jesus was raised from the dead. As multitudes heard the gospel and placed their faith in Jesus, they were baptized in his name.

There's a lot of confusion and debate about baptism among religious people, but the New Testament teaching about it is beautiful and encouraging. We who claim to follow Jesus should rejoice in the opportunity to be associated with him through this ancient ritual in which Jesus himself participated. It is not about working for salvation or earning anything by our obedience. It is about trusting, obeying and identifying with Jesus. It is inconsistent to name him as Lord, but refuse to obey this initial command given to those who would follow him.

Day 4, Matthew 4

Have you ever stood on the top of a mountain or at the mouth of a cave and called out to hear your own voice echo back? Or maybe you're a music lover who recognizes a repeated melody as a recurring theme in a composition.

Repeating sounds and themes are very much involved in Matthew's report of the temptation and the early ministry of Jesus in chapter 4. The first clue of this is the report of Jesus' preaching, which echoed the words of John: "Repent, for the kingdom of heaven is at hand." The keynote of the fiery wilderness preacher became the message of the carpenter turned itinerant preacher. But this repetition is in the context of other echoes.

The temptation account itself is an example of this. Granted, the temptations had to be and were custom-designed challenges to tempt the Son of God. But underneath the "dress" of the special situations, we can see the same devices Satan has employed since Eden. The temptations are familiar: "Are you sure you can trust God? Do you really believe he means what he says? There's a shortcut, an easier way to get what God has offered you." The same lying, empty promises are still echoing in our ears today. We need the same defense Jesus demonstrated: complete confidence and loyalty to God as our shield of faith against his darts, and competence with the Word, the powerful sword of the Spirit.

I hear other echoes as I read the chapter again. Matthew resounds with the words of the prophets from centuries past as Jesus' words and deeds brought their prophetic vision to life and fulfillment. Jesus traveled through the towns and villages of Galilee, echoing again and again the kingdom good news, healing the sick and casting out demons as evidence that the light of the kingdom was indeed dawning in their midst.

And the whole business of calling disciples resonates with the echo of his call: "Follow me." Peter, Andrew, James, John and others heard the repeated call and left everything behind to follow their new Master. Soon they would be echoing the call to others as they obeyed Jesus' command to go make disciples. The call to discipleship echoes around the world and through the centuries to you and me. Will we listen? Will we follow? Will the words of the Master's invitation continue to sound through us?

Day 5, Matthew 5

Many leaders throughout history are remembered for one specific speech—a message that defined them and became the keynote of their leadership. Before sound bites in a newscast became the tools by which politicians announced their positions on the issues, lengthy public discourses that appealed to an audience's powers of reason were common. Dynamic leaders shared their vision and stirred listeners to join or support their cause through impassioned speeches.

Jesus' longest recorded sermon begins in Matthew 5 and continues through Matthew 7. Matthew tells us at the beginning of the account that Jesus is addressing his disciples. The opening lines we now call "The Beatitudes" are a series of statements that must have come across to the first hearers as jarring incongruities. How can the poor, the hungry, the meek and the mourning be considered blessed? How can persecution possibly be a blessing? Modern expositors explain these things, but Jesus didn't.

The prominent themes of the sermon are the kingdom of heaven and righteousness. Jesus talked about the disciples' influence on the world around them. Israel had mostly failed to exert a positive outward influence on their Gentile neighbors, but Jesus said his kingdom's citizens would be salt and light to the world.

He said he came to fulfill the law and that unless the disciples' righteousness exceeded that of the very best law keepers they knew (the scribes and Pharisees), they would not enter the kingdom. Again, we probably can't feel the shock of these words as the first audience did. Either we know nothing about these scribes and Pharisees, or maybe we know so much about them we're not surprised to hear that our righteousness must be different from theirs.

Jesus then cited specifics of the law and traditions with which the disciples would have been familiar, and focused attention on the attitudes and not just the actions prescribed or prohibited by the law. He went beyond murder to deal with anger, beyond adultery to condemn lust, beyond the technicality of oath-taking to a lifestyle of telling the truth. He described a way of living not based on retaliation for every wrong done, but on love, even for our enemies. He cited

God the Father as the greatest example of showing love to the undeserving, and challenged his hearers to be like him.

Is Jesus being cruel by calling his disciples to a standard of righteousness we could never attain or sustain on our own? Or is the one who will die to become our righteousness showing us all how much we need him? I believe Jesus is preparing his disciples to embrace a righteousness he would provide that would stand in stark contrast to legalism and self-righteousness.

Day 6, Matthew 6

Why do you do what you do in the practice of your religion? Giving to a needy person, praying to God and fasting are expressions of your spirituality. But why do you do these things?

Jesus warned that all these good acts can be done for the wrong reasons. If we do what we do to get other people's attention and win their approval, Jesus said there's no reward from God the Father for doing it. But if our devotions are performed in a quiet, understated way, he said the Father who sees in secret will reward us.

This is a special temptation for preachers and other church leaders. Wanting to "set a good example," we may want to tell about our righteous deeds. It may be embarrassing to admit it, but most of us want to be liked. We hunger for acceptance, approval and recognition of our efforts. A pat on the back is nice, but receiving praise should not be our motive for doing spiritual things.

Psychologists say many people are driven to do what they do by a desire to please their fathers. Famous athletes, successful business people and ordinary men and women raising their families often attribute their success or their over-achievement to a deep desire to win their father's approval. Some grown-up kids carry life-long emotional scars from trying to please a parent who could not be pleased. There is healing in knowing our heavenly Father sees and rewards the things we do for him.

When our acts of righteousness are done before an audience of one, and we realize whatever good we do is because of his enabling grace, pride and self-righteousness melt away. We become less conscious of how we look or who sees us. It's fine if others approve, but we're not seeking their applause. If others fail to appreciate our efforts, we are not deterred by their criticism. We do not quit if we are ignored, because we weren't doing it for attention in the first place. There is both power and freedom in this design.

That same Father would save us from the crippling effects of worry. He promises to provide whatever we need if we make his kingdom and his righteousness our highest priority. Just as he sees what we do, God knows what we need. He loves us and wants us to have what we need. Jesus calls us away from anxiety to a life of trusting a faithful Father who feeds the birds and clothes the wildflowers.

Imagine the real, tangible benefits of knowing a Father who sees and rewards those who serve him, who knows and provides for those who put him first.

Day 7, Matthew 7

Jesus said those who heard his sayings and put them into practice were like a wise man who built his house on the rock. When the wind, rain and rising waters of trouble threaten and destroy life-houses built on lesser foundations, Jesus promised that disciples who heard and did what he said would weather the storms and stand firm.

Two builders, two houses, two foundations, the common storm, and two results. The picture is simple and pointed.

Surely we want to build our lives on a good solid foundation. We want to make wise decisions, not foolish ones. Yet so many people reject the wisdom Jesus offers in favor of doing it their own way. They judge people around them while never acknowledging their own faults and failures. They live by a double standard, treating people in ways they would not want to be treated themselves. Those who insist on doing it their own way instead of Jesus' way may imagine themselves to be individuals, thinking for themselves. But Jesus describes them as workers of lawlessness.

With practical wisdom and spiritual insight, Jesus offers a higher perspective on the challenges and problems of life to those who will listen. His teaching passes the test he suggests: examine the fruit to evaluate the tree. What kind of neighbor do I want? Wouldn't my neighbors be blessed if I lived more like Jesus said to live?

When the sermon was over, the crowd was astonished. They had never heard anyone speak the way Jesus did. He had challenged their thinking and their conduct. He had redefined what righteousness was all about. And his voice had the unmistakable ring of authority.

Being a citizen in Jesus' kingdom requires both humility and discernment. To refrain from judging others by a standard we would not apply to ourselves, to acknowledge our dependence and ask God to supply our needs, to consciously treat other people as we would want to be treated—all these things call for seeing ourselves and others clearly. But far from being merely an attitude or a mental exercise, Jesus calls us to tangible, real-world demonstrations of our devotion to him.

Day 8, Matthew 8

It must have been exciting to see the miracles. Imagine being among the band of disciples traveling with him as Jesus touched, yes, touched a leper, and the unclean one was cleansed. He commended the faith of a Gentile soldier who believed Jesus could heal his servant with an authoritative word and without being in the sick man's presence. Jesus granted the request. Later at Peter's house, many sick people (including Peter's mother-in-law) and demon-oppressed people were healed by his word and by his touch. It was happening just as Isaiah said it would in the old prophecy: Messiah "took our illnesses and bore our diseases."

Imagine the crowd of desperate people, curiosity seekers and genuinely interested fledgling disciples who would be all around him as news spread of what was happening. He warned would-be followers that the price was high for those who chose to go with him. They would share in his poverty and be called to put him ahead of the dearest relations on earth if they chose to follow him.

The core disciples must have been on an emotional roller coaster when the storm threatened their lives, only to hear Jesus calm the winds and sea with a word. Then came the confrontation with the demon-possessed pair at Gadara. Were the disciples scared like the people of the region when the pigs drowned in the sea after Jesus allowed the demons to inhabit the swine?

The disciples' question in the aftermath of the storm was a good one for them to ponder, and for you and me. "What sort of man is this?" Like the eyewitnesses, we have some decisions to make about Jesus after reading about the amazing demonstration of his power.

Were the people who got well, or who were set free from cruel demon possession, blessed by God? Could anyone do these things without God's power? Were the claims made by John and echoed by other witnesses true? Would we be persuaded to follow regardless of what it cost us? Or is it possible we'd be more like the Gadarenes, who were terrified about what had happened, but instead of accepting his claims, begged him to go away and leave them alone?

I want to think I'd be right behind him, leaving everything to be his disciple. But I do honestly wonder if skepticism, fear of change, peer pressure from unbelieving leaders and a host of other impediments might have blinded me to what seems so obvious. I wonder because some of the same factors are still discouraging people from faith and discipleship today. In the face of compelling evidence, some people are still asking him to move along.

Day 9, Matthew 9

Jesus saw the faith of the people who brought their paralyzed friend to him. At first we may think their faith was visible because, after all, it was Jesus who was doing the seeing. Just as he knew the thoughts of the scribes who were standing there thinking he was blaspheming, we may assume that faith is visible to him. And it is. But it's visible to us as well.

This chapter has several episodes that illustrate James' words: "I will show you my faith by my works." The actions of the paralytic's friends are described in greater detail by Mark and Luke, but it was what they did that showed what they believed. When the ruler of the synagogue came and knelt before Jesus to ask for his help in what already seemed a helpless situation, his faith was showing in what he did. When the woman reached out and touched the fringe of Jesus' garment, she believed she would be well. Jesus said her faith had made her well. When the blind men received their sight, Jesus asked if they believed he was able to do it, and then told them that it was done according to their faith. Faith is much more than an intangible philosophical position or mental assent to a statement. Faith motivates action, and the action makes the faith visible.

Another common thread in these stories is the confidence faith has in its object. These people not only believed in Jesus, they believed he could do something about their desperate situations. The friends who carried the paralyzed man's stretcher, the synagogue ruler and the woman all sought Jesus because they believed he was able to help them. They all by their actions made the same confession the blind men made when Jesus asked if they believed he was able: "Yes, Lord."

These lives and others were dramatically changed by the exercise of faith. A two-word invitation, at once accepted by Levi the tax collector changed the course of his entire life. It can be no other way. As Jesus explained, his kingdom rule can't be tacked onto our present way of life like a new patch on an old garment. The new wine he came to give cannot be poured into the old wineskins of how we used to live. Faith is a catalyst that produces changed lives.

Jesus sees our faith, and we can see one another's. Our faith leads us to believe he is able to do something about our problems. Faith is the motive for following him, realizing things will be new and different in our lives as we do so.

Day 10, Matthew 10

Have you ever started a new job and been overwhelmed by all you had to learn? If you've been through an orientation for a new position, you may remember that the people who trained you gave you an intensive compacted introduction, covering all kinds of information about the company or department you were joining.

The disciples' call and commission as we read it in this chapter reminds me of an orientation. Jesus described their mission, defined the limits of their task and warned about dangers they would encounter along the way. Not everyone they met would be delighted to hear about Jesus and his coming kingdom. The Master painted a sober picture of what lay ahead for the disciples—there were arrests, trials, possibly even death on their itineraries. But Jesus told them to be faithful and fearless. He promised their defense statements would be provided, and that the Father was intimately aware of who and where they were.

Have you ever felt alone or abandoned in your attempts to serve the Lord? Have you ever faced hostility because of your faith and discipleship? It's encouraging to read about the Lord's choice of these followers to become the leaders of his people. The call to discipleship is an honor. But the call is just the beginning. Those who answer the call and accept the mission are equipped for the task and under God's care throughout the journey.

The call, the mission, the supply and the reward are all of grace. We are selected, enabled and blessed by the Lord, so there's no room for self-serving pride. We do not need to be anxious about our assignment, even when we face threatening opponents. And there is no doubt that the promise of reward is good. When adversity comes, our peace is based on our relationship with the Father, not some external circumstance. If members of our own family do not understand or share our faith, Jesus has already made it clear that he, not family, must come first in our lives.

Jesus placed a tremendous responsibility on the shoulders of the twelve. They would take the good news across the world as they knew it. It was obvious (probably to the disciples themselves) that they were not up to the task. But the promise of his presence gave them courage to persevere.

Many of these words are instructive and encouraging not just to the apostles, but to all disciples in every age as well. If we take our commission seriously, persist despite opposition and rely on his help, there will be a reward for us, too.

Day 11, Matthew 11

Most of us have been through discouraging times of trouble. When circumstances are less than ideal, when we seem to suffer for doing the right thing, when our hopes have not been realized or when we don't understand what's going on around us, it's likely that questions and doubt may flood our minds. We may be able to identify with John, who from prison sent word to Jesus. John wanted to know if Jesus was the promised one, or if he should be looking for someone else. Of all people on earth at the time, John probably had the best grasp of who Jesus was. But he seemed to struggle with the apparent conflict between the reports he heard about Jesus' deeds and what he thought Messiah should be doing.

Jesus didn't excommunicate John for asking the question, or send a stinging rebuke about unbelief back with John's disciples. Instead he reminded John of the prophets' descriptions of what Messiah would do, the very prophets John had cited earlier in identifying himself as the harbinger of Messiah, and Jesus as the one of whom the prophets spoke. Jesus then told the crowds John was a prophet and more than a prophet. He said there was no one greater than John, and that John was the one the prophets had described as Messiah's messenger.

It's not a sign you're unspiritual when you are discouraged. Questions don't mean you've lost your faith or that you doubt God. Jesus offers ample evidence for seeking hearts to make a good decision about his identity. The rebuke that follows the question from John is related to this. Jesus chides the people in the crowd for being impossible to please, like children. He denounced some of the cities in Galilee that did not repent when they heard the message. They had seen, in their own cities, mighty works that should have motivated them to turn to God, but they refused to repent. Jesus said some infamous cities would receive more leniency in judgment than those who saw and rejected the evidence.

Are you like the "wise and understanding" ones Jesus said could not see the truth about the kingdom? Or are you willing, like a little child, to humble yourself and trust in him? Instead of cruel labor, he promises an easy yoke. In the place of impossible loads, he says his burden is light. Jesus offers rest to all who are weary and burdened. If you're struggling and tired, this is a beautiful invitation. What would keep you from following a master like Jesus?

Day 12, Matthew 12

Jesus had numerous conflicts about the Sabbath with the Pharisees. As hostile observers, they often charged Jesus and his disciples with breaking the rules about the day of rest. It's important to note that Jesus never really broke the law (sinned) about the Sabbath or anything else. Had he sinned, he could not have died for anyone else's sins. He did violate the traditions, and it infuriated the orthodox. He told them, "If you had known what this means, 'I desire mercy and not sacrifice,' you would not have condemned the guiltless." Jesus' suggestion that these experts didn't know something about the scriptures was a stinging insult.

Legalism condemns the guiltless. The Pharisees pronounced Jesus guilty when he wouldn't bow to their traditions which they equated with God's law. Just so, legalists bind what God has not bound, and pronounce condemnation on all who disagree with their interpretation.

The Pharisees also despised Jesus because he exposed their hypocrisy. They made exceptions to their rigid rules for their own selfish interests, but would not give any consideration to people they condemned. Modern legalists are no different. God says none are without sin, and that people who offend in one point are guilty. Those who trust law-keeping for their righteousness must overlook their own sins while denouncing others.

Jesus would die so all sins could be forgiven. But he warned about one particular sin that would never be forgiven. Jesus said whoever spoke against the Holy Spirit would never be forgiven. I think that's because the Holy Spirit would be the source of the apostles' message about salvation in Christ and the power behind the miracles that would authenticate their words. If the hard-hearted Jews who refused to believe Jesus before his death refused the apostles' teaching after the resurrection, there would be no means of forgiveness available to them.

The demand for a sign was a hypocritical tactic employed by people who had already seen undeniable miracles. They were conspiring against Jesus instead of humbly acknowledging him. Jesus knew their hearts and refused to cater to their selfish demands. There had been plenty of evidence, and the greatest sign (the resurrection) was still to come.

Legalism may be good for emptying out the unclean from lives with its emphasis on "don't" and "stop." But there is nothing in such teaching to fill what has been emptied with wholesome life and goodness. So the vacuum is filled by more evil, and the end of the story is worse than the beginning.

When Jesus' family came looking for him, it gave him the perfect opportunity to define the basis of genuine relationship with him. It is by doing God's will, not being a physical, blood relative of Jesus that we become his family. As we recognize the folly of the Pharisees' legalism, we should not overlook the importance of genuine obedience.

Day 13, Matthew 13

Little children learn that a parable is "an earthly story with a heavenly meaning." Jesus explained eternal principles with everyday pictures. He used the commonplace to illustrate the cosmic. It's interesting that the parables were also designed to obscure meaning from some people while revealing it to others.

Remember math class in school, where the teacher would introduce a new skill or concept, give you an example problem or two to illustrate it, and then assign other problems to let you apply what you'd learned from the example to other situations? Jesus did the same thing with the parables as he taught the disciples. Although he told many parables (so many that Matthew said he didn't speak to the crowds without a parable), we only have a record of two instances when he explained the stories to the disciples. We are left to make meaning of the others by applying the principles he modeled in the two he explained.

Parables are soil tests for our hearts, to see if the word we hear is penetrating and producing as it was designed to do. We need to honestly answer the question Jesus posed to the disciples after this barrage of stories: "Have you understood?" If our answer is, "No," we probably need to go back and read them again, and ponder them some more. We need to see if the word we have received is bearing fruit, having the intended effect on our hearts and lives. The same problems that limited the crop in Jesus' ancient story are still in our lives today. Satan still wants to snatch the word away from our minds before it can do us any good. If our response to the word is shallow emotion without the deep roots of faith and conviction, we will not persevere when adversity threatens. Do you know anyone in whom the word is not producing like it should because it is being choked by anxiety and concern for more and more material things?

We also need to monitor our response when we do understand the parables and get a glimpse of what the kingdom of God is all about. The man who found the treasure in the field went and sold all he had to buy the field, and he did it with joy. The merchant who was searching for fine pearls recognized the value of the pearl he found and was willing to part with all he had to acquire the special pearl. When we know what God wants us to do, do we do it with a sigh of resignation, or with joy? When we understand how much it will cost to have Jesus as our King, are we ready to part with everything it will cost us to be in his kingdom?

Day 14, Matthew 14

Herod is not the one who gets beheaded in the story about John the Baptist, but his story is nonetheless tragic. His conscience bothered him when he heard of Jesus, and he told his servants that John was back from the dead. His conscience should have bothered him. Every line of this episode paints Herod in dark colors of evil.

It is wicked to persecute the messenger who tells unpopular truth. John was unflinching in telling a powerful man his marriage was against the law of God, and Herod imprisoned the preacher instead of repenting. So the one Jesus had identified as a prophet and the greatest man who had been born was sentenced to death for telling the truth a guilty man didn't want to hear. He joined the ranks of the old prophets who died at the hands of angry people who were supposed to be the people of God, but didn't want to hear from God.

This sad story also teaches we should be very careful about the promises we make. Herod rashly vowed to do anything his dancing stepdaughter asked, and she was prompted by her vengeful mother to ask for John's head.

It's weak to allow people around you to tell you what to think and do, and you'll almost always be sorry for where they lead you. Herod was afraid of his wife, the people who recognized John as a prophet and the guests who heard his vow. All the pressures backed him into a corner where he felt he had no choice but to have John beheaded.

As a parent, I'm also struck by the line that says the girl brought John's head on the platter to her mother, who had asked for it. Do we realize we are training our children by our actions, words and attitudes to bring back to us what they heard and learned from us? The sober responsibility of training our children compels us to think about the verbal and nonverbal direction we give our kids.

It's not clear exactly why Jesus withdrew when he heard the news of John's death. Maybe he went to mourn, or to pray. Maybe he withdrew because it was not yet time for the final confrontation that would lead to the cross. I'm sure it wasn't fear that caused him to move. He went right on with the mission, feeding multitudes, healing sick people and building more faith in his disciples that he was indeed the Son of God by walking on and calming the sea. It may have looked like Herod the tetrarch was in control, but Jesus was doing the things that proved who was the real King of the Jews.

Day 15, Matthew 15

Legalism binds tradition and opinion as if the words of humans were the word of God. Legalism also teaches law-keeping as a means of salvation. Since no one keeps the law perfectly, legalists make certain commands the "important ones," making sure they keep a certain list of rules, while creating a loophole to excuse disobeying the other ones.

The Pharisees were legalists in all the above senses of the word. They repeatedly accused Jesus and his disciples of breaking the Sabbath rules. They were incensed that Jesus and his followers did not embrace their rigid ceremonial traditions. The Pharisees also believed they were righteous because they were better at keeping the law than the people around them they deemed to be sinners. They specialized in picking commands to measure their righteousness and others' sinfulness. They emphasized external, physical acts of obedience to meticulous rules.

Jesus was not subtle in his response to the Pharisees. He called them hypocrites. In multiple skirmishes with them, he exposed their inconsistency and their materialistic attitudes. He showed how far from God they were in their hateful exclusivism, and told them their external forms were empty, meaningless rituals. They might appear righteous to people around them, but on the inside where God saw them, Jesus said they were unclean and far from God.

The Pharisees were big on ceremonial cleanness. They saw potential ceremonial defilement lurking in every meal and marketplace situation. Jesus debunked their theory of holiness, pointing out it was not what was going into the mouth that defiled a person, but what was coming out of the heart.

Jesus went on healing the sick and feeding the hungry. He showed the compassion of God for the people he taught and touched, in stark contrast to the Pharisees who judged and despised everyone in sight.

Do you know any sincere and devout religious people who are more like the Pharisees than they are like Jesus? Legalism is still alive in the church today. If you've been a victim of the legalists' tactics, it's easy to be skeptical of church people. Just remember such attitudes are not from Jesus or from people who are really following him. If we've been guilty of treating the Bible and people around us like the Pharisees did, we should repent. We must carefully compare what we do to Jesus and what he did. It's easy to see the hypocrisy in others, but not so easy to see it in ourselves.

Day 16, Matthew 16

Storm warnings are routine in our technologically advanced age. Weather forecasters predict coming storms with remarkable accuracy. Television meteorologists have radar tools that show not only the location of a storm, but its intensity, wind speed and track as well. These forecasters and their tools help many people get out of harm's way.

People who lived when Jesus was on earth looked to the sky for clues about approaching weather conditions. They didn't have technology to produce a ten-day forecast. (Modern ten-day forecasts aren't all that good, either.) But the ancients had methods already old in their time to anticipate what was ahead. And still today, red skies in the evening or morning are folk wisdom's forecasting tools.

There are "red sky at morning" clues in today's passage about the approaching storm Jesus was destined to face. Jesus dropped a veiled hint about his coming death and resurrection as he told the Pharisees and Sadducees the sign of Jonah would be the only one they would receive. After Peter's remarkable confession of Jesus as the Christ, Jesus began telling the disciples what lay ahead in Jerusalem. Suffering and death were in the forecast for Jesus, but the disciples could not believe Messiah would ever face such a dark prospect. Peter voiced it for all of them: "This shall never happen to you." But it would happen, Jesus knew, and he next began to tell them that they too would face crosses and lose their lives for his sake. The kingdom would come, and they would see it. But the storms would come as well.

You and I are blessed to live on the "empty tomb" side of these dark events. It is hard for us to imagine the darkness and terror of the storm Jesus endured at the cross, not because we don't know the story, but because we do know it, including the beautiful morning of the resurrection. We look back on that storm from the calm place where we are assured of his triumph over the storm of hatred and violence that rained down on him that day.

But we are mistaken if we think there are no storms on the horizon for us as modern day disciples of Jesus. He has been forthright in the warnings—they hated him, they will hate those who follow him. The demands of discipleship still call for each of us to take up the cross and follow him. The red sky warning of impending storms is still there, even if we know the enemy cannot win.

The forecasters and their instruments have saved many lives through their predictions. It's smart to pay attention to weather warnings. It's also smart to save ourselves from needless loss and pain by listening to Jesus and staying close to him.

Day 17, Matthew 17

From Simon Peter's journal...

There's not been much time for fishing lately, and I was glad when Jesus told me to go down to the water and catch a fish. I needed some time to think.

That thing that happened while James, John and I were up on the mountain with Jesus really affected me. All that light! I saw Moses and Elijah, standing there talking to Jesus. It was just so, so...holy. I couldn't help blurting out that idea about making booths for them. The words weren't out of my mouth before the cloud came and the voice spoke. We were terrified, but we understood the words: "This is my beloved Son, with whom I am well pleased; listen to him." Nobody had to ask whose voice that was. I remember Jesus' hand touching me, telling me it was safe to get up, that I didn't have to be afraid. Moses and Elijah were gone when we looked up. He told us not to tell about it yet. I know I'll never forget it.

It's still hard to understand everything Jesus is telling us. We're learning, though. Now we know John Baptist was "Elijah" the prophet was talking about. Now he has come, and everything is ready for Messiah's kingdom. But Jesus is still talking about dying! I believe he's the one, but I don't see how that fits.

My brother Andrew and the others were having some trouble when we came down. A stubborn demon was torturing a young fellow who had been brought by his father. Jesus rebuked the demon, the demon left and the boy was better—just like that! Jesus said they failed because of a lack of faith, and we could move mountains and nothing would be impossible with faith. It was pretty obvious to us all that we're not there yet.

When we got back in town, the tax collector questioned me about whether or not we were going to pay our taxes. He may have been looking for an excuse to accuse Jesus. I told him we were going to pay it. When I got back to the house, Jesus knew before I told him what had happened. He sent me down here to fish, and said I would find a fish with a coin in its mouth. Of course, it turned out just like he said.

I don't know if I'll tell them where this shekel came from when I get to the tax office or not. I'm pretty sure they wouldn't believe me if I did tell them. I just know he's in control of every situation, and he knows everything before we say it or before it even happens. Some of what he's saying scares me, but I trust him.

Day 18, Matthew 18

Since the days of Solomon, it's been true that the borrower is servant to the lender. But most of us are in debt of one kind or another. We have mortgages on our houses and enjoy things bought on credit. A credit card company once advertised that you could have it all and you could have it now. If you're one of the millions who've used easy credit to borrow more than you can afford to pay back, would you be interested in an offer to forgive all the debt? Of course you would.

I'm not sure how the unmerciful servant got as deeply into debt as he did. An ESV footnote tells us a talent was worth about twenty years of a worker's wages. This fellow owed ten thousand talents. I'm no math major, but I think that's about 200,000 years' wages. And you thought you were in trouble! When his master pitied the debtor and forgave the impossible debt, he gave the man his life back. You remember the story. The man with the new-found freedom went out and looked up a fellow servant who owed him about three or four months' wages. As he demanded payment from his debtor, he should have heard the echo of his own recent plea to his master: "Have patience with me and I will pay you." But the one who had been shown so much mercy was merciless toward his fellow. After other servants saw and told the master what had happened, the forgiven man's debt was reinstated and he went to prison for the rest of his life.

Jesus said that's what it's like to be forgiven by God and be unforgiving toward one another. We're taught to pray, "Forgive us our debts, as we also forgive our debtors." We're supposed to let go of bitterness and forgive one another, even as Christ forgave us. We can only understand the necessity and propriety of forgiving undeserving people who've hurt us in the context of our own forgiveness. We didn't deserve it, either. But God was willing, at the cross, to cancel our debt. Because Jesus paid for our sins with his own innocent blood, God is willing to look at us and say, "You don't owe anymore. Debt forgiven."

The story is about monetary debt to help us understand. The indebted servant could have begged for a payment plan and begun a futile attempt to whittle down the balance owed. Our debt to God cannot be represented with complete accuracy by any material expression. We lack the currency to make even a token repayment. When God's grace extends an offer of forgiveness to us, we cannot afford to be harsh toward those who "owe" us about lesser matters. Enjoy the freedom God has granted you by sharing the mercy with others.

Day 19, Matthew 19

The glowing video display cast a blue-gray hue onto the walls and the people gathered in the small consultation room. The picture on the monitor was indistinct at first, but as the cardiologist identified the pulsating heart and which arteries were blocked and which were flowing, it became obvious my friend had a serious problem. The test results showed open heart surgery was needed immediately. None of us knew the answers to our questions: How does a visitor to our country have open heart surgery while he is here on a short-term visa? How can arrangements be made to pay the surgeon and hospital bills? What will the immigration officials and diplomats in both countries do? The cardiologist said, "I don't know what's going to happen here or how we can get this done. But God already knows what he's going to do. Let's pray about it." We joined hands, and the doctor, a man of small stature, prayed a big prayer of faith. My friend had surgery, and is doing well today, back in his homeland.

Jesus knew heart trouble when he saw it, too. He could look into the spiritual heart, diagnose the problem and prescribe the cure without the aid of diagnostic technology. When the Pharisees came with their questions about divorce, he knew they were testing him, not seeking spiritual guidance. He identified the reason Moses had permitted divorce when it was not God's original design—because the hearts of the Israelites were hard. The disciples wanted to shoo away the parents who were bringing their children to be blessed (a very rabbinical thing for Jesus to do). Jesus told those disciples with their own selfish agendas that the kingdom of heaven was more about those little children than their own prideful hearts. And when an admirable young fellow wanted to know what he could do to have eternal life, Jesus was able to identify the problem in his heart and prescribe the remedy the young man could not accept.

When the Great Physician checks your heart, and he does, what does he find there? Is there hardness that looks for the way to circumvent God's will for your life? Is there pride that promotes self and dismisses others? Is there covetousness that makes you cling to the gifts God has given you more than to him, the giver of the gifts? The results of such a penetrating examination may not be good news, but it's critically important to know. He knows exactly what needs to be done and how he's going to do it. When we're willing to submit to his diagnosis and treatment, we'll be fine, and someday, we'll be in our homeland, with him, forever.

Day 20, Matthew 20

One of the psalms tells us God is in heaven and does as he pleases. We try to control ourselves and the people around us. We tend to think we can determine our course and call the shots. But circumstances remind us there are many things beyond our control. In an old story, a little boy asks his father, "When will I be old enough so no one can tell me what to do?" We smile at the answer because we know it's true: "I don't know son, no one's ever lived that long."

God really is sovereign. His control is complete. His power is absolute. He is the master of the house who can say to those who grumbled at the pay window about his generosity, "I choose to give." Another psalm says he owns everything. So the master's words from the story are quite appropriate for God: "Am I not allowed to do what I choose with what belongs to me?" It's true that God will always act in a manner consistent with his nature. But who are we as creatures to assume we understand all about the nature of our Creator?

Because God is sovereign, his plans for his kingdom and our place in it are in his hands. When disciples or enemies had ideas about Messiah and the kingdom that were not in line with God's plans, they either bowed to or were broken by the sovereignty of God. When a mother asked that her sons be granted special places around the throne, Jesus said such things were in the Father's hands. Jesus himself was on his way to Jerusalem to die to accomplish God's plan. That was what God had prepared for his own Son, who taught his disciples that greatness in God's kingdom was to be found in serving, not controlling.

One of the wonders of God's sovereignty is that the God who does as he pleases is willing to receive our requests. He grants them if he chooses to do so. When Jesus asked people who came to him what they wanted, he listened. He did not always grant the request, but he sometimes did, and taught us as disciples to ask. There is tremendous encouragement in this for us. While we may not have the power to do as we please about everything, we have audience with the one who does. In addition to the power, he has the wisdom and the benevolent will toward us to do what is best for us whether we understand it or not. Trust God. Rejoice and rest in his sovereignty.

Day 21, Matthew 21

The last week before the cross began as the prophecy said it would, with Jesus riding into Jerusalem on a donkey. When he went to the temple the following morning and disrupted the thriving commerce of Passover week at the temple, the soundtrack playing in Jesus' mind was prophecy. The Jewish authorities were upset because the miracles were undeniable. They expressed their displeasure at all the incessant singing about the "Son of David." Jesus answered their complaint with another prophetic reference. When the posse of chief priests and elders questioned his authority, Jesus knew they wouldn't answer the question he asked in return about John, because they had rejected John, whom the people held as a prophet.

The weight of the prophecies was crushing the Jewish leaders. On top of the voice of prophecy, the parables Jesus spoke were bearing down on them as well. The stories were about them. In case they missed the point, Jesus told them tax collectors and prostitutes would enter the kingdom ahead of the pious religious authorities, and that

God would take the kingdom away from them and give it to others. Adding to their frustration was the tide of popular opinion that was at least saying he was a prophet, and some venturing to identify him as the long awaited Messiah, the son of David. So the prophecies were pointing to Jesus' true identity and vouching for his authority. The parables were revealing the attitudes and predicting the actions of the leaders.

When people oppose God's plan and reject his chosen one, what should they expect except a humiliating defeat? The characters were all in place. The week-long drama of the final confrontations between Jesus and the establishment would play out, and Jesus would be condemned, killed and buried by the end of the week. The hypocritical leaders would appear to have won for a very brief time. But the resurrection would bring them decades of trouble leading ultimately to the destruction of their whole way of life as well as their forfeiture of a place in Messiah's kingdom.

The barren fig tree Jesus encountered on his way into the city one morning is probably included to signify the barren situation of the Jewish leaders. But out of that dramatic incident, the Lord teaches his followers about the power of faith. The priests and scribes didn't believe when they had seen with their own eyes. Jesus promised those who did believe on him would do some more dramatic things. When they wondered how the fig tree withered at the word of Jesus, he taught them to expect to be able to do even more, saying, "And whatever you ask in prayer, you will receive, if you have faith."

Do Jesus' words convict you, or convince you? Do you hear a promise of punishment, or a promise of power?

Day 22, Matthew 22

Did you ever play the game called "20 Questions" when you were growing up? Have you answered the incessant questions of a preschool child? Have you sat in the tiny interview room on the Bloodmobile and answered dozens of questions about places you may have been and things you may have done that would disqualify you as a donor? Have you ever watched a presidential press conference and seen how the reporters pepper the president with questions? Has anyone ever tried to embarrass you by asking sensitive questions in inappropriate contexts? Have you ever been interrogated by an authority figure about your role in some situation? Are you tired of me asking questions yet?

During the last week of Jesus' life before the cross, it seems he had lots of questions posed to him by the religious leaders who hated him, feared him, wanted him discredited, wanted him dead.

Questions are good and appropriate in many situations. In the classroom or laboratory, questions are tools for exploring the unknown and gaining information. Questions can work like that in the spiritual realm, too. We learn by asking questions and seeking answers. But not all questions are quests for knowledge. Jesus' enemies and critics were not honorable in their intentions or honest in their inquiries when they confronted him with their queries. They wanted to entangle him in his talk, to pose a question that would force Jesus to say something they could use to accuse him.

When humans dare engage God in a match of questions, it is of necessity a mismatch. Creator versus creature will never be a level playing field. Remember how Job wanted to ask God some questions? Remember how the interview went when God asked the questions and Job ended up putting his hand over his mouth in silent shame? The Pharisees and Sadducees had rejected Jesus. Their lack of regard for him is clear in their tactics. But his answers to their malicious questions testified that he really was who they would not admit he was.

I do not believe Jesus' unanswerable questions back to his inquisitors were designed to destroy them, but they were intended to expose their hypocrisy and show them they were out of their league when they opposed him. They stopped asking questions when he succinctly answered theirs and they were unable to answer his.

What should we take away from this account of questions and answers? I hope you do not think we should never ask questions. An honest, well-framed question is a great way to learn. I suggest we should be very careful of our motives when we ask questions. Are we avoiding the obvious, or resisting what we already know to be true? And when we find a question from the Lord, I suggest we ponder it carefully, realizing that his questions are designed to accomplish his purpose of leading us away from self-reliance and drawing us to himself.

Day 23, Matthew 23

Jesus' strongest rebuke was addressed to the religious elite. The most advanced experts and the strictest practitioners of the law received the longest and strongest censure Jesus ever spoke.

Jesus called these people hypocrites and blind fools. What was it about them that drew such vivid, pointed criticism?

The scribes and Pharisees did not practice what they preached. They were good at burdening their hearers with regulations they did not keep themselves. These leaders had elaborate schemes to excuse their own disobedience while condemning people who did the same thing but were ignorant of the loopholes.

The Jewish leaders and teachers made a show of their religion. When they did some good deed, prayed or fasted, they wanted the attention and praise of people around them, so their religious activities had to be public.

These hypocrites specialized in the tedious details of how they expressed their religion. They made the minor points the major ones, and ignored the primary issues of genuine spirituality. Their devotion was expressed in things that could be listed and quantified, not in characteristics and attitudes that had to be lived out in relationship to God and others.

Not only did the sickening hypocrisy of these people keep them out of the kingdom of God, their sharp, judgmental attitudes turned others away from the kingdom as well. Hypocrites ruin themselves, but the damage also spreads to others around them.

Jesus said the scribes and Pharisees of that generation were the spiritual descendants of earlier generations who had persecuted and killed messengers from God. Hypocrisy and self-righteousness reacts with violent aggression against those who are bold enough to tell the truth about the lie they're living.

As we nod our heads in agreement with Jesus' criticism of the scribes and Pharisees and think we know someone who needs to read this chapter, it is probably wise to remember that these people were serious practitioners of their religion who imagined themselves closer to God than others around them. The poisonous fruit of hypocrisy is prominent in "church people." When those who claim to follow Jesus are more like the Pharisees than their professed Master, the same stern rebuke applies.

Many people who appear to be spiritual are not going to enter the kingdom of God because their religious pride keeps them from coming to God through Christ. The problem is not that the Lord is unwilling to save such people, but rather that they are unwilling to humble themselves and be saved. Let's not be guilty of the "Christian" version of the ancient Jews' hypocrisy. Jesus sees right through the act, and it makes him angry.

Day 24, Matthew 24

An old friend of mine would usually respond to an inquiry as to whether or not he was ready by saying, "I'm like boiled ham—always ready." Some army sergeant or football coach along the way had impressed the saying on him so deeply that it was a permanent fixture in his vocabulary.

I enjoy a nice surprise as much as the next guy, but I admit I'm not a big fan of folks just dropping by to see me. I like to know when someone's coming so we can put on some coffee and have the brownies ready. I want to be ready when the guests arrive.

Everyone who has grown up in a family or raised one of their own knows getting a family ready to go to church or out to eat or out the door for another day requires a great deal of coordination and preparation, especially if there are less bathrooms than people in the house. Every student who's faced some big exams in his academic career probably knows exactly how it feels to be ready (and not ready) for the test. Whether it's opening a new business or trying to get away on a vacation, we know the value of getting ready.

When Jesus told the disciples such a catastrophic upheaval was coming that not one block of the temple would be left standing on another, they could not imagine anything less than the end of the world causing such destruction. They wanted to know when it was all going to happen. Jesus warned them not to be deceived by charlatans and fakes who would brag about special knowledge, and told them to watch for certain things as warning signs. But he plainly told them no one—not the angels, not even he as he spoke to them, knew when it would happen. So, they were supposed to get ready and stay that way. He assured them his word would stand, even when the world they knew was passing away.

A smart homeowner would be ready for a thief who announced his intention to break into his house. A faithful servant is one who stays on task while his master is away, not knowing when he might return, but realizing it could be at any time. So Jesus counseled his disciples to be ready. Because his word is sure, we know he's coming. We know we want to be ready when he does come. But since we don't know and can't know when that will be, the only sensible plan is to be like old Boiled Ham—always ready.

Day 25, Matthew 25

Do you have a picture in your mind of what judgment will be like? Since I was a little boy (probably influenced by preachers I heard describing that day), I've imagined how it will be to stand before God in judgment. Jesus painted three word pictures of how it's going to be at the judgment. These stories should not only shape our mental images of judgment day, but shape our lives as well.

The first story is about being ready, making adequate preparation before the time comes. Knowing about the ancient marriage customs might enhance the picture, but the message is clear: those who are ready will go into the celebration, and those who failed to make adequate preparation or think they're going to rely on the preparation of others aren't going to be included when the door is shut.

The second story stresses being faithful stewards of what the Lord gives us. A steward manages someone else's property. He accounts for his management of the owner's goods. The master knows every servant's ability and hands out opportunity accordingly. Not everyone gets the same. But all are expected to be good managers of the gifts entrusted to them. The man in the story who is cast out instead of welcomed in claimed he was afraid. The master said he was wicked and lazy. But the good managers who brought the master a return on his investment in them were commended for their faithfulness, rewarded and welcomed.

The third story may be the most disturbing of this trilogy of judgment stories. I think on some level we realize we are supposed to make adequate preparation, and that we are responsible for what we did with what we had. But this one goes beyond general principles of readiness and good management to the practical difference following Jesus is supposed to make in how we treat others. The commended and the condemned in this story had one common characteristic: Neither of them recognized the king in his needy disguises. The ones who showed compassion and hospitality to people in need did it without knowing the king would take personally whatever they did for others. And the people who were hard-hearted toward needy people around them never imagined the king would take personally whatever they failed to do for needy.

My grown-up mental picture of the judgment is probably not much more accurate than the one I had as a kid. There are many things we just don't know. But these stories tell us what we really need to know, and remind us to behave as if we know it: Make preparation well in advance, put whatever God entrusts to you to good use and remember he knows how you treat the needy people in your path. Jesus says people who do those things are wise, faithful and blessed. Are you?

Day 26, Matthew 26

Jesus knew in advance what was going to happen. He knew by week's end he would be dead. As the days passed, he approached the dark events with confident, elegant dignity. He spoke with matter-of-fact calmness about torture, death and burial drawing nearer with each passing hour. It's almost all summed up in what Jesus told the disciples to tell the fellow at whose house they would eat the Last Supper: "The Teacher said, 'My time is at hand.'" In addition to the mistreatment and suffering he would receive at the hands of the Jewish authorities and Roman soldiers, he knew betrayal, denial and abandonment by those closest to him lay just ahead. Yet he walked through it, calm and under control.

He had lived his whole life under the Father's direction. This dark night would be no exception. He would not resist. He would not call down the angel legions to rescue him. He was somber, but there is no hint of reluctance or reservation in his words. Jesus commended Mary for anointing him, talked with Judas about betraying him and told the disciples about denying and deserting him—all in the same, even tone.

Later when his enemies came to arrest him, when the kangaroo court was perverting any sense of justice they might have ever entertained and when the high priest was forgetting his own dignity and making a spectacle of his accusations, peace characterized Jesus' words and actions.

What trust! What love! What mastery and emptying of self! Jesus was not enduring the horrific prelude to the cross by his own strength, but by the power of God in whom he trusted. He so loved his Father and us that he was willing to suffer to carry out the plan and to redeem us.

The Jewish authorities were plotting his death. The disciples were grumbling about Mary's extravagance. At the Passover table, he had to endure the duplicity of the one who'd already made a deal to hand him over to the enemies. It wasn't just Peter who was promising to die before denying; all the disciples said the same thing. At the center of the swirling darkness stood Jesus. The hands that had broken the bread and passed the cup at the supper table would soon be bound and blood soaked. But he was ready.

My admiration and appreciation for Jesus grows every time I read about the events of the last night. I fear I have been too much like the betrayer, the denier and the forsakers. I do not want to be anything like Jesus' cruel enemies. When adversity comes, I want to be like Jesus.

Day 27, Matthew 27

The greatest demonstration of love and a chilling exhibition of cruelty are on display in Jesus' trial and death. Film makers have employed both subtle understatement and graphic realism to convey the intensity of Jesus' suffering. If we must divert our eyes from the gruesome brutality, there are other places we might fix our gaze. As we zoom out from the shocking close-up of Jesus on the cross, there are other people in the picture we need to see. If we focus on some faces in the crowd, we may find ourselves, or someone very much like us.

We don't want to think so, but could we be Judas? Was he disillusioned with the direction the kingdom movement had taken? Was he trying to force Messiah to act? We don't know. But we do know he betrayed his Master for the price of a slave. We do know he perverted a gesture of love to mark Jesus for the enemies. Have we ever sold our Master cheaply, making a deal that betrayed our lack of loyalty to him? Have we been hypocrites—talking and singing about how much we love him, but bearing little evidence of that love beyond our words?

Pilate is another infamous character in the story. Pilate questioned Jesus, and was amazed at his silence in the face of accusations. His wife warned the governor to have nothing to do with him. As the crowd got louder, Pilate claimed he was innocent of Jesus' blood. Plenty of people in the crowd were willing to let the blood be on them. So he beat Jesus, and turned him over to soldiers with orders to execute him. Could we be the Roman governor, whose actions sealed Jesus' death sentence? Since he died on the cross for our sins, it would seem so. The writing above Jesus' head on the cross was in Pilate's hand, but the sin debt he paid by his innocent death was yours and mine.

I also think about myself when I see Barabbas, the notorious murderer who was released from prison when the crowd asked for him instead of Jesus. Jesus took Barabbas' place, just as he took ours when he died on the cross. The insurrectionist was set free, the shackles removed from his hands and feet because someone was going to die in his place. That sounds a lot like you and me, doesn't it? Do you think Barabbas stayed to watch what happened to Jesus, or did he just steal a glance over his shoulder at the bloodied prisoner before disappearing into the angry crowd?

Do you remember the song, "Were You There When They Crucified My Lord?" I know I was there in the sense that he was dying for my sins. But as I look at the faces in the crowd around the cross, I sense I have a lot in common with some people who were there the day Jesus died.

Day 28, Matthew 28

The first evangelist of the resurrection was an angel, but the first human carriers of the empty tomb story were the women who came early that morning. Their emotions had quite a workout that Passover weekend, and the fear and joy mixture they felt as they hurried to tell the news turned into worship at Jesus' feet when he appeared to them. All he had said about being Messiah was true! All evidence pointed to the truth, and his resurrection sealed their hearts in devotion to him.

When the eleven remaining apostles went to Galilee as Jesus had instructed through the women's words, most of these men who had walked with Jesus and knew him best bowed in worship, too. Oddly, some of them doubted, even in the presence of his resurrected body. Maybe it was hard to get past the last views they'd had, over their shoulders as they ran away in the garden. Had they watched from a distance as his trial went wrong, as he was tortured and crucified, and as his mangled, blood-soaked body was removed from the cross? He had mentioned resurrection, but who could believe that anyone could come back from such an ordeal? Now the words had moved from memory and theory to concrete reality. It must have been hard, at least for some of them, to believe.

The chief priests didn't believe before he died, and they weren't about to concede faith in him now. The men who were supposed to be the spiritual leaders of the nation chose to bribe wide-eyed guards and bury the story about what really happened at the tomb that morning under a lie about grave-robbing disciples. A character in one of Jesus' stories was told that people who wouldn't listen and believe the prophets' message also wouldn't believe if one they knew to be dead returned to deliver the warning to repent. Sure enough, when

Jesus did come back, they chose to lie rather than admit the truth about him.

The disciples were galvanized, fortified by seeing Jesus alive and well. The denial, the running away—all that was over. They would faithfully testify about him for the rest of their lives, and most of them would pay with their lives for doing so. They obeyed his parting orders to go make disciples. Because they did, we're blessed to know their story and Jesus' story. Put yourself in their sandals. How would you react? Ponder the record and the claim. Will you worship, or will you deny? Will you believe or doubt? Will you obey or refuse to recognize his call on your life?

Mark

Day 29, Mark 1

To a couple of brothers in the fishing business, Jesus said, "Follow me, and I will make you become fishers of men." Some important issues related to discipleship are addressed in this invitation to become a disciple.

Usually, a prospective disciple approached a rabbi and asked permission to become his follower. But Jesus invited the prospects he chose to leave what they were doing and become his disciples. He took the initiative in calling those first followers who would literally walk in his footsteps. So from the fishing boats and tax tables and wherever else he encountered them, Jesus selected a group Mark would later identify as "those whom he desired." These men, upon whose work and lives the expansion of the new kingdom would rest, were hand-picked for God's purpose.

No other rabbi could have ever said "Follow me" in the same sense Jesus did. They might have schooled their followers in the tradition they had themselves followed, indoctrinating them with the same influences that had shaped their own lives, quoting the revered traditions of the elders. But Jesus was not calling his disciples to a school of thought or a sectarian party. Instead he called them to follow him, personally, as he spoke with authority the very words from God to them.

Jesus invited them to be changed from what they were into something new. They would not transform themselves; Jesus would "make them become" this new thing. Their part in it was submission, becoming a follower. The invitation to discipleship is a picture of how God's choice and purpose can work in and through human choice. As they yielded to follow, he would make them what he wanted them to be.

Under Jesus' tutelage, they would *become* fishers of men. The process was just beginning when they left their nets to fall in behind their new Master. He would train and instruct them for years. They would listen and watch, learning to be like him by being with him. Jesus met them where they were, relating what they would learn to something they already knew. The relationship was established in a decisive moment, but realized over time. They had much to learn before they were ready for the mission that would shape the rest of their lives.

Do you believe you are called by God for a purpose? Are you following him, aware that your loyalty lies ultimately with him, not some school of interpretation, an ideology or a group? Have you surrendered control and direction to his will? Do you realize and appreciate that discipleship is a process, not an event? Thinking seriously about these matters will help you solidify your commitment, evaluate your progress and encourage you when you are painfully aware of your shortcomings.

Day 30, Mark 2

When Jesus said, "Your sins are forgiven," the scribes wanted to know why he talked like that. Only God could say that. So they were cornered by their own logic when Jesus not only said it, but backed it up with a spectacular miracle. When Jesus did the thing only God could do, they weren't ready to acknowledge the conclusion of their own argument.

When Jesus called a tax collector to be his disciple and then went to a party at his house with all his "sinner" friends, the scribes of the Pharisees demanded to know why Jesus would do such a thing. He used their inquiry to focus his mission. He came to call sinners. They could not imagine he was talking about them as well as the tax collectors with whom he was breaking bread at Matthew's table.

When people asked why Jesus' disciples weren't fasting like John's disciples and the followers of the Pharisee rabbis, Jesus explained that his message and mission could not be tacked onto or contained within the old forms. The wine of God's kingdom required new wineskins. There would be time for fasting, but his kingdom was about joyfully being with him, not mournfully struggling without him.

When the Pharisees wanted to know why the disciples "broke" the Sabbath by plucking a snack as they walked through the grain field, Jesus used an example from the nation's history to explain that the Sabbath ritual and regulation were created for the human family's good, and not the other way around. To the Pharisees, their interpretation of the law was more important than the people around them. Jesus demoted the Sabbath traditions from the high place they occupied in the minds of the devout by claiming that he was Lord of the Sabbath.

We understand about asking "why," don't we? We need understanding and clarification. We want the world around us to make sense, so we try to observe cause and effect. We try to make meaning and grasp the reason why both good and bad things take place. The irony of these "whys" people were asking about Jesus is that he was there in person, giving answers and showing credentials for those answers by the power he wielded. He more than once used their "whys" as springboards for important information about himself and the coming kingdom. The answers to the "whys" sometimes told his antagonists more than they were willing to accept at the time about Jesus.

But the healed paralytic who was able to take up his bed and walk away didn't need to ask why about what Jesus said and did. He and his friends believed and were blessed. Do you think Levi and his friends, basking in the sunshine of Jesus' acceptance, needed a big explanation about why Jesus was associating with them? As the enemies asked questions in protest and doubt, the followers were seeing the answers and embracing the truth with joy and faith.

Day 31, Mark 3

His family thought he was out of his mind. The religious experts declared he was in league with the devil. Some of the nation's leading citizens were plotting his destruction. But the crowd was attracted to Jesus. They were needy and he was meeting their needs, so they came out in big numbers to press close, trying to touch the one demons were confessing as the Son of God.

Crowd control was a potential problem for the little band of followers. So many people were so desperate to see Jesus that he had to have a boat ready to get away when the throng threatened to crush him. Wherever they went, the crowds followed. They were so busy dealing with the crowds that they didn't even take time to eat.

Jesus chose twelve to be "apostles," a special group he called to be with him to learn from him and to do the work he would send them to do. The apostles needed time to be with Jesus to learn the lessons he was teaching. They needed to watch how he lived and worked so they could walk in his steps. The training period was a necessary prerequisite to their ministry. Later we'll see the cycle end when the disciples return from a preaching tour with a report about what they did while they were away from Jesus. When they came back, Jesus insisted that they rest. Rest time was also a part of the cycle Jesus was teaching his disciples to live—be with him to grow and become, go out to do his work and teach his word and then come back to him to get some rest.

Would-be servants are often compromised and confused when they try to eliminate one or more of the phases in the cycle. We have nothing to say if we're not spending time alone with him. If we don't go out and fulfill our mission, we're just talking about it. We're hearing but not doing the word of the Lord. And those who think they're exempt from the need for rest will learn (perhaps the hard way) that our minds and bodies are engineered with a demand for down time.

This cycle fits a variety of time frames. All of life might be seen as a single cycle—preparation, work, rest. It could describe our annual or weekly schedules. It even fits a disciple's daily life. I need time with Jesus every day, preferably at the beginning of the day. I am so much better prepared to work with others when I have prepared myself through reading, meditating and praying. And when it's time for rest, I'm not always smart enough to remember that, and I push to do more when rest would prepare me to do better.

Day 32, Mark 4

The ill-fated *RMS Titanic* was touted as unsinkable. An official of the White Star Line, the company that built and owned the ship, boasted that God himself could not sink it. On April 14, 1912 on her maiden voyage, *Titanic* struck an iceberg and 1,522 died as the ship sank in the cold Atlantic.

Jesus and the disciples were on a much smaller craft than the *Titanic* one night when a storm seemed to threaten the boat and the lives of all on board. As a windstorm whipped the waves of Galilee so they were breaking into the boat and filling it, the seasoned fishermen turned novice disciples were terrified. They woke Jesus and asked, "Teacher, don't you care that we are perishing?" He spoke to the wind and waves in much the same way I might tell my little dog to quit barking. And the storm became calm. (That part's not always true about my dog.) Then Jesus asked the disciples about their great fear and small faith. The disciples were even more afraid after witnessing what had happened, and they wondered aloud to each other about their master's true identity.

The little boat that had been a pulpit earlier in the day was unsinkable, not because of who built it or who designed it, but because of who was sailing on it that stormy night. Were demonic forces involved in the furious storm? I don't know. Did God arrange the demonstration to build the disciples' faith? I don't know. But I do know Jesus made a big impression on the disciples that night by his easy mastery of a storm that threatened to swamp their boat.

As people of faith who claim to follow Jesus, is our first reaction still sometimes fear when we feel threatened by adversity? I do not have to know the name of the wind that's howling in your life to identify with the fear you feel when it blows. I understand about the wave breaking above your bow and making you cry out, "Lord, don't you care?" We need to hear Jesus asking us, "Why are you so afraid? Have you still no faith?" His gentle rebuke points to the source of our fear, like a doctor poking around to find where it hurts.

Our feelings may be wounded at the suggestion that a faith deficiency is at the root of our fears. But there's good news! The powerful, faith-building word of God is readily available. It's also good to know we are works in progress, growing and becoming stronger as our experience with and knowledge of Jesus increases. Dark spiritual forces are displeased by your decision to go with Jesus on your voyage through life. But we really are sailing on an unsinkable ship when we're with him.

Day 33, Mark 5

Her life had been miserable for twelve years. The constant loss of blood had drained her physical vitality. The embarrassment, inconvenience and social ostracism she suffered because of the blood flow had taken a different, but no less difficult toll on her psychological well-being. The doctors made her worse instead of better, taking all her money in the process. She was desperate.

She heard what Jesus had been doing, healing all kinds of diseases and conditions. The reports kindled a spark of hope and faith within her. She braved the surging crowd, struggled to get close enough to touch him, believing that doing so would make her well. She was right, and she knew it right away. Jesus knew it, too, and turned around to see her. His motive was not to humiliate her for what she did, but to commend her faith. He pronounced her healed and dismissed her to go in peace.

Faith comes from hearing the message. The woman's faith was not crafted through extensive theological training or hermeneutical exercise. (The people with those credentials weren't coming to faith, even when they saw the miracles with their own eyes.) She simply heard the reports spread by word of mouth about all the sickness, injury and demon possession Jesus had healed and cast out. She made a personal application to her own desperate situation. Her faith went beyond believing it had happened to others to seeing how it could happen to her. Faith trusts that the message is true, and acts to receive the blessing. More than physical strength or bold courage, it was faith that led her through the crowd to reach out and touch the one she believed could heal her.

The synagogue ruler had a similar exhibition of courageous trust. He did not care what the Jewish establishment might think or do about his display of confidence in Jesus. His daughter was dying and he was desperate. He fell down before Jesus, asking what he trusted Jesus could do for his sick little girl. Such faith pleases God, and he knows who approaches him in trusting faith. He has no trouble sorting out the touch of faith from the incidental contact of the curious. The onlookers may dismiss our request as impossible or even laugh, but the trusting ones keep looking to the one they trust to accomplish what they're asking him to do.

Aren't we more likely to come to Christ when we know we have no other alternative, when all else we've tried has failed? As long as I think I can handle my problem, or believe there are many possible alternatives to explore, I'm not going to see Jesus as my only hope. If you and I are worried about what others may think or what consequences we may face at the hands of unbelievers, we're not close to the level of trust this woman and man showed.

Day 34, Mark 6

Homecoming is an old tradition in many schools, churches and communities. A special time is set aside to honor returning graduates, former members and people who grew up in a town but have since moved away. Reunions are held to bring folks together who've not seen one another in years. Although there are usually some somber moments remembering people who have passed away, the celebration is generally a happy time of honor and friendship.

Jesus' return to Nazareth was not exactly a happy homecoming. The hometown people remembered him, which actually turned out to be part of the problem. The wisdom and works which were so evident in Jesus did not square in their minds with what they thought they already knew about him. How could the carpenter's son be this eloquent rabbi? How could Mary's son and the brother of the other family members they knew so well be doing the powerful works they'd heard so much about?

As Daniel J. Boorstin put it, "The greatest obstacle to discovering the shape of the earth, the continents and the oceans was not ignorance, but the illusion of knowledge." What the people of Nazareth thought they knew was the obstacle that stood in the way of discovering the Messiah. Their presuppositions about Jesus blinded them to what they could have been blessed to know. Their prejudice cost them the opportunity to receive great blessings. By taking offense at Jesus, they robbed the village's most famous resident of the honor he was due.

Across Palestine, the response to Jesus' message and miracles was far from uniform. While some put their faith in him as Messiah when they heard and saw him, others seemed to be hardened in their unbelief by witnessing the same things. Jesus was no stranger to rejection and skepticism. Not every miracle was tied to the faith of the one who was healed; however, some of them were. But at Nazareth he marveled at their unbelief. It's interesting to note he did not do many miracles at Nazareth. I think we should understand it was no limitation on his part, but the overwhelming rejection that kept any more than just a few sick folks from being healed.

The citizens of Nazareth missed what people in other places received because of their faithless prejudice. Could that same thing happen to you and me? Might we fail to receive what the Lord is so able and willing to give because of what we think we know? Could we miss the richest gifts he desires to give because our faith is weak or absent? It is to our benefit and his glory that we observe closely and trust deeply.

Day 35, Mark 7

The Jewish leaders who opposed Jesus, scrutinizing and criticizing every action and word, were meticulous in their ritual observances. They were good at following the rules they emphasized. The outward show of piety was probably impressive to those who witnessed their painstaking observance of the traditions handed down from their elders. When they criticized the disciples for eating with defiled hands, it was not a sanitation issue, but a ceremonial one.

The Pharisees and their associates made a serious error in judgment when they asked Jesus about his disciples' non-conformity. He responded, calling them hypocrites, and they were. Their 'obedience' was more about allegiance to a code of external, visible acts of piety that did not engage their hearts at all. Their doctrines spawned incessant debate and ruthless judgment and were really only human traditions, not the actual law of God.

Jesus accused them of robbing the word of God of its effect by putting loopholes in their traditions to escape the law's demands. Their spirituality was cold and heartless. They felt no pain at denying aid to helpless, aging parents. They claimed any resources that could support mother and father had already been pledged to God. With one clever twist of tradition, their self-calibrating consciences excused them from honoring their parents.

Jesus sounded like one of the old prophets, exposing the emptiness of their external rituals and the wickedness of their hearts. He told the people that true holiness was not determined by regulations about clean and unclean food. We're used to it because we've read it lots of times. But to a Jew who had lived under the influence of dietary restrictions of the law and the massive extensions of them in the traditions, it was radical teaching. Jesus said defilement didn't come from taking in food, which only passed through the digestive tract. Instead, he warned that what came out of the heart was what defiled someone.

Could our worship be vain, too? A preoccupation with form and ritual could mask the unconverted heart of a so-called Christian. We can still sing, give, fast or pray for show, while hiding from our peers (but not from God) a heart that is cold, dead and far from the one we're supposed to be worshiping. It is so easy to make our tradition as binding as what God commanded, but we have no more authority to do that than the Pharisees had when they did it long ago. Most traditionalists probably mean well, building helpful restrictions and strengthening the rules to hedge in the faithful. But human tradition tacked onto and taught as the word of God makes worship worthless.

Let's resist the urge to measure spirituality by displays of righteousness that may have nothing to do with our hearts. Hypocrisy is offensive to people who find it in us, and to God who always looks at the heart.

Day 36, Mark 8

Do you suppose Jesus was sometimes exasperated with the lack of faith and understanding he found among people while he was here on earth? Do you think Jesus grew weary of the Pharisees' arguments and hard-hearted rejection? When the disciples seemed slow to learn or believe what he was teaching them, can you hear the frustration in the question, "Do you not yet understand?" Mustn't it have been at least a little discouraging to hear Peter's beautiful confession so quickly followed by a rebuke when Jesus began to teach them about the coming cross?

I suspect the same compassion Jesus showed for sick, blind, grieving and misguided people kept annoyance at bay for some time. He was after all God, and God is long-suffering. As Creator, he perfectly understands the limitations of the creature. So he often repeated himself. As we read the gospel, it seems that he gave abundant, even redundant evidence to followers and enemies alike to compensate for skepticism.

There are several lessons in this. First, Jesus models the patience we need to deal with one another. Who are we to be impatient with people who don't immediately subscribe to what we want them to believe? How dare we be short-tempered with people we find to be slow learners? Are you a mature believer with a well developed understanding of the Lord's will? Did you come to that understanding overnight? Was someone patient with you? Every parent and leader needs to remember the example of Jesus in showing patience. Every would-be soul winner, eager to share the good news about Christ should remember not everyone is eager and ready to hear what we're so sure is true. With fellow believers, we know it's unreasonable to expect everyone to have the same level of maturity and understanding, regardless of diverse backgrounds and varying levels of experience. If I need the Lord to be patient with me, I should be patient with people around me.

But I also should remember that even God's patience has limits. Jesus knew the hearts and thoughts of everyone. He knew when the Pharisees were being obstinate and when the disciples were afraid or exhausted. And he gave warnings and made allowances for an appropriate period of time before he left them to the consequences of their stubbornness or unbelief. But when the right amount of time had passed and opportunity had knocked long enough, he went ahead with the plan. He did it with the whole world back in the days of Noah, and with the nation of Israel when he allowed their defeat and captivity after generations of warnings and discipline.

It's good to know God is patient. It gives us hope in our weakness. But it's important to also know that, in his perfection, he knows when enough is enough. We'd best not presume upon the patience of the Lord.

Day 37, Mark 9

Who's the greatest? The twelve men upon whom the future of Jesus' movement rested were quarreling among themselves like children on the playground about who would be greatest in the kingdom. I doubt they were saying things such as, "No, not me! Your faith is so much stronger than mine. You are the greatest!" I suspect the quarrel sounded more like, "Oh, yeah? Well, he called me first. I am so much more spiritual than you. Jesus likes me best. I'll be sitting at the right hand, not you." Like kids in the back seat of the car on a trip, the disciples had argued on the way back to Capernaum.

Jesus knew all about their quarrel when he asked what they had been discussing, just like God knew Adam and Eve were hiding in the bushes when he asked where they were. Even parents use this tactic, asking questions, not for their own information, but to confront their children about some situation where the kids need to face what they've said or done. The apostles didn't really want to talk about it; it was humiliating for Jesus to know about their fuss. So the Son of God who emptied himself to come into the world as a servant and a sacrifice taught them the way to the front of the line was to go to the back, and the way to be counted great in his kingdom was to be a servant. He held a child and taught these men with visions of grandeur that how they received helpless people indicated whether or not they were receptive toward Jesus and God the Father.

The disciples' desire to be great is alive and well in their modern spiritual descendants. The peace and unity of a body of believers is often disrupted by brothers and sisters vying for prominence and recognition in God's family. We are so much influenced by the world and the ways of the self-indulgent culture around us that we forget Jesus' standard for true greatness, and chase instead after a glitzy counterfeit. Most of us would still rather be served than be a servant, except when we're reading or singing about being servants like Jesus. Pride is the root of the selfish spirit, and I test positive for pride if I think others aren't on a par with me or if I think simple tasks of humble service are somehow beneath me. Some are better suited to certain tasks than others because of certain gifts they've been given. But no one walking in Jesus' footsteps can claim to be "too good" to render selfless service in his name to the least of those around us.

Let's not let him catch us quarreling.

Day 38, Mark 10

Both were eager. One ran to Jesus; the other sprang up when called. Both seemed sincere. One wanted to know what to do; the other, seeking mercy, wanted Jesus to do something for him. Both were blessed to have personal interviews with Jesus. One walked away from Jesus with tear-blurred vision; the other was crying before the interview, but afterward saw clearly for the first time, and followed the man who had made him see.

One was rich, and one was a beggar. One talked about his law keeping and what he had done; the other expressed his faith in what Jesus could do.

What a striking contrast between the rich young man and blind Bartimaeus! There's much to learn from their diverse backgrounds, requests and results.

It's important to note that Jesus loved the rich young man. Of course his love for all of us is what brought him here and led him to the cross. But Mark made a point of telling us Jesus loved this man, even as he told him what he lacked and what to do about it. The young man was disheartened by what Jesus said because what he needed most to hear was the last thing he wanted to hear. It's probably the same with you and me—the Lord challenges us to abandon some stronghold in our heart which divides our loyalty and keeps us from fully following him. He does it out of love, knowing what we need, wanting what's best for us.

When Peter said the disciples had done what Jesus called the rich man to do, Jesus promised whatever they left behind to follow him would be repaid a hundredfold now, and with eternal life in the age to come. Even if I can't grasp all that means, I can trust the promise that I will gain, not lose by following him.

I think about Bartimaeus sometimes during prayer requests. He didn't need time to gather his thoughts and decide on a request when Jesus asked what he wanted. He was direct: "Lord, let me recover my sight." He had heard enough sitting on his beggar's blanket on the outskirts of Jericho to believe Jesus of Nazareth was Messiah, the Son of David. Had he heard of other blind people receiving their sight? Whatever he had heard prompted him to plead for mercy. Rebuked by the crowd, he would not stop seeking a blessing from Jesus. He knew his opportunity was passing by, and he was not going to let it go quietly. Jesus bragged on his faith, and said his faith made him well.

Is your faith strong enough to keep anyone or anything from blocking your vision of his loving call on your life? What means most to you? Does your faith prompt you to act in the moment, unhindered by what others say or do? When you know you've been blessed by the Lord's mercy, do you follow him?

Day 39, Mark 11

It must have been an incredible week. Thousands of travelers poured into Jerusalem for Passover. The disciples started the week by doing something under orders from Jesus that made them look like horse thieves. They "borrowed" a colt, and just as Jesus told them to expect, they were questioned about it. They answered just as he had told them, saying, "The Lord has need of it and will send it back here immediately." It worked, just like he said it would. Zechariah's prophecy about Messiah arriving sitting on a donkey, on a colt the foal of a donkey, was coming true before their eyes—even if at first they did not understand all that was happening. Some of the pilgrims on the way into Jerusalem recognized him and started blessing Jesus and shouting "Hosanna!" about the coming kingdom of David. There would be no more delay. The time for the confrontation had come.

The following morning Jesus disturbed the money-making machine the Jewish leaders had established at the temple. The pilgrims could not bring their sacrifices on the long journey from home, so sacrificial animals were available for sale (probably at exorbitant prices). The pilgrims' money was no good inside the complex—they had to change their foreign currency into the temple currency at an outrageous exchange rate. If the parade the previous day had somehow escaped the leaders' attention (we know from Matthew that it did not), I suspect the disruption of the cash flow was the catalyst that shifted the plans of the chief priests and scribes into high gear to destroy Jesus.

When the leaders confronted Jesus in public the following day with questions about his authority, Jesus used the classic tactic of responding with a question of his own, knowing that the hypocritical leaders wouldn't answer. To admit that John was a heaven-sent messenger would equal admitting their wickedness in rejecting him; to claim he was just a man was a politically incorrect position they didn't wish to take. Never out of control of the situation, never responding from desperation, Jesus in essence said, "We understand one another perfectly."

More questions and public showdowns lay ahead. By the end of the week, in the grossest display of injustice in the history of the world, Jesus would go to the cross. But as we journey toward that day, it's wise to remember these dark events didn't "just happen" to Jesus. There was never a step along the way when he was trapped or outwitted. The public confrontations were necessary. The chief priests and their henchmen didn't "win." Jesus went to Jerusalem and followed the plan, knowing he would be killed and buried by the end of the week. The plan had been in place since the beginning of the world. He was willing to know hunger, rejection, pain and death for you and me, because he loved us so much.

Day 40, Mark 12

The Pharisees wanted to quarrel about the legality of certain aspects of daily life, like paying taxes to the despised Roman government. The goal of such questions was not to learn how to please God while under the dominion of a foreign power, but rather to trap Jesus into saying something they could use as a formal charge against him. They underestimated Jesus. He gave them a profound answer without giving them a single word they could use in their plot. The Sadducees used their interview time to filibuster about one of their pet doctrines. They didn't believe in the resurrection, so they came to Jesus with a ridiculous story they believed would thoroughly confound Jesus and show the folly of the idea of a resurrection at the same time. Imagine how his words must have stung these experts when he told them they knew neither the Scripture nor the power of God. He showed them how, from words they knew by heart, that the dead are alive as far as God is concerned, and finished his answer by telling them they were quite wrong.

If the scribe who asked about the most important command was trying to test or trap Jesus, it seems that after he heard and agreed with Jesus' answer he might have had second thoughts. Jesus said loving God with all our being was the most important command, and loving neighbor as self was second. The questioner acknowledged Jesus was right. He admitted these things were much more important than offerings and sacrifices, which were often emphasized as proof of love and devotion. Jesus saw that spark of recognition in the scribe and told him he was not far from the kingdom of God.

The condition of your heart is revealed by the nature of the questions you ask. The questions aren't bad in themselves, but the motive behind asking them may be. A good question may reveal a seeking, thoughtful heart as surely as a loaded question unmasks a heart of unbelief or rejection.

How often do we pass our words, thoughts and actions through the filter of the Great Commands? If everything else I'm supposed to do is somehow expressed in that pair of commandments, I should check my heart and life against the simple requirements of these laws. Do my thoughts, words and deeds reflect loving God most of all? Does my conduct and speech show love for my neighbor, that I really want what is best for him? These directives would put a stop to the mean and hateful patterns of behavior that characterize too many lives.

The scribe knew Jesus' answer was good and right when he heard it. He was able to apply it and see that following these commands meant more than any ritual show of obedience. Do we recognize the truth when we heart it? Do our lives show it?

Day 41, Mark 13

In the days before mandatory car seats for kids, an old friend of mine allowed his six year-old son to sit on his lap and "drive" as they traveled along I-75 in Florida in the middle of the night. The boy's hands were on the wheel, and Dad's foot was on the gas pedal. After a long time, the little boy woke his dad, saying, "Daddy, I'm tired. You drive now." The man had fallen asleep with his foot on the gas pedal, and the little boy had driven the car for many miles!

Maybe you've driven a long way after a long day, knowing it wasn't the safest thing to do. You've been in other situations where you had to stay awake. Most of us have stayed up with a sick family member, watching them, watching the clock, looking out the window for the first sign of graying dawn. Maybe your biggest challenge to stay awake comes during a sermon at church! But whatever the circumstance, we know how it feels to force ourselves to stay awake when we want to sleep. You just want to rest your eyes, put your head down for a 30-second power nap. Then someone punches you because you're disturbing the peace by snoring, or you wake up with drool on your sleeve.

When Jesus described certain events coming at an uncertain time, he told the disciples to stay awake. Anticipation is a big part of preparation for such eventualities.

We need to stay awake because our duty is so important. Disciples deal with spiritual matters, things of eternal significance. Our style may be casual, but our attitude toward making disciples should never be. Our own spiritual well-being and that of others may be at stake. We cannot afford to be lulled into complacency. Drowsy indifference about our ministry suggests we don't really think following Jesus is all that important.

We need to stay awake because our enemy is real and powerful. A few years ago when the circus came to town, I stood in front of the lions' cage and felt the ground shake when those big, ferocious creatures roared. They were well-fed, in a secure cage and I could see them clearly. It was still scary. Imagine a lion in the wild—a hungry, prowling predator. Do you think you could stay awake when you heard that roar? I do not think I could lie down for a little nap in that circumstance, do you? That's the picture the Bible presents of the devil—a roaring lion, seeking someone to devour. I have no intention of being a lion's lunch. I will avoid getting into a physical situation where that's possible. I should take greater care to be wide awake when our adversary is on the prowl.

Let's stay awake out there. Failing to do so could be the ultimate illustration of the truth in the old adage: "When you snooze, you lose."

Day 42, Mark 14

What's the most expensive gift you've ever given? Why did you give it? Perhaps it was a piece of exquisite jewelry, an automobile or maybe something even more costly. If it was a genuine gift, you probably gave it as an expression of your love.

Jesus was just a couple of days from giving the ultimate gift of his own life. He would give his body and blood for your sins, my sins, even the sins of those who would call out for his death and drive the nails into his hands. And he would do it for love.

But before all of that, before the rejection, treachery, denial, abandonment and abuse he would endure for us, one disciple who loved her Master did something as a gift to him. Mark doesn't call her by name, but we know from John it was Mary (sister of Martha and Lazarus) who did it. At a dinner in Simon the leper's house, she anointed Jesus with pure nard (an expensive fragrant ointment imported from the Far East). The gift was extravagant. The witnesses estimated the ointment was worth more than a year's wages. She broke the flask, holding none of the gift in reserve, and poured all the ointment on Jesus' head.

The people who saw it, even the other disciples, were upset over what they called "waste." They were quick to point out the practical good that could have been done with the proceeds from the sale of the perfume. They scolded Mary for her extravagant demonstration of love.

Jesus defended her, saying what she had done was "beautiful." He said she had done what she could, and counted it as anointing his body for burial, another chilling reminder of events that lay just ahead. He predicted the story of her love would be told along with the story of his love all over the world.

Have you ever had occasion to do something very costly out of love for the Lord Jesus? Can you understand Mary's heart and motive for doing what she did? Then you may know that not everyone appreciates or commends sacrificial giving. There are far more critics than people willing to give. When you give your time, talent or treasure, do not be surprised if you are criticized or if your motives are questioned. But know and believe that Jesus receives such gifts and sees the beauty of sacrificing something out of love for him. Trust that nothing you give out of love for Jesus is ever wasted. The indignant critics may suggest pious-sounding alternatives that could have been chosen. But take comfort and find joy in knowing when you do what you can for the Lord, he acknowledges and remembers it.

Day 43, Mark 15

The story of the crucifixion is told in somber understatement by the gospel writers. Perhaps it was unnecessary to describe crucifixion in graphic terms to the first readers of the gospel because of their tragic familiarity with that method of execution. But the accounts of violence inflicted on Jesus in those final hours of his life leading up to his death on the cross are not sensationalized. The events themselves are sufficiently dramatic that a straightforward account conveys plenty of intensity.

I think it's interesting to note some things Jesus did not do during the trial and crucifixion. When the chief priests were making multiple accusations against him before Pilate, Jesus answered Pilate's direct question about whether or not he was the King of the Jews by saying, "You have said so." But then Jesus amazed Pilate by offering no other response to the priests' charges. That would be difficult for most of us. We want to rise to our own defense when we are accused. If the charges are false, we want to deny them. Even if they're true, we want to explain. But Isaiah had long before predicted he wouldn't open his mouth to the accusers, and he didn't.

It's also amazing that Jesus didn't retaliate when the soldiers were mocking him. They ridiculed and abused him for sport. But Jesus didn't call for the angel legions. He didn't strike them blind or dead. Peter would later describe it: "When he was reviled, he did not revile in return; when he suffered, he did not threaten...." He also explained how Jesus was able to do this: "he continued entrusting himself to him who judges justly." When we think we're being mistreated because of our relationship to Christ (and even when we really are), we are not enduring more than he did on our behalf. When we want to repay evil with evil, his incredible example of forbearance should instruct and restrain us.

Was the real "last temptation of Christ" in the words of the chief priests and scribes who taunted Jesus on the cross? They suggested if he was the Christ, he should come down from the cross to save himself and prove his claim to them. When the thieves on either side were joining the chorus of mockery, must it not have been tempting to pull one hand free, then the other, and pull the plug on the mission of redemption? The hard-hearted, self-righteous religious leaders had repeatedly demanded a sign, ignoring the plentiful evidence provided by the undeniable miracles done in their presence. True to their rejection to the very last, they taunted a tortured, dying man, spewing out their hatred, forgetting the dignity of their high positions. But he stayed on the cross, and died for their sins. He didn't come down from the cross.

Truly, the things Jesus did were astounding. But it's also amazing to think about the things he didn't do.

Day 44, Mark 16

Most Bible readers know something about the resurrection. A casual acquaintance with Jesus' story would likely include some knowledge of the empty tomb and the fear and astonishment it brought to the first disciples to discover it. Because we've had a lot longer to think about it, it's not fair to judge the disciples whose first response to the resurrection news was unbelief.

True, Jesus told them (many times) it was going to happen. True, Mary Magdalene should have been a reliable witness, since she knew Jesus and the disciples knew her. Even after the next witnesses confirmed what Mary said, the disciples still didn't believe.

Perhaps the traumatic past three days had clouded their thinking. From the arrest in the garden to the trial, crucifixion and burial, it had spiraled down from bad to worse. Judas had killed himself. They had run away or watched what happened from a distance. Maybe the horror of witnessing the torture and death of Jesus left them so numb they couldn't remember all Jesus had said.

The women who went to the tomb did not expect Jesus to be gone. They brought the spices to finish the burial, not to check on the resurrection. The disciples were gathered to mourn his death, not to celebrate his resurrection. Mary's news and the other early reports that came to the disciples were incredible in the truest sense of that word. After Jesus appeared to the eleven, he rebuked them because they had refused to believe the first eyewitnesses. It's interesting that the eleven would become witnesses themselves, telling others the same good news as Jesus sent them out to preach the gospel.

What can we take away from all this? For one thing, let's take it easy on Thomas. He's not mentioned here, but in John we learn he was missing the first time the apostles saw Jesus. He refused to believe it until he saw it for himself. That's no different from any of his apostolic brothers, is it? They didn't believe the first reports, either. It seems unfair to call him Doubting Thomas. (Jesus told Thomas there was a blessing for those who believed without seeing. That includes you and me.)

Also, let's give people time to examine the evidence and sort out what they think when they hear about Jesus' death and resurrection. Across the Roman Empire, audiences scoffed at the story of a God who died and dismissed the story of the resurrection as folly. It takes time to process the information.

And let's take courage if we've ever struggled in our faith. The apostles overcame their initial unbelief to be bold preachers of the resurrection. Peter had denied Jesus, but the angel specifically sent word to him that Jesus would meet him in Galilee. We are blessed with plenty of evidence to come to faith. Faith in the resurrection should change us and motivate us, just as it did the first followers.

Luke

Day 45, Luke 1

Who can imagine Gabriel's "to do" list? We don't know all he does, but we do know God sent him to Daniel to explain some visions. In today's portion, Gabriel is on duty as a messenger again with these interesting assignments: "Go to the temple in Jerusalem and tell Zechariah, an old priest, that he and his old wife Elizabeth are going to be the parents of Messiah's forerunner. Then go to Nazareth and tell a young virgin named Mary she will have a baby who will be the Son of God." That's not exactly your everyday routine list of errands, even for an angel.

After Gabriel's interview with Zechariah, the old man was rendered mute until all Gabriel told him came true. Gabriel gave him the silent treatment after Zechariah questioned and explained why the message from the angel couldn't be right. Mary also asked a question when Gabriel brought her big news, but she wasn't silenced for doing so. Why the difference?

I think it's because their questions came from different places of the heart. Gabriel said Zechariah didn't believe. Elizabeth said Mary was blessed because she did believe the angel's message to her from the Lord.

I'm not saying Zechariah was a bad person or an unbeliever. On the contrary, Luke tells us that he and Elizabeth were both righteous before God. They walked (lived) in obedience to God's commands. But he did not believe what Gabriel said about the baby. So Gabriel muzzled him for a few months, setting up a dramatic confirmation of the name the boy was to be given. On the other hand, Mary didn't know how she, a virgin, could conceive a child. Gabriel used the example of how Elizabeth was too old, but nevertheless was expecting a baby, because nothing is impossible with God. Mary was so full of trust in God that she said, "I am the servant of the Lord; let it be to me according to your word."

Which are you more like, Zechariah or Mary, when it comes to trusting God about something he says that you don't fully comprehend? Do you explain why that can't be right in your circumstances? Or do you humbly say, "I trust you, Lord. Do just what you're saying in my yielded life"?

You may be thinking of another thing Gabriel has on his to do list: blowing the trumpet that will signal the second coming of Christ and the end of the world. Did you know the Bible doesn't actually say that? That might be an interesting subject for another day. But when whoever blows the final trumpet does so, I want to have lived like Mary—believing and trusting God's word, even if I don't fully understand it, and submitting myself to him and his plan for me. Then, like her, we'll have a fabulous song of praise for God's goodness to us, too.

Day 46, Luke 2

The birth of Jesus is a celebration of the certainty of God's word. The prophecies were fulfilled and the promises came true. He was born in Bethlehem, to a virgin, when the time came. The details such as finding the baby wrapped in swaddling cloths and lying in a manger are "correct" because everything God had said about it in advance was "correct."

Some of the "as it had been told" things about the birth of Jesus were just a few hours old when they were verified—the angels' words to the shepherds, for instance. Other details had been spoken months in advance, such as Mary and Joseph being told the baby's name would be Jesus before he was conceived in the womb. Had old Simeon been waiting for years, decades maybe, for the glimpse of the Christ he knew he would see before he died? And the promises kept when Jesus was born had been stacking up for centuries! Adam and Eve, Abraham, David and all the prophets had heard he was coming for so long. When the time was exactly right, God sent Jesus into the world, just as he said.

Of course the birth of Jesus shows us that God loves us. But it also certifies the trustworthiness of God's word. All the other prom-

Like Israel's prophets, John called for changed lives as evidence of changed hearts. Repentance is proved in practical, everyday conduct, not in minute points of doctrinal orthodoxy. When the people asked what the message of repentance meant to them, John told them to share with people in need. He told them not to cheat, and not to misuse authority. That's what Isaiah, Malachi and the other prophets had called Israel to do, exposing their ritual worship as hypocrisy because their lives did not match their worship and professions. Like the old prophets, John insisted on a practical, observable difference in someone who believes and turns to God.

John's plain speech was also like the prophets. Not all preachers will stand before powerful people and say exactly what God tells them to say. Imagine calling the religious elite a "brood of vipers." People who trusted their physical kinship to Abraham did not like to hear that God could raise up children for Abraham from the stones. John said God's axe was on the root of Israel's tree, and the fruitless nation was headed for the fire. He rebuked the king's sin. Like his predecessors, John went to prison and died for speaking God's truth to powerful people who did not want to hear it.

John also reminds us of the old prophets by pointing to Jesus. The ancient prophets spoke about one who would come centuries later, specifying details about his birth, life, work, death and resurrection. John stood at the end of that line and had the privilege of identifying Messiah to his contemporaries. He vividly described God's judgment of those who rejected heaven's message delivered by heaven's messenger.

When John baptized Jesus, the Father's voice and the visible presence of the Holy Spirit validated Jesus' identity and John's identification of him. Messiah had come, just as the prophets said. The kingdom was at hand. And John, at the end of a centuries-long line of witnesses, pointed to his carpenter cousin and told the nation, "Behold the Lamb of God."

Day 48, Luke 4

The word "authority" produces a reflexive resistance from some people who hear it. Perhaps those who react this way have suffered abuse at the hands of an authority figure. Some parent, school official, boss or church leader so misused their authority that the victim now recoils with anxiety and dread whenever the subject is introduced. I've known a couple of people like that. I've also known some people who were bent on rebellion and despised any sense of authority that might restrain them, much like a two year-old's insolent refusal to do what Mommy says.

Most of us know authority is not a bad thing. We want and need some authority structure in our lives. We're not fans of anarchy. We know the weak will be victimized by the strong without the restraining influence of authority.

It's interesting that Satan offered to give Jesus authority over all the kingdoms of the world. Some people think what he offered Jesus was his to give after Adam and Eve abdicated their rule over creation in the Garden of Eden. Others say since Satan always lies, he was offering Jesus something that was not his to give.

If anyone who ever lived on earth had authority, Jesus did. The crowds who heard him speak marveled at his authoritative teaching. Unlike the religious teachers they were accustomed to hearing, Jesus didn't just quote what other rabbis had said. He sounded like the "author" himself, and of course, he was. As he responded with the word of God to every temptation Satan put before him, it was as if the one wielding the sword had forged it himself. And of course, he had done so. When demons and disease left at his command, it seemed to the people who witnessed these miracles that the very power of God at work. And of course, it was.

If anyone ever modeled both the perfect use of authority and submission to it, Jesus did that, too. Jesus, whose words and works were so authoritative, was himself submissive to the leading of God's Holy Spirit. He went to the wilderness when the Spirit led him there to face the tempter. He came back from the wilderness into Galilee under the Spirit's power. When he spoke in the synagogue at Nazareth, Jesus knew the Spirit of the Lord was upon him. When he went to a desolate place and people came to him and tried to make him stay with them, Jesus told them he had to go other places because that was the purpose for which he had come. He was conscious of a God-given purpose guiding his actions.

In matters of using and submitting to authority, Jesus is our perfect example. We would do well to study and imitate him about this and every other part of life.

Day 49, Luke 5

After Jesus borrowed Peter's boat for a pulpit, the carpenter took the fishermen out to catch some fish. It went against conventional fishing wisdom, and followed a frustrating night of failure. The fishermen were cleaning the nets to try again the next night. But Peter, because Jesus said so, went out into the deep and let down the nets again. In a way fishermen would understand, Jesus told them, "I can do what you can't." Soon, the nets were breaking, and the boats were sinking. Peter fell down in fear and astonishment at Jesus' knees (was the boat knee-deep in fish?) and acknowledged the holiness of Jesus. When they returned to shore, that demonstration of Jesus' power led a group of professional fishermen to leave the catch of a lifetime behind to follow him.

The disciples saw the power displayed in awesome ways in the following days. In compassionate response to the pleas of a leper, Jesus touched the unclean man (how long had it been since the afflicted man had been touched?), said he was clean, and he was. When the friends of a paralyzed man tore through the roof to get their friend to Jesus, everyone was amazed when the fellow got up, rolled up his mat and walked home.

Not everyone was thrilled by the displays of power or by the things he said. When Jesus told the paralyzed man his sins were forgiven, the Pharisee observers were unwittingly close to confessing Jesus as God. They said, "Who is this who speaks blasphemies? Who can forgive sins but God alone?" They were so close! But their preconceived notions about their righteousness and what Messiah should be kept them from connecting the obvious dots about his identity. They separated themselves from the "sinners," but Jesus called a tax collector to be one of his disciples, and then had the audacity to go to a party at his house with all his sinner friends. Jesus explained it to them, but they couldn't fathom associating with such sinful people.

Two general reactions to these remarkable displays of power and wisdom emerge in Luke's narrative. He described the first general reaction among the public with words such as astonishment, amazement, awe and glorifying God. People were celebrating and admitting they had seen extraordinary things. The disciples were a special category of positive response, leaving behind the lives and livelihoods they knew to follow this Galilean. But the Pharisees had a different reaction. They accused Jesus of blasphemy. They grumbled about his associations and demanded that he conform to their frame of reference and practice.

As you read the story and see the polar opposite responses to Jesus, which do you think yours would have been had you been there? Which response is showing in your life right now? Are you following him?

Day 50, Luke 6

God gave the Sabbath to Israel to teach them to rest and trust in him. As given, the Sabbath was a great blessing. But the Jews turned the blessing into a burdensome curse. They made up hundreds of traditional rules to interpret the law, and made their traditions and interpretations equal to the law itself. Sabbath observance became a merit badge, proof of the good Sabbath keeper's devout righteousness.

No wonder the Sabbath became a lightning rod issue between Jesus and the Pharisees. The disciples were getting a snack, not harvesting a crop when the Pharisees accused them. When Jesus and his disciples didn't follow their traditions, the Pharisees accused them of law-breaking. Jesus responded that David and his men ate the bread of the Presence (when it was technically "unlawful" for anyone but a priest to do so). He cited the example to show that ceremonial laws were not absolute and arbitrary in matters of human necessity. I don't know if they understood his point or not. But I suspect they got it when Jesus said the Son of Man (a messianic title from Ezekiel) was lord of the Sabbath. He was claiming to be greater than their favorite command!

The Jewish leaders had not accused Jesus of Sabbath-breaking earlier when he cast a demon out of a man in the synagogue at Capernaum. But now Jesus' Sabbath activities became opportunities to find fault and accuse him. Jesus didn't evade the issue. Knowing he was being watched, he told the man with the withered hand to stand. He then focused attention on the real issue: "Is it lawful on the Sabbath to do good or to do harm, to save life or to destroy it?" Then he spoke to the man, telling him to stretch out his hand, and it was restored. He technically did not "work" on the Sabbath; he only spoke. But it was enough. The Pharisees were furious, and started making plans to get rid of Jesus.

Meticulous Sabbath observance is not a burning issue for us today. But some principles do apply. We could make the same error the Pharisees made by judging and condemning people who do not follow our emphases and interpretations. Jesus was sinless. He always obeyed God's law. The Pharisees were wrong when they accused him of doing something unlawful.

Let's remember the Law could never justify flawed, weak human beings. It convicts, but cannot redeem. It shows our sin, but cannot save us from its condemnation. If righteousness could have been legislated, there would have been no need for Jesus to come and die on the cross. We need to remember these things when we're tempted to trust our goodness or obedience as the basis for our justification. Obey God out of love. Obey him out of gratitude. Obey him out of reverence and awe. But don't ever think you obey him to earn his favor.

Day 51, Luke 7

Since faith plays such a vital role in a Christian's life, I'm very interested in the faith of the centurion and the faith of the sinful woman, whose stories bookend this chapter. Jesus bragged on this Gentile soldier's faith, saying he had not found such faith among the

Israelites. What was it about the centurion's faith that Jesus commended? The Lord said the sinful woman's faith had saved her. Why?

The centurion's faith was based on what he had heard about Jesus. That's like you and me, and all who hear the gospel and believe the testimony about Jesus. He had a problem he couldn't solve. His servant was dying. This Roman heard that Jesus had helped people in similar situations. In humility, he did not make a demand or even go in person to see Jesus, but sent emissaries to ask for Jesus' help. The Jewish elders were commending this Gentile to Jesus when they said he was worthy, but the centurion himself sent word he was unworthy to have Jesus come into his house. He recognized the authority structure of Jesus' life—Jesus had authority over sickness and demons like the centurion had over his soldiers. Yet he also recognized that Jesus was under some higher authority, as he was to his superior officer. Jesus marveled at the man's faith and healed his servant without going to the house where the servant was sick.

The sinful woman didn't need Simon the Pharisee or anyone else to tell her about her problem. She knew she was a sinner who needed mercy from Jesus. Again, humility shines through, even in her bold actions. She came to Jesus with a flask full of ointment, eyes full of tears and a heart full of worship. Simon had been a rude host, neglecting to show common courtesy by providing water to wash dusty feet. But this woman, in deep humility, washed Jesus' feet with her tears, wiping them with her hair, kissing and anointing his feet with the ointment. She knew her debt was great, and the sense of pardon and hope she found at Jesus' feet released the floodgates of her worship.

Jesus explained the difference in the woman's adoration and Simon's discourtesy with a story about two forgiven debtors, noting that the one who got more forgiven would love the forgiver more. To the woman who'd heard plenty of condemnation, Jesus spoke forgiveness. Simon's guests questioned who could say such a thing, but Jesus dismissed the woman in peace, assuring her she was loved and forgiven.

Sometimes Jesus' compassion led him to do things, such as raising the widow's son at Nain, without any request or comment about the faith of the people involved. But sometimes he said or did something specifically in response to someone's faith. Whenever he compliments or comments on the faith of the people he's blessing, I want to have a faith like theirs.

Day 52, Luke 8

"For nothing is hidden that will not be made manifest, nor is anything secret that will not be known and come to light." It's reasonable to expect the one who knew the secrets of the hearts and was himself the light of the world to bring secret things to light.

Jesus spoke in parables to reveal the secrets of the kingdom to his followers, but to conceal them from the hard-hearted rejecters. When he explained the parables to the disciples, the mysterious realm of the spiritual and eternal became as real to them as the everyday matters of sowing seeds and gathering harvests. The potential was in all the seed; the condition of the hearts into which it fell determined the success or failure of the crop.

When Jesus asked questions, it was to clarify the situation for the people involved, revealing the truth they needed to see. To terrified disciples who thought they were about to drown, he asked, "Where is your faith?" even as he rebuked the threatening wind. To the demon possessed man of the Gerasenes, he asked "What is your name?" In the press of the crowd, Jesus asked "Who was it that touched me?" Jesus was not seeking information unknown to him when he asked such questions. All these and others he asked brought secret, hidden things to light. He saw the weakness of the disciples' faith and the strength of the woman's. Everything is manifest to him.

Some are called by name, others are not, but the women who supported Jesus and his disciples are forever remembered for their personal, practical support of the mission. Although their role would be viewed by some as secondary or behind the scenes, it became manifest, well-known, when Luke wrote it down for Theophilus and for the ages.

The good news about the kingdom and his mighty demonstrations of power were just impossible to keep quiet. The man who had been possessed by demons became a living manifestation of the power of Jesus as he modeled his new way of life and told people throughout the city how much Jesus had done for him. The woman who was healed when she touched his garment came forward to explain why she did it and what happened when she did it. And though the little girl's parents were told not to tell, how long do you think it took for the news of the little girl's return from death to be known among those who were so sure she was dead they had laughed at Jesus when he said she was sleeping?

Today, know that the condition of your heart soil, the strength of your faith and the faithfulness of your quiet service are manifest to him. Know that the Master of the elements, of demons, of disease and of death itself sees you, knows you and will make everything known.

Day 53, Luke 9

Talk about the cross was not vague metaphor to the Jews under Roman occupation in Palestine. Many Jews were crucified by the soldiers appointed to keep order among the local population. The people in the towns of Galilee and Judea were familiar with the gruesome sight. When Jesus talked about "taking up the cross," no one would have associated his words with a fashion statement or a jewelry fad. An execution device is not a likely candidate to become a fashion accessory in the context where its function as an instrument of death is well-known.

So when Jesus talked about taking up the cross and said he was headed to the cross himself, anyone who heard his words would have known he was talking about death. The first conditions of becoming a follower of Jesus are to deny self, take up the cross and follow him. His words challenge something central within those who would follow him. There must be surrender—a resignation occurs before a new disciple falls in step behind his leader. Those who balk at the first step aren't likely to go along with the rest of his requirements for discipleship.

When the disciples weren't able to help the demon-possessed boy and his father, it was because they were relying on their power, trying to do the work of God with human strength. They quarreled about who was greatest and tried to keep others from serving in Jesus' name. As they clamored for high position and exclusive monopoly over who could and couldn't work in his name, it was obvious they were still preoccupied with themselves. Their threatening words against the Samaritans show they were still too caught up in self to have a heart of compassion like Jesus for Jew and Samaritan alike.

The potential disciples who professed commitment but wanted to limit it weren't ready to deny self. One made no reply after Jesus explained his impoverished lifestyle. The other two wanted "me first" things of one kind or another. No doubt Jesus' words about the dead burying the dead and who was unfit for the kingdom of God sounded harsh to some who heard them. I think the words were for shock value. They underscore the truth that Jesus and following Jesus must have undisputed, unlimited first priority in a disciple's life. Whatever or whoever gets ahead of Jesus in our hearts becomes our idol.

These first followers were just beginning to hear about Jesus' approaching death. They were learning about losing their lives to save them. It took bold courage to go against the grain of the religious establishment and identify with Jesus. The invitation, now two thousand years old, still challenges all would-be followers of Christ. Do we have the courage to deny self, take up the cross and follow him today?

Day 54, Luke 10

You're not ready to turn to Christ until you're ready to turn away from yourself. The lawyer who asked Jesus what he could do to inherit eternal life illustrates this point.

This lawyer was not an attorney, but an expert in the Law of Moses. His first question sounded noble enough, but the underlying motive was not—he wanted to put Jesus to the test. When Jesus responded with a question, the lawyer was the one facing a test. His response showed he had a good grasp of the law's requirements and was able to summarize the law in the same way Jesus did on another occasion. Quoting from the law, he said "Love God supremely, and love your neighbor as yourself." Jesus told him he was right, and then stated the problem we encounter, even when our understanding is correct:

"Do this and you will live." The problem is we don't always do what we know is right. Law can only reward exact and complete obedience. Anything short of perfect obedience inherits death, not life.

The lawyer's second question gets to the heart of the matter. He wanted to know, "Who is my neighbor?" Seeking to justify himself, he wanted to qualify the command and limit its scope so his conduct would be approved. He was looking for the loophole. Just how far did all this neighbor-loving go? Jesus didn't immediately expose the man's self-serving motives. He didn't define the terms and launch into a debate about what persons and relationships are governed by the law of loving neighbors. Instead he told a story in which an unlikely hero modeled the virtue of loving his neighbor. The unfortunate victim of the robbers may not have acted wisely, but he was still a neighbor. The command crossed racial and cultural lines, building a bridge over a history of hostility between Jews and Samaritans. Jesus contrasted the stranger's loving conduct with the indifference of two religious professionals who passed by without offering to help. The Samaritan invested time, money and effort to show love for a fellow human being in need. The priest and Levite saw the robbed man, but took no action. If they claimed to love their neighbor, they missed a good chance to show it.

Jesus finished his response to the man's second question with another question of his own: "Who proved to be a neighbor?" Again, the lawyer answered the question correctly, and the implications would come in Jesus' comment on his answer. He used the word "do" again, telling the lawyer to go and emulate the Samaritan's compassionate demonstration of love for his neighbor.

Forget the fine print and technicalities that might frustrate our quest for righteousness by law-keeping. The simplest statement of the law's requirement sets the bar so high that no one can "do" it for merit. That dissolves self-righteous pride and points us to a Savior in whose perfect obedience we can trust.

Day 55, Luke 11

It's no coincidence the disciples asked Jesus to teach them to pray after they saw and heard him pray. All rabbis taught their students to pray. But these followers saw and heard something in Jesus' prayers that made them want to pray like he did.

Have you ever considered how blessed we are that they asked, Jesus answered and Luke recorded what he said? Words we love, phrases that have comforted untold millions and the clearest instructions anywhere about how we should pray are here in these lines.

The simplicity of the prayer Jesus taught makes it an ideal pattern to keep in mind as we compose our own prayers. We should declare the greatness of God, submit ourselves to his sovereign rule and express our dependence on him to provide for our needs. Our lists of needs and requests fit in right after we exalt him and humble ourselves. That's compact and complete. While other passages teach about prayer and many books have been written on the subject, this model prayer is a concise summary.

Jesus included another point by adding a story to the example prayer. The message of the story is: "Persist! Don't stop praying!" The story is not saying God is annoyed like the man who finally got up to give his friend bread after repeated requests. Instead, Jesus contrasts the loving Father's delight in hearing and answering the requests of his children. We keep on asking, seeking and knocking, all the time trusting God's great love and wisdom to answer by granting what's best for us.

Have you evaluated your prayer life in light of this teaching? It's good to know and recite this prayer. But the real gift of it is learning how to pray your own prayers by following this basic template. Think about how these words can help you pray.

God is glorified and your confidence in him grows when you magnify his name! When you do a good job with this part of the prayer, you see God as very big and powerful. You won't hesitate to ask about big or difficult things when God is magnified in your prayer.

It's good to remember that he is God in control and you are not. Praying about his kingdom rule reminds you that you want his will to be done in this world and in your life. Come in humble submission to him, surrendering your whole life to his reign.

Don't forget to ask for what you need. Yes, he already knows, but it's good for you to ask. It reminds you of your dependence and instills gratitude for what you've already received. And don't be shy about asking again and again. God isn't hassled by your requests; he's honored by them.

Have you prayed this way, on purpose, every day, for some period of time? Why not try it today and this week? It might transform your prayers forever.

Day 56, Luke 12

Every day we're told the same lie. It comes to us meticulously crafted, appealingly packaged and maddeningly repeated. "You need, you lack, you could have more; your life is pathetically limited and less than cool as long as you do not have our product. People will like you if you use our product. Our product will make you an object of desire. You're not really living if you don't have what we're selling. And we accept all major credit cards."

We think we're too sophisticated to fall for it. But we find ourselves caught up in the idea we need more—more to be happy, more to enjoy life. So we spend and buy on credit and mortgage our future to acquire things, chasing the elusive butterfly of fulfillment and significance. The next gadget, the newest model, the boldest fashion—surely some of it will make us feel complete and validated.

And it's so easy these days! One of my favorite online merchants has "one-click shopping." I just click the mouse, and my next purchase is on its way to me.

Jesus offered a vaccination against the insidious, creeping plague of materialism in his warning: "Take care, and be on your guard against all covetousness, for one's life does not consist in the abundance of his possessions." He exposed the fallacy of thinking that real fulfillment or meaning can be bought, sold or acquired in a material thing.

It's easier to see how others are believing the lie than to realize our own vulnerability. We shake our heads at sad stories about wealthy people who are not happy. We see people desperate to get more, because they're not content with what they have. But how many of us who know what Jesus said are also struggling with too much debt and confused priorities, unsure of what we want, but eager to get the next thing?

The rich man made several errors in judgment. He thought a lot about himself. He thought security could be stored in a barn. He thought material things could satisfy his soul. He thought he was going to be around a long, long time to enjoy all he had amassed. According to Jesus, the man was laying up treasure for himself instead of being rich toward God.

All this has a very modern, contemporary feel, doesn't it? The rich man's values are the values of many people in the world and in the church today. People really haven't changed much in 2,000 years. Technology has advanced, bringing more and more sophistication to the things we collect and our methods of acquiring them. But we're still susceptible to the painful emptiness of trying to find meaning and life in the things we call our own. Jesus offers real significance to his followers. But he says lasting satisfaction is found in self-denial, not self-fulfillment. Abundant living is in relationship with him, not in a pile of possessions.

Day 57, Luke 13

How could Israel miss the Messiah their prophets had been talking about for centuries? How could Jesus tell them they were in danger of being left outside, looking in at Gentiles enjoying the banquet with Abraham, Isaac and Jacob in the kingdom? What was causing the gap between Jesus and the Jewish leaders to grow deeper and wider? There are several clues in this passage.

The Jewish leaders had rejected John's message and were rejecting Jesus because the keynote of both men's preaching was "Repent." Jesus stressed the alternative to repentance was perishing. The Jews viewed the tragic deaths of the people they cited as evidence something was amiss in the lives of those unfortunate individuals. But Jesus said the victims were no worse sinners than anyone else, and called everyone to repent.

The story of the barren fig tree points to the spiritual barrenness Jesus had found among the Israelites, the long time God had been patient with them, and the short time his patience would continue. The door of opportunity was closing. Their fruitlessness would bring God's judgment on them.

The legalist Jews despised Jesus because they despised grace. Jesus healed the woman in the synagogue on the Sabbath who had been afflicted by a disabling spirit for 18 years. But the ruler of the synagogue did not share her joy or join in the praise. He indignantly chastised the people for coming to be healed on the Sabbath! Jesus exposed the hypocrisy of the "no healing on the Sabbath" point of view, showing they cared more about an animal than a suffering human being.

The kingdom was coming. It would spring up and grow like a plant from a seed thrown out into the garden. It would spread like leaven spreads through flour in which it is placed. It was coming whether the Pharisees and other Jewish leaders wanted it to or not. It was coming and would include people the Jews could not imagine in it. And when the kingdom came, it would be too late for those who had rejected the king.

The very heart of God toward these stubborn, unwilling people is in Jesus' words of lament over Jerusalem: "How often would I have gathered your children together as a hen gathers her brood under her wings, and you would not!" That sad cry also summarized why they were not going to be in the kingdom. God was willing, but they were not.

Day 58, Luke 14

Can you sense the irony in the controversies between the Pharisees and Jesus? The one who was holy was judged unholy by people who thought they were holy. The Lawgiver was accused of law-breaking by people who thought they were law-keepers. When Jesus healed on the Sabbath, it was a double insult to them. He was not honoring their tradition, and every public miracle affirmed the truth they were denying. Jesus of Nazareth was the Messiah. But they sought to discredit and destroy him because he did not fit their theology.

One Sabbath day at a leading Pharisee's home, where the Jewish leaders were watching, Jesus asked a question to focus the controversy. I doubt the man with dropsy would have been on the Pharisee's guest list. His condition made him ceremonially unclean, and contact with him would have defiled them, according to their thinking. Was it a set-up, to catch Jesus in another Sabbath violation? Jesus wasn't seeking a ruling from them when he asked, "Is it lawful to heal on the Sabbath, or not?" It was time to press the issue, and Jesus would not back down. He healed the fellow and sent him away. Then he exposed their hypocrisy and selfishness by citing their own exception. An emergency (such as an ox in a well) allowed some leniency in the prohibition against working on the Sabbath. The Pharisees couldn't reply, but it was clear—they cared more about an ox than a person.

Jesus showed the foolish risk of self-promotion by noting some dinner guests clamoring for the best seats. Seeking honor, they were humiliated when the host gave their place to another guest. Perhaps he said this for his disciples' benefit, too, since they often quarreled about being the greatest in the kingdom. Isn't it still hard for us to believe what Jesus said about humility being the way to exaltation?

Jesus also unmasked the selfishness of many hosts who seemed to be hospitable and generous when they invited dinner guests. But the guests were equals who could reciprocate. Jesus advised inviting outcasts, down-on-their-luck poor people who could never repay. He said God would bless and repay such hospitality.

The people who rejected the banquet invitation dishonored the host by their selfishness. The master filled his banquet with people the Pharisees would never invite. The substitute guests could not boast; they were beggars, there only by grace.

Self-preservationists in the crowd found the cost of following Jesus too high. Family, possessions, even one's own life must come after allegiance to Jesus. It's tempting to make this denial a nice metaphor, but Jesus' words are clear. He demands first place love and allegiance. A disciple lacking devotion is like salt lacking saltiness—good for nothing.

The call to selfless surrender still thins the crowd today. We may deceive ourselves, but Jesus knows our hearts and sees if we're willing to pay the price to follow him.

Day 59, Luke 15

Does grace upset you? Your answer depends on how you see yourself. Jesus attracted tax collectors and sinners who knew they were unworthy and broken. But the Pharisees (who saw themselves as righteous) grumbled when Jesus associated with people they despised. Their "righteousness" prohibited contact with such sinners, lest their "holiness" be defiled.

In three stories, Jesus showed how the Pharisees who imagined themselves very near God were really far from him. Teachers often liken the intensive search for the lost sheep and coin to God's great quest to restore sinners. I don't think that's the point. The stories contrast the Pharisees' concern for lost things with heaven's concern for lost people, and the Pharisees' joy at finding a lost sheep or coin with heaven's joy when a sinner repents. The Pharisees cared more about possessions than people. They were not like God at all.

In the same way, "The Prodigal Son" isn't really about the younger boy. It's not even about the father, except to show the difference between him and the older brother. The Pharisees were the targets of the story, and the older son's actions and attitudes mirrored theirs toward sinners and Jesus who accepted them. The older brother represents the Pharisees whose duty to God was cold and loveless. They were distanced from their 'sinner' brothers, but they were also far from the loving Father. They thought service earned something, that God owed them for obedience. They failed to see what they wanted for their service was theirs to receive as sons. But that would relate them to the brothers who received it by grace, and they could not stand that. They saw their brothers' sin, but denied their own. They resented God's grace that invites and celebrates our repentance.

We identify with the prodigal or the father, based on our experience. Every sinner who knows he's a sinner can see himself in the prodigal. No wonder he's the title character. His folly reflects what sin has cost us. Our hope of restoration lies in the Father's grace for returning prodigals. We who are parents feel our hearts beating in sync with the father's great heart. We love our children so much! We want them to know and rejoice in our love for them. But we need to get the point of the story. The older brother shows that God's acceptance is not granted as compensation for our service, but because we are his children. Self-righteousness is the way of misery, pouting outside the party, refusing to embrace the unreasonable extravagance of grace.

So let's shed some tears as we identify with the wasteful, rebellious son. Then let's dry those tears and rejoice in the Father's willingness to receive us when we return to our senses and come home from the far country. But let's keep the poisonous plant of self-righteousness from taking root in our hearts. Its ugly fruit is judging our brothers, despising grace and distancing ourselves from the Father's love.

Day 60, Luke 16

It's a story right out of today's papers, but Jesus told it 2,000 years ago. Graft and corruption are nothing new. Wasteful mismanagement of entrusted funds has been going on a long time. When the boss found out about his manager's dishonesty, he fired the guy and ordered a review of the accounts. The clever fellow in this story created his parachute by further cheating his master, discounting accounts receivable, so his partners in the deception would "owe" him after he was fired. That's the one detail from the story Jesus chose to apply to his disciples—using money in a way to make friends. But Jesus suggests using material things to spiritual advantage, using wealth (which is temporary) to help bring people into the kingdom of God, so that when you leave this material world there will be friends waiting to welcome you in eternity

Did Jesus commend the shrewd dishonest manager? The servant's master in the story did, but I don't think Jesus told the story to commend shrewdness, but rather to contrast the thinking and conduct of the dishonest manager with what he was commending—faithfulness.

Jesus' words about faithfulness are sobering. We're fooling ourselves if we think we'd handle more differently than we handle less. The material things we're given to manage in this world are not true riches compared to what the Lord says is waiting for us in eternity.

The things we hold in this world do not even belong to us. Money is a heart check to find out if we really love God most of all.

People of God's kingdom should not be surprised when people of the world do not understand and even ridicule our perspectives on material wealth. The Pharisees, who judged by externals such as riches, ridiculed Jesus' financial advice. When Jesus told the story of the rich man and Lazarus, the first hearers would have been shocked at the idea that a son of Abraham and a wealthy one at that would not be in the kingdom of God. (We could easily misapply the story and make the opposite misjudgment, thinking it was the beggar's poverty that brought him reward, and that all the wealthy will share this rich man's fate.) Jesus told the story to show the Pharisees their tendency to judge by externals and not the heart would lead them to wrong judgments.

Are you faithful in managing what God has put into your hands? Many of us ask to be entrusted with more. Are you showing by your faithfulness that you're ready for more? If you've made a career and maybe a life out of being shrewd, wouldn't you rather be known for your faithfulness? Are you using your material wealth to do spiritual good? Do you judge by externals like the Pharisees? It's smart to re- member that God looks at the heart, and his values are not the values of the world around us.

Day 61, Luke 17

After Cain killed Abel, God asked the first murderer where his brother was. Do you remember Cain's retort? "I do not know; am I my brother's keeper?" Genesis does not tell us God's direct answer to that insolent question, but Jesus' words about stumbling blocks and forgiveness remind us the answer is "Yes." He addressed two issues about sin in the lives of others where we have responsibility. Every individual is accountable to God for his or her actions. But God also made us to live in community with mutual responsibilities toward those with whom we share our lives.

One of those responsibilities is a "don't" and the other is a "do." The negative one is to do nothing that would cause another person to sin. As Jesus said, temptations to sin are inevitable. We live in flesh in a fallen world. We have an adversary who wants to delude and destroy us if he can. But Jesus pronounced a woe on those who become stumbling stones to others. No follower of Jesus should ever be the stumbling block in anyone's path. We should never discourage anyone who wants to do right, and we should never lead anyone to do wrong. Jesus didn't specify in this place what terrible fate awaits those who cause others to stumble. But he did say it would be better to be drowned by having a big rock tied around your neck and being tossed into the sea.

Not only does Jesus say we should avoid causing others to fall, he also gave a positive duty: restore those who do sin. He gave three challenging commands to accomplish this—rebuke the sinner, forgive him and repeat the process as necessary. Rebuking someone is not simply "getting them told" about what they've done; it's helping them see that what they've done is wrong and encouraging them to turn away from the sin. The Pharisees were good at finding sin in others, but restoration was not their goal. Forgiving others is a necessary part of our own spiritual well-being. But it's also an important part of restoring someone who has sinned against us.

In between these two admonitions, Jesus said, "Pay attention to yourselves!" This is essential to obeying both parts of watching out for one another. We avoid causing others to sin by guarding our own words and actions. And our attempts to restore others have no credibility when we're not monitoring our own lives.

Why are we supposed to be our brother's (or our sister's) keeper? One reason is that sin and its consequences are serious. Also, we are all susceptible to influence. But the best reason why we should look out for one another is because Jesus said to do it. Our culture values independence and privacy, but no follower of Jesus can opt out of the plan to look out for one another.

Day 62, Luke 18

Isn't it odd that religion, which seems to be a highway for approaching God, very often becomes a roadblock on our path to God? This is true because human pride sees an opportunity in the ritual of religion to perform, to earn, to merit approval by getting it right and doing it well and often. It's true in many churches today. It was true among the most diligent practitioners of religion in the days when Jesus walked among them.

The controversy between Jesus and the religious establishment with all the accusations about Sabbath breaking, association with undesirables and loyalty to human tradition came down to this: the self-righteous spirit of the scribes and Pharisees would not allow them to receive the teaching of repentance from Jesus. Having no sense of being lost, they weren't looking for a Savior.

We learn from the context of some parables and the content of others that Jesus frequently addressed the Pharisees in his stories. The story of the Pharisee and the tax collector who went to the temple to pray is especially pointed. One of the characters is named "the Pharisee." That wasn't very subtle, was it? And Luke's introduction to the story makes the original audience and intent of the story quite clear: "He also told this parable to some who trusted in themselves that they were righteous, and treated others with contempt."

Self-righteousness and contempt for others are companion vices. When one is present, the other is not far away. We're used to sound bites on the news telling us a lot about a person in only a few words. The same thing happens when we listen to a few words of the Pharisee's prayer. In about 30 words, he compared himself to others, made a catalogue of others' sins and called God's attention to his diligent execution of religious duty.

In contrast, the tax collector, a sinner of such disrepute to Pharisees that they had their own special category, was humble and broken about his own sinfulness when he prayed to God. He was not telling God how wonderful he was or how terrible other people were. His prayer was a simple plea for mercy and an acknowledgment of his need for it. And Jesus said the tax collector was the one who went home right with God. Jesus' kingdom principle of humiliation as the way to exaltation is at work in this story. One of the epistle writers would say, years later, "God resists the proud, but gives grace to the humble."

Where is your trust? What is your opinion of yourself? How do you see and treat others? These questions are interrelated in a dynamic way. What would a 30 word sound bite from your prayer tell us about your answers to these questions?

Day 63, Luke 19

Zacchaeus was an unlikely prospect for discipleship. But the tax collector was eager to see Jesus, and responded with joyful obedience when Jesus called him down from the sycamore tree. When Jesus came into his home and life and called him a son of Abraham, Zacchaeus was a changed man. He committed himself to generous charity and strict repayment of any fraudulent collections.

Zacchaeus' joy is set against the grumbling of some who were displeased (again) that Jesus was (again) associating with sinners. Jesus told them he was on task—he had come to seek and save the lost.

Jesus' story about the nobleman who went away to receive a kingdom meant the kingdom was indeed coming, but not yet. The story showed the polarization between the subjects who were trusted servants, and the rebels who said, "We do not want this man to reign over us." When the king returned, he rewarded the faithful and destroyed the enemies who rejected his authority. Jesus' foes probably got the point.

Even among the servants in the story, there is a dichotomy. Some of them took the money the master gave them and made a remarkable return on it while he was gone. One had a 1000% increase, another 500%. Both were commended and rewarded for their faithful efforts. But the master was not so pleased with every servant. One brought back what he had been given without any return on the master's investment. His fear kept him from acting, reflected an unhealthy attitude toward his master and robbed him of a reward.

I don't know all God has given you to use in serving him and others. I do know you are accountable for what you do with what you received. He has also commissioned us to do business until he comes. Do not allow fear and a negative attitude toward the Lord to keep you from serving him, being productive and receiving your reward!

I hope you are not bold enough to reject his rule over your life. He is Lord of all, whether we confess him or not. We will one day bow before him. We can do it now, be faithful servants and enjoy a reward. Or we can wait until we are forced to acknowledge him, when it will be too late to serve, and too late to be rewarded.

Our attitude toward grace will go a long way toward determining whether or not we'll be willing, productive servants of God. Are you aware of his grace in your life? Do you find joy in knowing that Jesus came to seek and save people like us? Or do you grumble over love and mercy being shown to undeserving sinners? Let's appreciate grace and be willing servants. The same grace that saves us will empower us to do what he calls us to do. Fear should not keep us from being faithful, productive servants.

Day 64, Luke 20

One night a few months ago, I was surprised to find Snow White on the front porch when I answered the doorbell. Later the Incredible Hulk and Barney stopped by. Dora the Explorer and the Power Rangers came to the door that night, too. I feigned mystification with each super hero or cartoon character that rang the bell. But I wasn't really fooled. I knew each visitor was a little kid in a costume, pretending to be someone else. They thought I'd never guess their true identity because of their clever disguises. But I saw through the ruse. Besides, they were all too short to be real princesses or ninja.

We expect neighborhood kids to wear costumes for Trick-or-Treat. But who would think the chief priests and leading scholars of Judaism would play masquerade? They wanted to destroy Jesus, but they feared the crowd who seemed to support him. So they sent play-actors, pretending to be sincere, trying to make Jesus say something they could use to accuse him before the Roman authorities. But Jesus perceived their craftiness and answered their questions, giving them no basis for an accusation.

It's ridiculous to try to trick Jesus, right? How can you fool someone who knows what you're thinking? But do we ever engage in the same game, pretending to be sincere when we're not?

How about worship? Have you ever attended church, sung the songs and bowed your head during prayer without even paying attention? Our praise songs can be as insincere as the compliments the spies heaped on Jesus. We can be present for the Lord's Supper, give our offering and look interested in what the preacher's saying, but be absent in mind and spirit. Maybe our play-acting fools our fellow congregants, but no one has ever fooled God.

How about repentance? Have you ever prayed for forgiveness with no intention of turning away from the sin? Have we ever been sorry, not for sinning against God, but for getting caught or for the consequences we brought on ourselves by disobeying him? God knows our hearts. There's no way to pretend we're sincere about turning from sin. We may even fool ourselves about this, but no one has ever fooled God.

How about the Lordship of Christ? It's one thing to say "Jesus is Lord," and quite another to deny ourselves and do what he tells us to do. Sometimes people fret about hypocrites in the church who say they're Christians, but don't live obedient lives. Don't worry. Hypocrites in churches today are as unmasked before Jesus as the ones in the temple and synagogues were 2,000 years ago. Our concern should not be with them, but with matching our own lives to our professions.

I gave the costumed kids the candy they came to collect, even though I knew they were not who they were pretending to be. The stakes are much higher for pretending before God. You can't afford to play that game.

Day 65, Luke 21

Is it a vase, or two profiles in silhouette? In another popular example, the ink drawing depicts an old woman; but upside down it looks like a beautiful young lady.

Different viewpoints aren't always optical illusions. To a stranger, Granny looks like an old woman. But to her children and grandchildren she is beautiful. An old dresser looks like a piece of worn-out junk to me, but my wife may see a valuable antique. Sometimes beauty truly is in the eye of the beholder.

I heard a story from years ago about an evangelist who left his family at home and rode a train across the country to preach in an evangelistic meeting. He arrived on Saturday evening, and was a guest in the home of one of the church's elders. After the Sunday morning service, they were having dinner at the elder's home. The table conversation came around to the contribution that morning. The elder had counted the money and reported with dramatic disdain that someone had the gall to put a single penny in the collection! With humility, the evangelist told the elder he was the one who had given the penny, and it was all the money he had after paying his own train fare to come to the revival.

Jesus said the widow who gave two small copper coins out-gave all the rich people who put their gifts in the offering box. No human accountant would be likely to see it the way Jesus saw it. But the Lord knew the woman was giving all she had to live on to the treasury (which probably supported her). It was generosity out of poverty, and it weighed a lot more with God than a token contribution from the wealthy. The size of a gift depends on the perspective from which it is viewed.

We shouldn't be surprised when God's perspective is different from ours. His thoughts and ways are higher than ours. He looks at the heart while we see what's outside. The disciples saw the magnificent temple, adorned with noble stones. Jesus saw forty years into the future and said not one of those stones would be left on top of another after the Romans destroyed Jerusalem. Jesus told the disciples that some of them would be put to death. Two sentences later he said, "But not a hair of your head will perish." From a human point of view, it's a contradiction. But the eternal Christ saw existence and well-being consisting of far more than life in this physical body.

Messiah's enemies would see death and destruction in the events Jesus foretold, but the persecuted disciples would see deliverance and vindication. The same cataclysmic occurrences would produce two very different outcomes, depending on perspective.

When you find yourself disagreeing with God, it's wise to try to "see it his way." By his grace, God offers us a better way to see him, ourselves and the world around us.

Day 66, Luke 22

In the borrowed upper room where he ate the last supper, Jesus told the disciples, "I have earnestly desired to eat this Passover with you before I suffer." I hear a longing in those words older than the hunger of that day or the anticipation of the week leading up to it. The longing was older than the time of his public ministry or even his life on earth. I can imagine God the Son watching Israel eat the Passover from the first time in Egypt down through the centuries, knowing the day was coming when he would become the real Passover, the Lamb of God slain to set God's people free.

Now, with the arrest just hours away, it had come down to an intimate meal with the men responsible for carrying out the mission. The Passover meal, rich for every Jew in the symbolic significance of each part of the ritual, unfolded with the cups of wine, the unleavened bread, the bitter herbs. And out of it, Jesus took two elements of the meal and infused them with rich new meaning. The bread and the wine would become a new meal with new significance to every disciple of Jesus. The bread was supposed to remind them of his body, which would be tortured in the hours to come as he endured multiple trials and the execution itself. The wine would remind them of his blood—blood of a new covenant between God and his people, blood shed to redeem. His memorial would not be a statue or a building, but a simple meal whose elements would recall his death for those who would partake of it.

Jesus shared the meal that night with the innermost circle of followers, the apostles. Was his heart breaking by knowing one of them would betray him with a kiss into his enemies' hands? Did their quarrel at the table that very night about who would be the greatest in the kingdom get on his nerves more than usual? Did Peter's boastful overestimation of his loyalty bring tears to his eyes? Later in the garden, they would sleep while he prayed in agony, and run away when the guards seized him.

We look back at that gathering in the upper room the night before the cross, and see not one of those who ate with Jesus that night deserved to be there. And we know that no one who gathers around to eat the Lord's Supper now deserves a place at the table, either. We, too, are guilty, self-centered and unworthy. But we, like they, are welcomed to eat, drink and remember. It was Jesus' earnest desire to accomplish our redemption, to do for us, in our place, what had to be done to atone for our sins. How can we be less than earnest about meeting with other ransomed ones to eat the bread and drink the wine of remembrance?

Day 67, Luke 23

To play politics, according to the dictionary, is "to act for political or personal gain rather than from principle." It's no compliment to say someone is playing politics. The lying shenanigans that surrounded the trial and execution of Jesus illustrate the unsavory side of politics.

The Jews despised the Romans who occupied their land. They wanted Messiah to free them from Rome's tyranny. But the chief priests put their hatred on hold when they needed Rome's authority to kill Jesus. They used phrases calculated to stir the governor's interest in what he could have dismissed as an ethnic quarrel over religious customs. The charges were lies, but they knew how to get Pilate's attention—"forbidding us to give tribute to Caesar...saying that he himself is Christ, a king...he stirs up the people." The Romans wanted no impediment to the revenue stream, no rival to Caesar's rule and no riots. The chief priests crafted the charges accordingly.

Pilate sent Jesus and his accusers across town to Herod when he heard Jesus was from Galilee. He handed off responsibility for hearing the charges against Jesus to the Idumean puppet king as a matter of jurisdiction. Herod found in Jesus nothing more than amusement—hoping for a miracle show, settling for contemptuous mockery. Their mutual distaste for dealing with Jesus became the basis for a new friendship between two politicians.

Pilate tried to appease the Jews by beating Jesus, torturing an innocent man for political gain. When that failed, he caved in to the shouting crowd, released Barabbas and ordered the crucifixion of Jesus to prevent open rebellion.

Not everyone who encountered Jesus that dark day was playing politics. The penitent thief defended Jesus from the insults of his fellow thief. Through the blood and humiliation, the thief saw a king who would come into his kingdom when no one else, not even the closest disciples, imagined the kingdom was still on Jesus' schedule.

Jesus recognized his faith and promised he would be with him that day in Paradise.

The centurion who took in the whole spectacle praised God and proclaimed Jesus' innocence. Joseph of Arimathea begged for Jesus' body and gave him a decent burial. Like the donkey Jesus had ridden into the city earlier in the week, Joseph's new tomb would only be borrowed for a little while and then returned. But Joseph didn't know that when he showed sympathy and respect for Jesus.

So the politicians used Jesus to further their own agendas. That still goes on in the world today. But all the political posturing missed the point of who he was and what his death would mean. The broken-hearted disciples gathered spices to finish the task of burying Jesus after the Sabbath. Joseph's tomb contained (at least for moment) the body of a man who was a victim of ruthless politics. Jesus' friends and foes alike thought it was all over. They were in for a big surprise.

Day 68, Luke 24

It's fun to watch the 24-hour cable news channels as news is breaking to see how they react to every scrap of information, trying to make meaning of it live on the air. Even when they're reporting something tragic, there is an almost comic side of the confusion that often accompanies the first reports of a story.

It is sometimes necessary to tell people who've been in an accident or suffered some other trauma the same things over and over again until the confusion clears. When we receive news either too bad or too good to believe, we want to hear it again, and maybe a third time, giving us a chance to make sense of what we're hearing.

I sense some of that in the disciples' reaction to the first reports of the resurrection. The angels' announcement and Jesus' own words to witnesses of his resurrection were messages of reminder and reassurance. Jesus had told them in advance he would be put to death and raised from the dead. He told them about it more than once. In the aftershock of the crucifixion, the disciples needed reorientation. They were broken-hearted and disappointed that their Master had been killed. Their hopes and dreams of the kingdom were shattered.

Their hearts had a hard time trusting their ears and eyes when they heard and saw that Jesus was back.

Why did the risen Lord conceal his identity for a while from the two men on the road to Emmaus? Perhaps it was to give the men time to process the interpretation of the Scriptures and grasp the necessity of the suffering before they were bowled over by the reality of the resurrection. Why did he vanish as soon as they recognized him? Maybe it was to get them up and back to Jerusalem within the same hour with the report of what they had experienced.

When Jesus appeared that same evening to the little nucleus of disciples, he greeted them, asked why they doubted and offered convincing proof that it was really him and he was really alive. He opened their minds to understand, and promised to empower them to go and tell the news among all nations.

Do you need reminding from time to time? Are you ever slow to believe what he's told you? Is there sometimes an apparent disconnect between what you hoped for and what happened? Do you long for him to open your mind to understand the Scriptures? Then take heart in this account of the disciples' first reactions to the resurrection. Rejoice in the good news that Jesus' resurrection was real. Know that your resurrection is assured by his. Imagine sitting down in heaven someday with these men and women and hearing their stories first hand. I don't know for sure if that kind of thing will happen in heaven, but the reality of the resurrection makes it a possibility.

John

Day 69, John 1

Disciples of Jesus are commissioned to make other disciples. Today's chapter is a wonderful primer about disciple-making. What lessons can we learn about evangelism from these first examples of people leading others to Jesus?

John the Baptist told the people Messiah was coming, the one about whom the Old Testament prophets had spoken. When Jesus appeared at the place where John was baptizing, the forerunner announced, "Behold the Lamb of God, who takes away the sin of the world!" John testified about Jesus' identity, telling his listeners that Jesus was the Son of God. As a result, some of John's disciples started following Jesus.

Jesus asked those first followers what they wanted, and invited them to come and see. Andrew went and found Simon, telling him they had found the Messiah. After Philip was invited to follow, he went and got Nathanael to come and see. Nathanael turned from a skeptic to a disciple when Jesus knew all about him before meeting him.

Do you sense a pattern, a rhythm in these events? Those who were introduced to Jesus introduced others to him. Disciples told others and invited them to see for themselves. No one was forced to follow; they were invited to examine the evidence and decide for themselves.

You and I can learn a lot about disciple-making or evangelism here. The message of evangelism is clear: "Behold, the Lamb of God." It's about Jesus, not us. It's about who he is, not who we are. It's unwise and unbiblical to think we're busy making disciples when we're just trying to get people to agree with us about some point of doctrine or practice. He's the subject; he's the message of evangelism.

We also learn the action of evangelism. Disciple-makers tell others what they have found and learned. Andrew and Philip both said, "We have found him!" The telling flows from the joy of discovery and the desire to share what has been found. This is natural. We tell friends about good restaurants or some household product that works well. It should be just as natural and far more important to share good news about a Savior.

The spirit of evangelism is also clear. It is invitation. Some believe a contentious, debating spirit is a mark of faithfulness and the key to persuading others to put their faith in Jesus. But this text does not suggest that at all. Disciples invite others to try and see, to look for themselves. The spirit of invitation is neither high-pressure nor combative. It does not attempt to control, manipulate or bully others into compliance.

Does this kind of evangelism work? Look at the reported results: After John's declaration, his disciples followed Jesus. When Andrew told Peter they had found Messiah, he then brought him to Jesus. And when Philip invited Nathanael to come and see for himself, he confessed Jesus as the Son of God. That sounds like exactly the kind of results we're looking for.

Day 70, John 2

"Do whatever he tells you." That's the advice Mary gave the servants at the wedding after asking Jesus to do something about the embarrassing wine shortage. Jesus told the servants to fill some water jars on hand for purification rituals. They did. He next told them to take some of the liquid to the host. They did. Somewhere in the process, Jesus transformed the water into the best wine of the day. The disciples who were with Jesus believed when they saw the sign he performed.

I can't think of any better compass for our lives than to do whatever Jesus tells us to do. Jesus' advice about relationships and priorities, about everyday matters and eternal things is always the best counsel. With compassion and wisdom, he steers us away from self-destructive behaviors, and by his sterling example models the best way to think, speak and act. The strictest law keepers among the Jews made a confusing and impossible mess of religion, but Jesus showed the simplicity and importance of loving God most of all and our neighbors as ourselves. He taught us to honor our commitments, control our anger, tell the truth, and guard against lust and greed. He taught us how to overcome worry, and how to pray and rely on God instead of ourselves. Wouldn't our lives, homes and communities be happier if everyone would do as he said?

Jesus' followers learn from his teaching and imitate his example. The disciple's life lesson is summarized in Mary's words to the servants at the wedding. We're not really disciples if we're not following his example. We're not trusting Jesus if we ignore instead of obey what he says. The scope of his authority is as broad as our whole lives: "Do whatever he tells you."

Later on, Jesus would tell his disciples that those who know his teaching will be blessed if they do what he says, and that we are his friends if we do what he tells us. He said if we love him, we will keep his commands. In the other gospel records, Jesus said those who do the will of the Father will enter the kingdom, and the wise person hears and does what he says to do. He said those who hear and do the will of God are his family. Where did the idea come from that obedience is not part of our relationship with Jesus? It didn't come from his words on the subject.

Disciples are taught to obey everything Jesus commands. That's part of the self-denial to which we're called. That's how we follow him. Suppose Peter, Andrew, James and John had stayed on their boats when Jesus called them to follow him, or that Matthew had remained at the tax table when he received the call. Would they have been followers if they hadn't obeyed? Of course not. And if we won't do what he says, neither are we.

Day 71, John 3

Perhaps we could meditate on the beautiful mystery of the new birth. Maybe we should devote this day to exploring the magnificent grandeur of "For God so loved the world...." Then there is that chilling statement about the judgment that comes to people who love darkness and will not come to the light.

But today let's focus on something John the Baptist said about himself and Jesus. As Jesus and his disciples began baptizing, some of John's disciples reported the news to John. They were concerned that many people were following Jesus. John reminded them he had said all along he was not the Messiah. He rejoiced in his role as the friend of the bridegroom. Then John summarized his life, his mission and his attitude about the growing prominence of Jesus: "He must increase, but I must decrease."

These words are a descriptive chorus for the life song of everyone who would follow Jesus. The handful of words expresses a heart full of submission that should characterize every disciple's life.

John's words model the self-denial of real discipleship. Jesus told crowds who came to hear him that those who wanted to follow him had to deny themselves and take up the cross to do so. The presence of Christ with us and in us should transform us until we can say with Paul, "I no longer live, but Christ lives in me." As we do more of God's will, we'll do less of our own.

Look at the double "must." Talk of self-denial and surrendering our will may make us think of the most dedicated super-Christians. But John's acceptance of Christ's necessary increase should be a pattern for all disciples, not just extraordinary ones. Jesus did not establish some system for ranking disciples. The self-denial is not optional. It is a primary condition, a must for those who would trust in Jesus and commit themselves to him.

John's words about increasing and decreasing remind us that our development as disciples is a process. The New Testament describes the disciple's gradual development, a pattern of growth toward maturity. We are being transformed into the image of Christ. We grow up into him in all things. We cultivate the fruit of the Spirit and add qualities of spiritual maturity to our faith. He begins a work in us he promises to complete. This implies we should be patient with ourselves and others as we are all works in progress. It also reminds us that we should be able to look back over our past experience and see the growth toward maturity. When we remember we're pilgrims on a journey, we are comforted about past failures, and hopeful about doing better in days to come.

John said this process of decreasing while Jesus increased was a joyful one. We should seek signs of his increase in us and a corresponding decrease of ourselves with joyful anticipation, not sorrowful resignation.

Day 72, John 4

Jesus becomes more precious to me when I see him sitting by the well at Sychar. Tired and thirsty, he sits beside the famous well to rest at midday. What a Savior! Our all-powerful God put on human flesh, willing to know the weariness of physical exhaustion. The Creator of water was willing to be thirsty to satisfy our thirst for the Water of Life.

Jesus met this woman of Samaria where she was. When the text says he had to pass through Samaria, it was not because there was no other route. The Jews so despised the Samaritans that they would take the time and effort to go around Samaria rather than travel through it. But Jesus had a harvest of souls to gather from this unlikely field. He had to go there to meet this woman and set events in motion that would lead to many Samaritans believing in him. That's a miniature of the whole Incarnation, isn't it? He was willing to come here, quite out of his way, for us. It's also true about each of us he came to redeem. He meets us in the way of our daily lives, speaks to us in ways we can understand and offers to enrich and transform us, as well as use our testimony about him to draw others.

Jesus asked her for a drink of water to start the conversation, and offered to give her living water. He then led her through an escalating appreciation of who he was, finally revealing himself as Messiah. The master teacher took her from what she understood to what she wondered about to what she could not imagine. When the Lord asks us to give or give up something, we need to remember this principle. What he asks us to give does not compare with what he offers to give us.

Jews wouldn't have associated with her because she was a Samaritan. Men wouldn't have spoken to her because she was a woman. (Remember the disciples marveled when they found him talking to her.) The "righteous" people wouldn't have had anything to do with her because of her broken life. But Jesus cut through the prejudice and hypocrisy to introduce her to her Savior, and to send her on a mission to bring her neighbors to him.

Jesus was gentle and frank about her troubled life. Above all people, Jesus knew the seriousness of sin. He would die to pay the penalty for all sin. No one is holy, compared to him. But his holiness was not diminished by engaging this woman to capture her heart and redeem her life. How dare we treat people ensnared by sin with scorn when the Savior did not do so? And when we realize our own unworthiness and need of grace, we can be glad to know he will deal frankly and gently with the sin in our lives, too, if we will open our hearts and turn to him.

Day 73, John 5

All the gospel narrators show the conflict between Jesus and the Jewish religious leaders. But nowhere is the cause for the friction clearer than in John. Twice in today's portion John writes, "This was why..." about the Jews' persecution of Jesus.

After healing the invalid at the pool called Bethesda, Jesus told the man to pick up his bed and walk. The Sabbath enforcers accused the man of breaking the Sabbath. His reply to their charge said more than he realized: "The man who healed me, that man said to me, 'Take up your bed, and walk.'" That's great, isn't it? The person who had the power to heal him on the Sabbath could say what he could or couldn't do on the Sabbath. After he met Jesus, he went back and told them who had healed him. When Jesus disregarded their Sabbath tradition, they intensified their hateful opposition to him.

In a classic case of throwing gas on the fire, Jesus then claimed to be doing the work of his Father. That's when John writes the second "This was why." It wasn't that they didn't understand Jesus' claim to be the Son of God. It was because they understood it perfectly. He was calling God his Father and making himself equal with God.

Some modern writers say Jesus never claimed to be God's Son. It's hard to imagine what else the long quote from Jesus could mean. He said he and the Father were doing the same work, and that they equally held the power of life, death, resurrection and judgment. Jesus said that Moses and John the Baptist testified of him, along with the works the Father gave him to do.

One of the most sobering statements Jesus ever made to people who claimed to know the word of God is found in this speech. He said, "You search the Scriptures because you think that in them you have eternal life; and it is they that bear witness about me, yet you refuse to come to me that you may have life." The Scriptures cannot give life, but they do point to the life giver. Law can only condemn; it has no power to redeem. But it was designed to make us aware of our need for a Savior, and to introduce us to him. The Jewish leaders (as well as most of the nation they influenced) refused to accept Jesus as the one to whom the Scriptures pointed, choosing instead to trust themselves and their ability to know and keep the law. Seeking justification, they embraced the very thing that condemned them. Needing a Savior, they chose to ignore the compelling evidence that Jesus was the one their Scriptures predicted would come.

We can be blessed by being careful students of the Word. But let's not make the same mistake the Jewish leaders made. Eternal life is not in a list of rules; it is in a relationship with the Son of God.

Day 74, John 6

It's a staple of life around the world. Grind some grain into flour, mix with oil, add a little salt and perhaps some yeast. Bake the mixture for a while, and you've got bread. Bread has many forms and variations across cultures, but it is symbolic in all of them of basic sustenance.

The great "I am" passages in John are easier for modern readers than the original hearers. We see the dramatic sayings as part of the package of evidence John recorded to produce faith in Jesus. When people first heard "I am the bread of life," the words were full of promise, mystery and a very tall claim.

Jesus used a figure of speech that would speak to every race in every age. After he fed a multitude with a boy's lunch, the satisfied followers were ready to make him king. Jesus got away from them, recognizing their interest was in more fish sandwiches, not in the kingdom of God. He told them they should be more interested in food that endured to eternal life. Among their questions was a demand for a sign or a work to make them believe. They had seen a wondrous demonstration just a day earlier, but now they were hungry again. They remembered Israel's wilderness manna. Perhaps they expected Messiah to provide their literal daily bread.

For bread to be such a universal image, there was a lot of confusion about the way Jesus used it. The crowds heard the opportunity to get free food. The Jews tried a literal meaning, speculating about how Jesus could give his flesh to be eaten. They did not believe Jesus was the "true bread from heaven" because they thought they knew all about his background.

Even some disciples who had been following Jesus were offended by the concept, calling it a hard saying. Jesus told them they did not really believe, and said no one could come to him unless the Father granted it to them. After others left, Jesus asked the Twelve if they would also go. Peter's response was right; there was nowhere else to go for eternal life.

The story about Jesus feeding the multitude reminds us that when the Lord asks us a question, it's for our benefit, not his. He knew the plan, but he wanted Philip and the others to learn that he was the supply for the challenges they faced. I suspect we are sometimes like the disciples scrambling to meet overwhelming needs, and calculating about how to do what he's told us to do with our own meager resources. I doubt we consistently remember and understand that God who once sustained Israel in the wilderness has now promised us the life-bread of Christ to sustain our souls for eternity. That sustenance can never come from our own resources. It is a gift from the Father, through Jesus and our faith in him.

Day 75, John 7

Opinions about Jesus were diverse. Some people thought he was a good man, but others thought he was leading people astray. Some said he was Messiah, "the Prophet" Moses said would come. But others said he was possessed by a demon. His own brothers did not believe in him during his earthly ministry; yet many who heard Jesus speak in Jerusalem put their faith in him.

Some people had already made up their mind. Others listened and were impressed by what they heard. Some thought for themselves, while others were steered by the religious elite who told them what to think and berated all who disagreed with them.

It seems little has changed in the marketplace of ideas about Jesus. That same spectrum of opinion ranging from trust to ridicule is expressed in conversation, books and on web sites today. One unhappy wrinkle I have observed in our time is that some who claim to be following Jesus have adopted the bully tactics of Jesus' ancient opponents—insulting honest inquirers and pressuring people to agree with them or else. If you have met some professing disciples who behaved this way, I urge you not to judge Jesus or all who follow him by such spirit and action.

If people listening to Jesus weren't clear about his identity, their lack of clarity did not stem from any evasiveness on his part. Jesus' claims about who he was and where he came from were unmistakable. He claimed his teaching came from God, and that those who wanted to do the will of God could know it. He said he knew God, came from God, God had sent him and he would return to God. His words revealed no ambivalence or uncertainty about his identity.

His opponents' words reveal a lot about them as well. From the taunting of his brothers to the scathing insults of the Pharisees, people showed what was in their heart by what they said about Jesus. The chief priests and Pharisees ridiculed the officers who had been sent to arrest Jesus when they returned without him, saying no one had even spoken like Jesus. Look at the tactics of these men: They implied that anyone who didn't agree with them was deceived. They claimed their opinion was the authoritative standard. They cursed the people they were supposed to be leading when the people didn't agree with their position. When one of their own (Nicodemus) asked the council a fair question about a point of order, they insulted him, didn't answer the question and showed their prejudice and ignorance by their comment about no prophet coming from Galilee. Jonah was from Galilee.

Listening to the evidence, weighing it carefully and articulating your decision clearly are the components of honest conviction. Refusing to listen, rejecting any idea different from your own and rudely attempting to manipulate others to agree with you are tell-tale signs of hypocritical dishonesty.

Day 76, John 8

Have you ever known any religious people who were quick to "pick up stones" to throw at others? The scribes and Pharisees were like that. Today's reading begins and ends with them holding stones, and ready to throw them.

The Pharisees brought a woman who had been caught "in the act of adultery," saying the law commanded them to "stone such women." The actual demands of the law and their own accusing words tell us the woman should not have been brought in alone. John tells us they were setting a trap for Jesus. They thought it was a situation where whatever Jesus said could be used against him. Can you feel the tension build as Jesus bent down and wrote on the ground while they accused her? Jesus finally stood and said, "Let him who is without sin among you be the first to throw a stone at her," and stooped back down to write. Jesus avoided their trap, defused the situation and perhaps saved the woman's life. With gentleness, he pardoned her and sent her away with instructions to change her life.

Some people doubt this story's authenticity, but I'm so glad we have it! It gives fresh hope to every one who has felt the stinging shame of guilt. It shows the compassionate heart of God who loves and longs to forgive, not condemn. It strikes a sharp and needed contrast between some religious people and the God they claim to serve.

The next stones came up (literally) after a heated conversation about paternity. Jesus told them again about his relationship to the heavenly Father. He also said the devil was their father, not Abraham. You can see why this conversation didn't go well. The Pharisees resorted to insults and name-calling, which is usually a sign that a disputant has no valid point. When Jesus said another "I am" that made an unmistakable claim for his divinity, they were ready for the rocks again. Jesus got away before they could stone him. It wasn't time for the final confrontation. He would die, and they would participate. But the death would not be by stoning. The prophecies had to be fulfilled. And they would not be rid of Jesus after he died. Their troubles with the Nazarene and his followers would be just beginning.

The religious bullies didn't get to throw any stones that day. Jesus was in control. His objectives were accomplished: he showed God's love and mercy to a broken, guilty sinner, and exposed the character of the hypocrites who made themselves his enemies. He saved the woman from judgment and punishment. He offers to do the same for you and me. Was Jesus soft on sin? No. At the cross, Jesus paid for the woman's sin he forgave, along with yours and mine. Through his death, Jesus demonstrated that he was both just ("the sin debt has to be paid") and the justifier ("I'll pay it myself") of those who trust in him.

Day 77, John 9

Imagine the heartbreak. Your son is born blind in a world without educational or vocational opportunities. There's also the stigma from your culture's understanding that handicap or illness is payback for some secret sin. Your son grows, but does not attend synagogue school, does not run and play. As his peers become apprentices, he becomes a beggar, dependent on the charity of passersby for a coin or some food.

Then one day the neighbors tell you, "Your son can see! He can see!" In startled disbelief, you go outside and there he is, talking to a crowd. Some say it's not him, but he insists he is the one they've seen begging on his blanket for years. He says Jesus made mud, put it on his eyes and told him to go wash. The Pharisees reject the story of how Jesus healed him. Their prejudice about Jesus has run headlong into undeniable evidence that a blind man has been healed.

So they call you, the parent, to testify. Your joy over your son's new sight is replaced by fear. These ruthless inquisitors are not looking for truth, but for some way to discredit the obvious fact that Jesus healed your son. They've threatened to excommunicate anyone who follows Jesus. Expulsion from the synagogue will make you a social leper. It won't even be easy to buy groceries. So you admit he's your son, affirm that he was born blind, and then deny any knowledge of how this glorious change took place. You're not proud of your performance, but you were so afraid.

Like detectives wringing a confession from a suspect, they badger your son with questions. Like attorneys cross-examining a hostile witness, they demand answers. They make a show of telling what they "know." What your son says could not have happened. And then, in a moment of simple, shining eloquence, your son gains the upper hand. He says, "One thing I do know, that though I was blind, now I see." He gives the teachers a lesson in their own logic. The more he says, the worse the Pharisees look. His conclusion is that Jesus has to be who he claims to be, or he could not do what he's done. Outwitted and out-argued by your son, the spiritual leaders do the only thing they can to save face: they excommunicate him!

When Jesus introduces himself, your son confesses his faith in Jesus and worships him. Your son believes from firsthand experience that Jesus is Messiah. Thrown out by the religionists, he is taken in by Jesus.

Jesus' summary statement of the event challenges you and everyone who knows about it to decide. By giving sight to the blind, he calls you to see who he is. As he told your son, "You have seen him, and it is he who is speaking to you." His question to your son is a good one for you, too: "Do you believe in the Son of Man?"

Day 78, John 10

There is no more loved image of God's provision and care for his people than Psalm 23: "The Lord is my shepherd." Rest, peace, healing, direction—we crave all the things the shepherd provides. Assurance of his presence fulfills a deep longing within us. His provision and blessings sustain us. Anxieties fade as we find contentment in our relationship to the shepherd. No wonder multitudes passing through their darkest valleys have found comfort in these words.

Jesus chose the same image to describe his sacrificial love and provision for his followers, his sheep. A relationship with him provides security and peace that comes from knowing and being known. The sheep do not wander; instead, they follow him. He gathers them into one fold to be under the care of one shepherd. He gives the sheep life by laying down his own life.

The shepherd motif is also in Ezekiel, where the spiritual leaders are called shepherds. God pronounced stern judgment on those shepherds who failed to lead and feed his sheep. He held them responsible for the perilous danger into which the sheep had fallen. That shepherd picture is also in Jesus' words. The Jewish leaders had proven to be strangers and hired hands who did not care about the sheep at all, who did not guide, protect or save the sheep from danger. Jesus' claim to be the good shepherd who cares for the sheep is a contrast to the failure of Israel's shepherds. He said the sheep could tell the difference, and they would follow the real shepherd, not the thief.

Jesus mixed no words about the Jewish leaders being excluded from his flock. He said there were other sheep to be brought in, but the leaders did not believe because they were not part of his flock. As a consequence of rejecting Jesus, they would miss the gift of eternal life that the sheep in his Father's hand would enjoy.

Whenever Jesus talked about his relationship to the Father, the Jews cried "Blasphemy!" and tried to stone him. Even in the face of their hateful rejection, Jesus still appealed to them to believe the works if not the words. While many who saw and heard him did believe, these leaders were not going to acknowledge the obvious source of Jesus' power.

It is humbling to be a sheep, to admit we do not trust our ability to guide or provide for ourselves. To have a shepherd means we do not trust ourselves to find our way. But it is also very fulfilling to know we're sheep of the Good Shepherd. The security and satisfaction he promises fill our lives with joy and meaning. He loved us enough to lay down his life for us, giving our lives significance. Knowing that the Shepherd had the authority to lay his life down and take it up again gives us confidence in his promise to give his sheep eternal life.

Day 79, John 11

Our faith seems strong when God blesses us with good things. As his children, we cherish our confident trust in a loving Father. But when we suffer loss and grieve over a loved one's death, our faith should mean even more. John's account of the resurrection of Lazarus teaches us a lot about faith, death, grief and resurrection.

In the face of death, Jesus called the disciples and grieving sisters to believe. He told the disciples he was glad they had not gone before Lazarus died, because their faith would be strengthened. He told Martha that Lazarus would rise again, and steered her from general faith in a resurrection to specific faith in him as the Resurrection and the Life.

When Jesus told the disciples that Lazarus had fallen asleep, they thought he was getting better. But Jesus meant Lazarus was dead. This is significant for those who trust Jesus about things we cannot yet know for ourselves. From this side we see death as final. But Jesus views death as sleep, from which he will awaken us as surely as we awaken our children each morning.

Children (and some adults) choose "Jesus wept" as their memory verse because it is the shortest verse in the English Bible. But this simple sentence is far more than a trivia answer or an easy memory verse. These two words are an eloquent statement of Jesus' compassion for those who grieve. Although Jesus had the power to bring Lazarus back and was just about to do so, he still sympathized with the mourners. Does he care about our sorrow? Can the eternal God sympathize with mortals grieving over death? The answer is yes; Jesus wept. Is there weakness in weeping? Does sorrow betray some lack of confidence in God's promises? The answer is no; Jesus wept. When your cheeks are wet with tears, trust that he knows about yours and cried tears of his own.

The people standing nearby could take the stone away, as Jesus told them to do. They could unbind Lazarus from the strips in which he had been wrapped. But only Jesus could do what happened in between. When he called Lazarus by name, the man who had been dead four days came out of the tomb still wearing his grave clothes. John said many believed in Jesus when they saw Lazarus alive again. But not everyone came to faith that day. Some went and told Jesus' enemies. Even as they acknowledged the many signs he had performed, they intensified their plans to kill Jesus.

As Jesus asked Martha, I'm asking you: "Do you believe this?" Do you believe Jesus raised Lazarus and has the power to raise you and your loved ones from the dead? Is your faith in Jesus strong enough to trust him about that? His death and resurrection give us courage to face our own death with full confidence that we'll only be sleeping until he wakes us for eternity with him.

Day 80, John 12

The tsunami of testimony about the resurrection of Lazarus surged across Jerusalem before Jesus arrived for the final week. The crowds swelled; people wanted to see the one who had raised the dead. They wanted to see Lazarus, too. Many people believed in Jesus after the miracle. But some people had a heart problem that kept them from faith despite this powerful demonstration of Jesus' claim to be the Son of God.

The Pharisees' heart problem was willful unbelief. Their desperation grew as more people turned to Jesus. Lazarus, sitting there at the dinner table back from the dead, was especially annoying to them. His resurrection was an undeniable, certified miracle. What could they do? This would have been a good time to admit their error in opposing Jesus, and confess their faith in him. But that wasn't going to happen. Instead of repenting, they added raised Lazarus to their list of "People In Our Way Who Need To Be Killed."

Some of the authorities had a different heart problem—fear. They did believe, but they were afraid to express their faith. If we feel anger toward the hard-hearted chief priests, perhaps we should feel some pity for these people. Not everyone among the rulers of the Jews was willfully blind to the glory of God radiating from Jesus. Some of them heard the words and saw the signs, and believed. But they were so afraid of the Pharisees that they dared not make a public confession of faith. They saw how others who came to faith were treated, and they had no desire to be expelled from the synagogue. They lacked the courage to be identified with Jesus. John said it was because they loved the glory that comes from man more than the glory that comes from God. It was the darkest kind of peer pressure.

The bullies kept them quiet, kept them from following the one who could save them.

Here are two barriers to faith we should never allow to hinder us from following Jesus. One is internal; the other external.

Guard your heart against willful refusal to see and know the will of God. Remember it was not the notorious outlaw sinners who were willfully rejecting Jesus; it was the most respected religious people of the community. Their pride and self-righteousness kept them from acknowledging their need and turning to Jesus. Humility and a willingness to grow and learn will help you remain open to God's message.

Know there will be peers who would lead you away from faith and discipleship. Some of them are even among professing followers of Jesus. Your best efforts to love and serve the Lord may be sharply criticized, even as Judas found fault with Mary's extravagant, loving gesture. You may already know how discouraging that can be. Please do not allow the nay-sayers and bullies in your circle to keep you from placing your faith in Jesus and giving him your very best.

Day 81, John 13

How well do we know ourselves? Are we as we see ourselves? Are we who we think we are? When Jesus told the disciples that one of them would betray him, they were uncertain of themselves and those around them at the table that night. Jesus knew who would do it. But the disciples didn't know. The events and dialogue of the last night suggest we may not know ourselves as well as we think we do.

Jesus gave the disciples (who often quarreled about who was the greatest) an unforgettable demonstration of humble service. He laid aside his outer garment, tied a towel around his waist, took a basin of water and washed the disciples' feet. The disciples needed to learn that if their Master would humble himself to do a menial task for them, they should never feel they were too good to serve one another. No follower of Jesus should feel any task of service is beneath him. I want to say I'm humble, and that I am becoming more like Jesus. Am I humble enough to perform the lowliest service for my brothers and sisters? Am I enough like Jesus to serve with the right attitude?

We find another way to check our true identity in the new command Jesus gave to love one another. If we claim to obey him, we cannot harbor hatred for one another in our hearts. This kind of love goes beyond the Golden Rule and even the second command to love our neighbors as ourselves. He commands us to love one another as he has loved us. We who call ourselves disciples must not miss what our Master says here. The evidence of our discipleship is not a score on a doctrinal test. The proof of our discipleship is not affiliation with some group or observance of some ritual. Jesus said others would know we are his disciples if we love one another. Am I really a disciple? Would my loving behavior toward others affirm my discipleship? Or would my obvious lack of love deny my claim?

Peter was sure his loyalty would pass any test. He would lay down his life for Jesus. That was an admirable profession, but Jesus knew and told Peter he was mistaken about himself. He would, in fact, deny Jesus three times before the night was over. Peter no doubt believed his devotion was deep and secure; he loved Jesus so that he would die for him. Jesus, who knows the hearts of his followers better than we know ourselves, had to tell Peter that his passionate vow lacked substance. Am I loyal to Jesus? Do I think nothing could separate me from him or make me deny him? Am I sure?

May we be so humble in our service, so loving in our hearts and so loyal in our devotion to Jesus that he will see in us what we want to see about ourselves.

Day 82, John 14

People study for decades, write long books and preach complicated sermons trying to understand and explain the concept of the Trinity—Father, Son and Holy Spirit as one God. To me, the inexplicability of the idea is neither troublesome nor threatening. God is so wholly other from us that we should not be surprised to find his nature shrouded in a considerable degree of mystery. No physical illustration I've ever read or heard has been adequate to give a helpful picture of God's three-in-one nature, and most of the analogies I've seen have glaring doctrinal flaws.

I have found help with this in Jesus' words spoken to the apostles the last night before the cross. His oneness with the Father who sent him and his identity with the Spirit he would send after him are stated in matter-of-fact simplicity. To know and see Jesus was to know and see the Father. The Spirit who was coming was then dwelling with them and would be in them. The day was coming when they would know Jesus was in the Father, they were in Christ, and he through the Spirit would be in them. The Spirit would be sent by the Father in the name of Jesus. They would come and make their home within Jesus' disciples. Jesus' perfect oneness with the Father was the secret to his perfect obedience to the Father's commands.

That concept of obedience moves us from the abstract and mystical words about the Trinity to the practical, measurable reality of our own oneness with God and our love for him. Jesus said it over and over in this setting: "If you love me, you will keep my commands... Whoever has my commandments and keeps them, he it is who loves me...If anyone loves me, he will keep my word, and my Father will love him, and we will come to him and make our home with him. Whoever does not love me does not keep my words."

There's not a lot of mystery about that, is there? We demonstrate our love for God, not in the ethereal mist, but in concrete obedience. It may be fine to ponder the incomprehensible, but it's better to do what he tells us to do. We're indebted to great minds among us who have studied closely and long to help our understanding of the deep things of God. But we non-theologians can never claim it's just too complicated to know if we have a relationship with him. Jesus said, "If you love me, you will keep my commands." If he dwells with us, we will keep his words. It is not your job to understand exactly what that means or how it happens. It is your job to obey him, and trust him to keep his promise.

Day 83, John 15

It's not unusual for a dying person to wish to be with loved ones and talk about matters that are important to them in life's final hours.

In the last hours with his closest disciples, the ones on whose shoulders the weight of the mission would rest when he was gone,

Jesus talked about the things that would matter most: abiding in him, keeping his commandments, loving one another and being hated by the world.

We are useful and productive in our service to God because we are connected to him, not because we have the power within ourselves. In the simplest terms, Jesus explained that the branch cannot bear fruit unless it is connected to the vine. All our grand schemes and high opinions of ourselves must be seen through the lens of his words: "apart from me you can do nothing." We enjoy tremendous potential in our prayers and efforts when we abide in him. Jesus didn't leave the idea of "abiding" in the abstract; he says those who keep his commandments abide in his love, just as he kept his Father's commandments.

In the last time of teaching and shaping the lives of the apostles before he went to the cross, Jesus was not outlining the cardinal doctrines or ritual observances of a religion, but was stressing what he had been saying all along: love God and love your neighbor. Obedience to the other commands would grow out of obeying these two. We demonstrate love for one another in sacrificing self. It is the same with our love for God; when we deny self to do what he commands, we are showing our love for him.

In all this love, it may hurt our feelings to discover that the world will hate those who are devoted to Jesus. Once again, the world is not the natural creation or all the people on the planet, but the rebellious element of the human family that defies God's authority and lives in opposition to him. Jesus reminds us not to be surprised that the world would hate us, because it hated him. The persecution the disciples would face grows from the same root that led to Jesus' persecution. And as he would overcome the opposition, we'll overcome, too, when we are loyal to him. The hatred of the world will not stop the mission. Indeed, as the Acts record shows and history has confirmed, opposition has stoked the spread of the kingdom and the gospel.

Would you enjoy the security and guaranteed productivity of a branch within the vine? Would you entrust your care to a vinedresser who will prune you to make you more productive? Would you live without fear of what the unbelieving world can do to harm you? Then learn what it means to abide in Christ. Loving obedience is the key to this life of reliance and trust. We can abide in him only if we are surrendered to his will.

Day 84, John 16

I've heard it so many times among grieving families: "I don't know what I'm going to do without him." Or, "How can we go on without her?" When faced with the fact that a loved one who means so much to you is gone or is about to go, it is normal to wonder aloud how your life can go on or what it will be like without that person.

The disciples had similar anxiety as they heard Jesus talk about leaving them and returning to the Father. To help them through the difficult transition, Jesus reassured them about several matters.

There was adversity ahead for the disciples. Knowing it in advance would keep their devotion strong when it came. They would remember his warning, and not think the mission had gone wrong or that God was out of control.

He promised to send the Spirit to be their helper, teacher and guide. What Jesus had been to them by his physical presence, the Spirit within them would be, and even more. The task before them was enormous. They could only accomplish the mission by the power of the Holy Spirit working in them and through them. Jesus guaranteed they would not be left alone.

Jesus also said they would pray to the Father in his name, a new thing for them to do. It would not be that Jesus would ask the Father on their behalf, but that they could personally approach the Father, ask in Jesus' name and receive what they asked from a Father who loved them.

Did it hurt their feelings when Jesus replied to their statement of faith with a prediction they all would run away and hide? Even this revelation was designed to give them peace later, when they reflected back on what Jesus had told them in advance.

It's a challenge for those of us who've read it before to read these lines and sympathize with the disciples because we already know how it's going to turn out. We know about the resurrection and how it fits with seeing him, not seeing him and seeing him again. People who've read Acts know the impact the Spirit is going to make on these men and their service to God. We get the figurative speech because we're aware of the events Jesus is describing.

The real question for us is whether or not we believe in his presence and power in our lives today. When adversity comes, do we trust and rely on him? Do we realize the reality of the Spirit of God within us, strengthening us, guiding us? Do we take the privilege of prayer for granted, reducing "in the name of Jesus" to a formula to signal the end of a prayer? And when we've failed, do we find peace and confidence to get up and go on, realizing he knows our frailty and weaknesses, that he knew them in advance and loved us anyway?

Day 85, John 17

Do you ever have the opportunity to listen to other people's prayers? I frequently have the privilege of praying for others. Occasionally, someone prays for me, in my presence. What a blessing! It's encouraging to know we've been lifted up to God by people who love us and are seeking God's special blessing for us.

Through John's words, we can listen to Jesus' prayer just before his arrest, trial and crucifixion. Facing the humiliation and agony of the cross, he asked the Father to glorify him. He made special requests for the disciples God had given him—that God would keep them, give them joy, protect them from the evil one and set them apart from the world. And then he prayed for you and me. What did Jesus ask on our behalf? What blessings from the Father did our Savior seek for us, just before he went to the cross?

Jesus prayed that those who followed him after hearing the apostles' teaching would be united. That's us. As a member of the body of Christ, I feel some shame when I read the words, "that they may all be one." The factious spirit that divides the body of Christ today over petty differences is an insult to the Lord who prayed for our unity. Beyond the cultural and theological differences we have allowed to divide us, we must wrestle on a more personal level with the attitudes and actions that separate and isolate us from one another. Jesus said our unity would be a testimony to an unbelieving world that he had come from God. Division among us silences that testimony. It may not be possible for us to fix the problem on some institutional, corporate level. But every follower of Jesus Christ can determine in his or her heart to live out what it means to be one in Christ with others who follow him.

Jesus also said our unity would testify to the world that the Father loves them. As we obey the Great Commands to love God most and neighbor as self in practical, observable ways, we put flesh and blood on the concept of God's love for the whole human family. If we have turf wars and strident quarrels about minutiae, our message of God's love is lost in the noise of our conflict, and our testimony is ineffective.

The other thing Jesus asked for us is that we might be with him where he is, to see his glory. The one who emptied himself of glory to come and live among us and die for us wants us to be with him, in heaven, where his glory is fully realized. He would endure the cross, despise its shame, experience a separation from his Father and die so his prayer could be answered.

This prayer is a look into the heart of Jesus just hours before he died. Isn't it good to know that we were on his mind?

Day 86, John 18

It was many dark nights ago, but I remember it as if it were last night. Judas came and told my master's associates that Jesus would be in a secluded place where they could arrest him. We went out into the night with lanterns and torches. The soldiers were armed. We followed Judas across the valley and into a garden.

I didn't expect Jesus to approach us, but he did. He asked who we sought, and we replied, "Jesus of Nazareth." When he said, "I am he," we went backward and fell on the ground. After Jesus identified himself again, the guards seized him. There was a struggle. I remember the flash of pain and the warm rush of blood on my neck. My right ear was gone, and the swordsman was aiming for more than my ear.

And then, Jesus touched me, but not in violence or aggression. He restored my ear, healing the wound with a gentle touch. His voice was calm as he told his men to put away their arms. He asked them, "Shall I not drink the cup that the Father has given me?"

We took him to Annas, then to my master's house, where we waited in the courtyard while they interrogated him inside. The pressure was enormous. The questioning was loud and violent. We built a charcoal fire because it was cold. One of the Galileans had protested at the gate that he was not with Jesus, and denied it again as he stood around the fire with us. My cousin from the arresting posse saw him in the flickering light and recognized him as the man who had attacked me. He accused him of being with Jesus, but the man denied it again, just before a rooster crowed. The guy ran away weeping. I guess the pressure got to him, too.

After daylight, we took Jesus to Pilate. We stood outside his headquarters so we would not be defiled before eating the Passover. We would beat an innocent man, solicit false testimony, falsely accuse him and call for his crucifixion. But we weren't going to be defiled by entering a Gentile's house. Looking back, the hypocrisy sickens me.

As it became obvious the accusations were baseless, Jesus remained calm. But Pilate felt the pressure. My master and those with him were going to cause trouble if Pilate didn't do what they wanted. Everyone seemed to feel the intense pressure, except Jesus at the center of it all.

Sometimes on dark, chilly evenings around a charcoal fire, I still touch my right ear with wonder undiminished by intervening decades. I remember his healing touch, and believe that Jesus is who he claimed to be. Earlier writers didn't reveal my name. But now, John has identified both me and the man whose loyalty to his Master caused him to lash out against me. The swordsman was Peter, and I am Malchus, servant of the high priest and a witness of the Savior's suffering.

Day 87, John 19

The trouble-makers arrived early and ruined his day with their demands. They hated this Jesus they brought to him for judgment, and needed Roman law to put him to death. Pilate declared him innocent at least three times, but the Jewish religious leaders were unyielding in their insistence that Jesus be crucified. I doubt Pilate knew his name would live in infamy as a result of his actions that day when he sentenced Jesus to die on the cross.

Then, tired of being manipulated by the Jews, Pilate refused to change what he had written on the placard above Jesus' head. It proclaimed "Jesus of Nazareth, the King of the Jews" in three different languages so everyone in the multilingual Passover crowd could read it. Did Pilate imply the insult the chief priests inferred from the words, advertising that the Romans had crucified their king? The Jews didn't like it, but Pilate would not change what he had written.

Long before Pilate wrote about Jesus on the cross, the prophets wrote details that were fulfilled by the events of Jesus' death. God's foreknowledge of what would happen enabled David to write a thousand years in advance that Messiah's executioners would gamble for his clothing and give him vinegar to drink. Some unbelieving critics claim that Jesus knew the prophecies and manipulated events to make it seem that he fulfilled them. That theory can't explain the many details of Jesus' birth, life and death predicted in the Old Testament. How could he manipulate events before his birth or after his death? Since the first Passover more than 1,400 years earlier, the lambs had been slain without breaking any bones, prefiguring what would happen when Jesus died. Five hundred years before it happened, Zechariah saw the one who would bring salvation to his people being pierced. The soldiers weren't aware of any script; their actions were foreknown and foretold by God's prophets.

The writing continued after Jesus died, too. In addition to the gospel accounts, the shadow of the cross stands across the rest of the New Testament. The cross and the empty tomb are the central themes of the Acts preachers. Writing decades after the events he described, John vividly remembered the blood and water pouring from Jesus' side and the other details he had witnessed. He wrote them down, knowing it was true, so his late first century readers (as well as those of us reading in the twenty-first century) could believe.

Far more happened the day Jesus died than the Romans, the Jews or Jesus' disciples could have imagined. To the disciples, it seemed the kingdom dream had ended in shocking, gruesome violence. The chief priests must have enjoyed celebrating the Passover that evening, thinking their problem with Jesus was solved. Did Pilate think it was over when he gave Jesus' body to Joseph of Arimathea to be buried? It wasn't over. It was just beginning. We're still writing and reading about it today.

Day 88, John 20

I don't like snakes. I know most of them are beneficial and not dangerous to humans. I still don't like them. When I'm in their environment, I'm always looking out for them. I understand effective anti-venom is available for most of the poisonous snakes in our area. It's good to know snake bites are seldom fatal. If I should ever be bitten, it's probably not the venom that would get me—more likely the heart attack from my fear.

Most households have chemicals useful for cleaning our bathtubs or fertilizing our geraniums that can be harmful or fatal if swallowed. I am glad Poison Control can tell us what to do if we accidentally ingest some poison, and that there are antidotes to most poisons.

The resurrection is like an antidote. Knowledge of it and faith in it saves people from a variety of pitiful conditions. The resurrection turned Mary's weeping and uncertainty to joy. The disciples' disillusionment and unbelief became strong vibrant faith in the presence of evidence that Jesus was indeed alive. When Mary, Peter and John looked into the empty tomb, the transformation began. Thomas moved rather quickly from "I will never believe" to "My Lord and my God" because of the convincing proof that it was in fact Jesus, wounds and all, who appeared in the locked room. It's a matter of seeing the evidence or hearing the testimony.

After telling about these disciples coming face to face with the risen Jesus, John said he wrote it down so we could believe. He said there was far more, but he specifically wrote what he did so that you and I could believe in Jesus the Christ, and that by believing we would have life in his name. Through his words we look with Mary and John into the empty tomb. We stand in the burial chamber with Peter and see the linen cloths that had been wrapped around his body and the cloth that was on his face. (Whatever the Shroud of Turin is or isn't, it doesn't match John's description of the cloth in which Jesus was buried.) Through our tears and struggles with faith, we are invited to see him raised, and find the antidote to our guilt, fears, confusion and uncertainty.

I love the greeting that Jesus spoke three times in this passage: "Peace be with you." Their lives had been anything but peaceful in the past hours and days. They were hiding because they were afraid. What if the Jews came for them, too? What would happen to them now that their Rabbi and Teacher was gone? Jesus quiets all that anxiety with his living presence, and transforms them into bold witnesses of his resurrection. There's a blessing for those of us who can take that step of faith without actually seeing. The antidote works by faith for us as well as it did by sight for them.

Day 89, John 21

Was Peter contemplating a return to the fishing business? Were those seven apostles on board that night uncertain about the future or just passing the time? For whatever reason, they spent a night on the familiar lake, and like most of my fishing outings, they caught nothing.

When the early morning grew light enough to see 100 yards to shore, a question came across the water to them from a man standing on the beach. It was the question unsuccessful fishermen do not want to hear: "Do you have any fish?" You can imagine the tone of their one-word reply: "No." But when they followed the suggestion of the stranger on the shore to throw the nets on the right side of the boat, they were suddenly back in business. As they strained to handle the bulging nets alive with fish, Peter and John felt the sense of déjà vu. This had happened before. Back at the beginning, Jesus had.... It was Jesus on the beach! Peter strapped on his clothes and went overboard while the others dragged the catch in to the shore.

Jesus had breakfast ready when they got there, fish and bread on the charcoal fire, waiting for them. After they had eaten, Jesus gently led Simon Peter through a reaffirmation of his love, giving him three opportunities to express his love for his Master, to cancel out the three denials Peter had spoken around another charcoal fire a few days earlier. Jesus re-commissioned the one he had nicknamed "Rock," and told him what lay ahead for him.

Peter, who had the gift of impulsive speaking (like some of us), wanted to hear something about someone else's future. Jesus refocused Peter' attention on his own assignment, telling him not to be concerned with anybody's business but his own.

I love so many things about this story. Hasn't it been your experience that we're not really very good at what we try to do without the Lord's help? I admit it, and rejoice that he blesses me again and again to do better than I could ever do on my own. Who does not know the sting and shame of failure, when through weakness or stubbornness we've not done what we promised the Lord we'd do? When I've failed, I'm so glad Jesus is willing to forgive me, and re-calibrate my heart to loving him most and putting him first in my life. And when you're an expert at monitoring other people's lives and responsibilities, Jesus' counsel to Peter could not be clearer guidance for you. All the comparisons, all the excuses, all the distractions that keep us from humbly serving him melt away into insignificance when we hear him say, "What is that to you? You follow me!"

Acts

Day 90, Acts 1

My eleven-year-old daughter hugged me in the airport concourse and cried, "I know I will never see you again." It was my first time (in her lifetime) to go away on a foreign mission trip. I was back home in three weeks, and she got used to my travels. But as children have a way of doing, she turned the tables on me. As she boarded a plane to go to Europe with her high school friends, I had a similar sense of dread about watching her fly away. When she left for college, we watched her little car until it was out of sight, and we cried. It was the same when her sister went to college. And after they left the wedding receptions with their husbands, we were happy for them and sad for us. We knew those departures were coming, but we still felt lonely when they came.

Have you stood at the big windows and watched a plane take off with your loved one on board—watched it climb, shrink to a tiny dot and finally disappear? Then maybe you can understand how the apostles felt as they watched Jesus rise into the heavens. With their necks bent and faces skyward, Jesus disappeared from their vision. Two angels assured them he would be back, returning as he left, just as he promised.

So the apostles went back to Jerusalem to wait and pray with about 120 of Jesus' followers. Jesus was no longer physically present with them. They did not know what lay ahead. But he told them to wait and they did.

We're all in the "waiting room" about something, aren't we? From kids waiting to grow up to old folks waiting to go home, each life has seasons of waiting. We enjoy some of the promises God has made here and now, but for others, we're waiting.

That little nucleus of disciples in Jerusalem models some significant characteristics of God's people who are waiting. First, they were together as they waited. They scattered when Jesus was crucified, but now they were back together. They weren't divided into factions or trying to go it alone. We need company while we wait.

They were praying as they waited. They knew their future was in God's hands. The mission would be impossible without God's help. They had to rely on God. Do your prayers show your dependence on God? Would someone watching you through a typical day see you appeal to God for help and guidance?

They obeyed instructions they had been given as they waited. They were told to stay, and they stayed. Obedience is the natural fruit of trust. We may say we trust him, but our obedience shows we really do. Disobedience equals distrust—rejecting God's counsel, preferring our own. As you wait for God to keep his promises, you keep his commands. Your obedience does not earn God's favor, but it does demonstrate your love and trust.

Day 91, Acts 2

The disciples didn't know what would happen when the Spirit came. But since Jesus said the Spirit would come, they knew he would and they recognized him when he did. The wind sound, the pyrotechnics and the miraculous ability to speak in multiple languages attracted a crowd. Like most crowds, this one contained both seekers and skeptics. Some were amazed and wondered what all this meant; others dismissed the tongue-speakers as drunks.

Peter denied the drinking charges and quoted the prophecy that was being fulfilled before their eyes. The miraculous demonstrations were predicted, but the prophet's point was the coming judgment of Israel and the salvation of those who called on the Lord.

We may miss the full impact of the Pentecost sermon because we already know the occasion, the sermon content and the results. If we could hear it as they heard it, Peter's words would glow with intensity.

The apostles were brave to stand in the city where Jesus had been crucified seven weeks earlier and say, "You knew that Jesus was approved by God. You saw the miracles. But you killed him!" Peter explained it was God's plan, described in the Scriptures, for Jesus to die and be raised from the dead. The crowd had been told that Jesus' body was stolen. But Peter said God raised Jesus from the dead, and made the one they had crucified both Lord and Christ.

The convicting message cut to the listeners' hearts. They wanted to know what to do. Peter responded with two commands and associated two promises with those commands. The commands? Repent and be baptized. The promises? They would receive forgiveness of sins and the gift of the Holy Spirit.

Repentance is a change of mind. People who had 50 days earlier cried out for Jesus' crucifixion now confessed him as the Son of God.

The Jews were familiar with ritual washings, and had seen baptism associated with repentance in the ministries of both John and Jesus. So baptism was a reasonable and familiar expression of faith and public identification.

Do you believe Jesus is the Christ? Have you done what Peter told people who believed it that first day to do? Have you turned away from sin, changing your mind from doing what you wanted to do to what he wants? Have you, as a believer, been baptized in the name of Jesus Christ? Don't think of baptism as a ritual that earns your forgiveness. Jesus did that work at the cross. Baptism is the means that Jesus and his apostles commanded for expressing our trust in him and identifying with his death, burial and resurrection. Don't debate him about it. Trust him. Obey him. He will keep his promises.

That first day, three thousand people believed the message, turned from their sins and were baptized. The Lord added them to the company of the saved. When you respond as they did, he will do the same for you.

Day 92, Acts 3

Most of history's influential leaders have been great communicators. They could get other people to follow them because of their persuasive skills.

A speaker is wasting his time if he does not establish common ground with his audience. This is especially true if he wants to change their minds about some important issue. The smart communicator knows he has to build a bridge and bring his listeners across to his side. Connecting precedes convincing.

Peter's preaching in the early days of the Jerusalem church is a masterful example of such bridge-building strategy. The miraculous signs were great attention-getters, but they only set the stage. He still had to connect and convince to bring his listeners to Christ. God used his words to convert thousands of people then, and millions since.

Peter started and finished the sermon in Solomon's portico of the temple with an appeal to Israel's strong ethnic heritage and direct references to Abraham, the revered father of their nation. When he said the God of Abraham was the one who glorified Jesus, and that Jesus was the one through whom the promises to Abraham were kept, he was plugging into their deepest identity and strongest allegiance. When Peter said Jesus was the one Moses and the prophets had foretold, he was tying the gospel message to the core of a message they already held sacred. He was telling them that putting faith in Jesus was in no way a repudiation of their scriptures and heritage; Jesus was in fact the realization of these things. All these words were constructing a bridge over which the message could be delivered.

There was not a hint of compromise in all this. Peter still told them they made a terrible choice in rejecting Jesus, giving them the glaring example of how they chose a murderer to be released instead of Jesus. He mixed no words in telling them, "You killed the Author of life." This brought him to his everyday theme: "God raised him from the dead. We are witnesses of this." Then he tied that truth to the wonder they had witnessed that very day—it was through the power of Jesus' name and faith in it that the man they knew to have been lame was now leaping around, praising God.

He then called for the change. He assured them he knew they had rejected Jesus in ignorance, and he urged them to repent. He cast the vision from their own scriptures of how blessed they would be by acknowledging Jesus as Christ, and what destruction awaited those who would not do so.

I doubt the audience was sleeping or checking the sundial while Peter was speaking that day. Everyone who would effectively communicate the message of the gospel needs to enroll in Peter's School of Preaching. What did he do? He got their attention, made the connection, spoke with conviction and called for decision. Now that's good preaching.

Day 93, Acts 4

Nothing caps a great sermon quite like the preacher being thrown into jail. The chief priests and Sadducees hated all that talk about Jesus and the resurrection. It was late in the day, so they did the only thing they could think of: they jailed the apostles—the first of many nights behind bars to come in the bold preachers' careers.

The next day, the Sanhedrin gathered for a hearing. A common plot in courtroom drama is that the slick lawyer underestimates a witness, and asks a question that allows the witness to give testimony that destroys the lawyer's case. That's what happened in the apostles' very first court appearance.

Let me put it in baseball terms for you. On the mound for the Sanhedrin, Annas the high priest was facing Peter, at bat for the visiting Apostles. Annas' first pitch was a hard fastball right down the middle: "By what power or by what name did you do this?" Peter swung at the pitch and drove it all the way into the cheap seats in deep center field. He realized in that moment what Jesus had promised about being given words to say when they were on trial. "You want to know about the good deed we did, healing a man who had been crippled more than 40 years? You want to know how we did it? By what name we did it? I'm so glad you asked! By the name of Jesus of Nazareth—you crucified him not long ago, but God raised him from the dead—by his name we did it! You men rejected him, but he is the only Savior."

And just like that, it was over. They couldn't deny the miracle; the man formerly known as the *lame man* was *standing* there right beside them. The whole city knew about it. They could only threaten the apostles and release them. "We're going to let this one slide. But you'd better not say anything else about Jesus." Peter and John hammered that one, too: "You decide if it's right for us to obey you instead of God. We can't help it; we've got to tell what we've seen and heard."

If you'd been arrested for preaching, what would you pray for when you got out? These men acknowledged that everything was happening just as God said it would. They did not pray for the opposition to go away. Instead, they prayed for boldness to keep preaching, asking God to certify their preaching with more miracles. What would you do, having been warned by powerful people to keep quiet? These men kept preaching the word with great boldness, defying the high priest's gag order.

Meanwhile, the new disciples were reflecting God's love to others, sharing with people in need. Their unity was strong and visible. The original 3,000 had become 5,000. The snowball was already rolling down the mountain. Arresting and threatening the apostles couldn't stop the number of disciples from swelling even more.

Day 94, Acts 5

Motives matter. Detectives seek a motive, asking why the suspect would commit the crime. Learning why is often more challenging than figuring out what was done and who did it.

The Jerusalem church was united and generous. Many disciples sold property and gave money to care for the poor. Joseph of Cyprus did it, and the apostles nicknamed him Barnabas (son of encouragement). Did Ananias and Sapphira want recognition for their generosity and some cash for themselves out of the transaction? They lied about how much they got when they brought the money. Instead of being praised, they were buried. Peter rebuked them for lying. They didn't have to sell, and were under no obligation to give the proceeds. Greed was the motive. It led them to lie and cost them their lives.

Jewish opposition intensified as the church grew. Why were they so determined to destroy the movement? Luke said they were filled with jealousy. Pilate recognized jealousy as the motive behind the plot to crucify Jesus. Now the same envy drove the Jews' hateful opposition to Jesus' followers. They seized and imprisoned the apostles. It's almost comical to read how the Sanhedrin called for the apostles to be brought from their cells, not knowing an angel had broken the apostles out of jail and sent them right back to the temple to teach. When the guards brought the apostles from the temple, the leaders asked what part of "don't teach anymore about Jesus" the apostles couldn't understand. They claimed the apostles intended to bring Jesus' blood (guilt for his death) on them. These same people had assured Pilate that Jesus' blood could be laid on them and their children. The apostles were celebrities, and the Jesus movement was getting out of hand. Jealousy drove the Sanhedrin to do unjust, ungodly things to try to stop the swelling growth.

The motives behind the apostles' actions are also interesting. When the high priest asked why they kept teaching, Peter and the others said, "We must obey God rather than men." They were committed to obedience and driven by allegiance to God. Peter used his court appearance to say it again: "God raised Jesus, whom you killed. He is Leader and Savior to all who will obey him." After being beaten and threatened, they left rejoicing and kept preaching the gospel. What was the motive? How could they rejoice? They understood that suffering for the Lord's sake somehow glorified him. Their song as they limped away, bruised from unjust punishment, is testimony to the power of motivation.

What motives drive our behaviors? Do we seek selfish recognition, cloaking our greed beneath a good deed? People may never know, but God will know our true motive. Do we ever criticize something good because we're jealous of the people who are doing it? Will we obey God, even under threat of negative consequences? If we are mistreated, is our primary concern God's glory or our rights? Motive makes a difference, doesn't it?

Day 95, Acts 6

Escalating persecution did not slow the rapid growth of the church. The outside pressure seemed to amplify the progress. But a situation developed from within that threatened to divide the group and distract the leaders from their God-appointed task.

Tensions are inevitable in a group of imperfect people. Someone will offend someone else. It doesn't matter if the offense was intentional or not. Cultural and language diversity (which should bring vitality and expansion opportunities to the group) can intensify the problems.

Feeding their widows was an appropriate part of the church's ministry. Poor widows were vulnerable to abuse in the ancient world, and God had taught the Jews to care for them. The Greek-speaking Jews complained that their widows were being neglected. Would internal conflict hinder the progress of the movement? The apostles avoided that possibility with a solution that worked. Their approach is a good pattern to follow when we deal with conflict.

The apostles addressed the problem instead of ignoring it. Avoidance is the number one tactic among peace-loving people when conflict arises. We'd rather not deal with it. Maybe it will go away if we don't pay it any attention. But ignored problems usually get worse instead of better.

The apostles didn't attack the complaining people; they attacked the problem they were talking about. Addressing the problem is more efficient than getting involved in personal conflict.

The apostles' plan of action was consistent with established priorities. Preaching the word of God was their task. Delivering groceries to needy widows would take time away from their real job. They were not "too good" to do benevolence work, nor were they idle. They were devoted to preaching the word and prayer. A division of labor was the most effective way to solve the problem. The modern church too often defines all church activity as "preachers' work" and gives the ministry of the church to paid staff. This strategy compromises the priority of preaching, and hinders the growth of the church.

The apostles appointed the right people for the job. They described the people needed, and told the church to find men who met the qualifications. It's no coincidence that men with Greek names were selected to deal with a problem in the Greek-speaking segment of the church. Problems are solved by getting the right person, not just anybody, to serve in ministry. The wrong person will only create more problems.

The apostles prayed for the selected helpers and gave them the authority to complete their assignment. The apostles wanted to grow the church, not control the people. They didn't micro-manage their helpers. They bathed the ministry in prayer. They wanted God's will done, not their personal agenda.

Did it work? The word continued to spread. The number of disciples multiplied. Even some Jewish priests who had opposed Jesus became disciples. The problem turned out to be a blessing because the apostles handled it well. When we imitate their strategy, we should get similar results.

Day 96, Acts 7

"You're just like your father!" Has anyone ever said that at your house? Maybe it's a compliment about physical resemblance. But it's usually a negative statement about some undesirable behavior in a child. Quarreling husbands and wives sometimes employ the phrase like a goad, implying that their mate's annoying character trait was inherited from the previous generation.

On trial before the Jewish council, a group composed mostly of Christ-rejecting hypocrites, Stephen told them they were just like their fathers. It was true, but they killed him for saying it.

Stephen had become a powerful influence through the miracles he performed and the wisdom with which he spoke as the Holy Spirit worked through him. His enemies attacked him with the same plan they had used against Jesus. They lied about Stephen, saying he spoke against Moses and God. They arrested him and brought him before the council, where false witnesses said he spoke against the temple and Moses. The high priest asked Stephen if these things were so, which opened the door for Stephen's amazing defense. His speech is a sweeping panorama of the nation's history and a succinct indictment of the Jews' rejection of the Holy Spirit.

Stephen expressed kinship and respect with his first words: "Brothers and fathers." Beginning with Abraham, he recited Israel's history, compressing decades and centuries into phrases. Over half the message is about Moses' life, including his Messianic prophecy that God would one day raise up a prophet like himself. He chronicled Israel's idolatry and rebellion. He talked about David, Solomon and the temple, but quoted Psalms and Isaiah to show that no physical building could be God's dwelling. Then he said they rejected Jesus just like their fathers rejected the prophets.

Enraged, the Jewish leaders stoned Stephen to death, after Stephen said he saw Jesus standing at God's right hand in heaven. As Jesus had done, Stephen prayed the Lord would not hold his murderers' sin against them, and asked the Lord to receive his spirit as he died. At the end of this sad account, Luke introduced a character we'll see again in this story—a young man named Saul who guarded the coats of Stephen's executioners.

What can we take away from this chapter besides a heavy heart over the first Christian martyr? Let's remember that religious people did this terrible thing. They stopped up their ears as they rushed to kill Stephen, but their minds and hearts were closed before they made the physical gesture. Let's beware the temptation to do ungodly things under the guise of being loyal to God.

Stephen is one of our great heroes. His courage was unflinching in the face of hostile opposition. His heart was unblemished by bitterness, even toward his killers. His faith was unshaken as he died. Ah, that you and I might live, and if necessary, die like Stephen did!

Day 97, Acts 8

Do you struggle with some temptation because of your past? Are you searching for God and wrestling with questions? There are some good examples for you in today's reading.

Stephen's death marked the beginning of intensified hostility against the disciples. Instead of quelling the movement, the opposition spread the gospel from Jerusalem. Luke shows how that happened in the adventures of Philip. When Philip took the good news on the road, he found people who received the message so many had rejected in Jerusalem.

The Samaritans believed the preaching about Jesus and the kingdom of God, amazed by the signs Philip performed. Superstition flourishes in the darkness, and Simon had tricked the Samaritans into thinking he had the great power of God. When they (including Simon) saw the real power of God in Philip, they were baptized in the name of Jesus. Simon knew the difference in his tricks and what

Philip was doing. When the apostles came, he tried to buy the power of the Holy Spirit. Peter rebuked him and warned him to repent. Simon accepted the rebuke and turned away from his bad idea.

Even when we have new life in Christ, our past may make us more vulnerable to certain temptations. New Simon was still thinking like old Simon about how he could use that power. Peter's stern censure was a necessary course correction for the former trickster.

Philip's next assignment took him out of the city and into the desert where the Holy Spirit got him a ride with a sincere seeker. The Ethiopian had traveled to Jerusalem to worship as a proselyte to Judaism. As he returned, he wasn't reading a magazine or playing chariot tag bingo to pass the time. Although it gives me a terrific headache to read while riding, this fellow was reading Isaiah in his Bible as he rolled through the wilderness.

When Philip asked if he understood what he was reading, the Ethiopian replied, "How can I, unless someone guides me?" I like his humility! Philip started in Isaiah 53 where the man was reading, and told him about Jesus. That's a good lesson about sharing your faith. You have to meet folks where they are if you want to get them where you want them to go. I also like the Ethiopian's eagerness to do what he learned. Instead of questioning the necessity of it, he asked to be baptized when they came to some water. He found what he was looking for and went home rejoicing, even though the preacher disappeared right after baptizing him!

Both these stories are about humility. If you've fallen for a temptation, are you humble enough to be corrected and repent? If you're looking for joy and meaning, are you humble enough to learn? When you learn the will of God, are you humble enough to obey? How often has pride kept us from learning what we need to know and doing what we need to do?

Day 98, Acts 9

The church was growing in Jerusalem and beyond as many people turned to Christ. An amazing change in one man's life would bring many more to Jesus.

Do you know anyone who's made a radical change? A conservative who's become a liberal? A Democrat who turned into a Republican? A chocolate lover who now won't even touch the stuff? (That's a little extreme, I know.) Those examples are mere positional shifts compared to the 180 degree change that came to Saul of Tarsus.

The rising star of the Sanhedrin distinguished himself through tenacious persecution of Jesus' followers. When disciples fled Jerusalem, Saul followed them with warrants to arrest and return any men or women he could find who were Jesus' disciples. Then, on one bounty hunt to Damascus, everything changed for Saul. The Lord appeared and spoke to Saul. His traveling companions led Saul, blinded from the encounter, to Damascus. He fasted three days and nights in the darkness, waiting for the promised instructions.

Imagine for a moment that you are Ananias. You've heard of Saul and you know he is on his way to Damascus to arrest any disciples he could find. Then the Lord gives you the ultimate dreaded visitation assignment: "Go over to Straight Street, to Judas' house. Saul is there. He knows you're coming. He's waiting for you." You tell the Lord what you've heard about this terrorist. He insists that you go anyway, and says this one is a chosen instrument to carry his name. So you go. You touch him. You deliver the message. Saul's sight returns. He is baptized. And then the persecutor is a preacher, proclaiming that Jesus of Nazareth is Messiah. You no longer wonder if it is possible for people to change.

The reactions to this transformation are predictable. The Jews go to their default plan for people who are persuading others to follow Jesus: they decide to kill Saul. Would-be assassins watch the gate day and night, waiting for an opportunity to kill the defector. After Saul escapes Damascus by the old "preacher in a basket" trick, he goes to Jerusalem. The believers there are understandably skeptical of his conversion when he wants to join them. Barnabas (who will later be Saul's mission partner) vouches for Saul and persuades the disciples to trust him. Same bold preaching. Same Jewish plot. Same escape maneuvers. But a very different Saul. The road warrior against Jesus is bringing the same tenacity to his new assignment—a road warrior for Jesus.

Why is this important to you? Maybe you're discouraged about someone who needs to change. You've waited, but it's just not happening. You wonder, "Does anybody ever really does change?" This story says the answer is "Yes." Maybe you're disgusted by your own lack of progress as a Christian. You begin to doubt you've changed, or that it's even possible to change. Take courage. When we, like Saul, settle the question of who we call "Lord," amazing changes follow.

Day 99, Acts 10

When Jesus commissioned the apostles to preach the gospel, the plan called for humans to tell other humans the good news. The Lord authenticated their testimony through miracles. God was working in the background—intersecting Philip with the Ethiopian, sending Ananias to Saul. But divine hands-on activity was needed for the next step in the expansion of the gospel beyond Judaism.

Cornelius was a good man who needed Christ. He was devout, generous and prayerful. But he was also a Gentile, a Roman soldier. An angel told him to send for Peter, who had something to say that Cornelius needed to hear. When Peter arrived, he wanted to know why he had been summoned to this Gentile's house. Cornelius told him about the angel and the message from God. After hearing Cornelius' story, Peter did not hesitate to tell Cornelius and his household about Jesus.

God had been working on Peter, too. A roof-top vision of a menagerie of clean and unclean animals wrapped in a sheet was accompanied by God's own voice, telling hungry Peter to kill and eat. When Peter refused, he heard, "What God has made clean, do not call common." After this happened three times, the men from Cornelius were at the gate, looking for Peter. Peter didn't have all the answers yet, but he was far enough along to receive the guests and go with them the following day.

After Peter preached at Cornelius' house, the Jews who had come with him were astonished when the Holy Spirit was poured out on Cornelius and the others there, just as it had happened on Pentecost. As the centurion and his friends learned how to be saved, the Jews learned that God intended for people of all nations to come to him through Christ. Peter had talked about it in the first sermon at Pentecost; now both preacher and audience were seeing it come true. No one present could object to these Gentiles being baptized in the name of Christ.

If you are not a follower of Jesus, the message for you is this: As good as Cornelius was, he needed Christ. No amount of kind benevolence, praying or any other demonstration of piety can take the place of knowing Christ as your Savior. Salvation is in him, not morality or good works.

If you are a Christian, does your conduct show God is interested in every person without partiality? Peter and his Jewish brothers were overcoming centuries of cultural conditioning to align themselves with God's plan. We can see the exclusiveness of the ancient Jews. Do we see it in ourselves? Our discrimination may be based on other criteria, but we need to acknowledge it exists, and overcome it with God's help.

Aren't you glad that God is working, drawing his people to himself? Will we be observant, and receptive to his guidance? Whose path will intersect with yours today or tomorrow to make an eternal difference?

Day 100, Acts 11

The news from Cornelius' house got back to Jerusalem before Peter did. The critics were waiting for him. (Expect criticism from people who don't want change when you do something innovative for the Lord.) Their prejudice was clear. They did not accuse him of baptizing Gentiles; they criticized him for eating with uncircumcised Gentiles. Peter told them about his vision, Cornelius' angel visitor, and the Holy Spirit falling on Gentiles, just as he had done on Jews at Pentecost. Peter concluded with a good question: "Who was I that I could stand in God's way?" He realized that Gentile inclusiveness was coming straight from the Lord, and that he could not set God's agenda or limit God's plan.

This is the same Peter who a few years earlier told Jesus the cross was never going to happen. When the Lord spoke of his approaching death and resurrection, Peter rebuked him for saying such things. Jesus' words must have stung Peter as his Master told him, "Get behind me, Satan! You are a hindrance to me. For you are not setting you mind on the things of God, but on the things of man." That wasn't Peter's last impulsive remark, but he learned from the experience. Peter had to get used to associating with Gentiles. When he realized it was God's plan, he knew better than to stand in the way.

After Peter's explanation, the critics stopped criticizing their brother and started praising God, saying, "Then to the Gentiles also God has granted repentance that leads to life." The leaders had to learn the lesson and live it before the followers could embrace it. Massive expansion into the Gentile world was coming. Antioch would become the new center as evangelistic missions to Gentiles went out from an integrated church where the disciples were first called Christians. But the church in Jerusalem needed to learn that Jews and Gentiles were equal in God's sight. They didn't get it perfectly. (Which of God's designs do you get perfectly?) Rocky controversy over Gentiles keeping the Law of Moses was coming. But these events positioned the church as much more than an extension of Judaism.

Not only Peter and not only Jews resist God's way. Don't we do the same when his will goes against what we think or how we've always done it? Maybe it's stubborn resistance to God's will about your personal life. Maybe it's grace being shown to people you don't think are worthy (as you forget for a moment your own unworthiness and need of the same grace). It could be learning that the kingdom of God is much bigger than the limitations of your understanding. Whatever the point of your resistance, I pray that you, like Peter, will see the futility of standing in God's way. Like a mighty locomotive speeding down the tracks, God's purpose is moving ahead. You can stand on the tracks and protest, or you can ride. My advice to you is: "All aboard!"

Day 101, Acts 12

The jail break stories are almost light-hearted reminders of Who's In Charge. Don't misunderstand. There's nothing pleasant about the beatings and executions. The persecution was serious and severe. But when rulers or jailers, Jews or Gentiles, tried to imprison people that God wanted out, no chains or bars could hold them.

James had left his father's fishing boat years earlier to follow Jesus. He was among the select few who saw and heard things that even other apostles were not privileged to share. For reasons unapparent to us, God allowed him to die under Herod's hateful sword. Herod was a ruthless bully who killed innocent people for political advantage. But Herod did not overpower God to kill an apostle, or snatch one away while God wasn't looking. Peter's deliverance proves that God was still in control.

Has anxiety ever kept you awake? You may marvel that Peter was asleep the night before his scheduled execution. The angel touched him and spoke to him, as if rousing a sleepy-headed teenager on a school morning. He told him each step to take about getting dressed and out the door. Peter thought he was dreaming or seeing a vision until he was out on the street and realized that the Lord had broken him out of jail again.

Peter's appearance at Mary's house also makes me smile. The disciples were praying hard for Peter's rescue. When he knocked at the door, their prayers answered, they thought Rhoda was crazy when she announced Peter was there! In her excitement, she had not opened the gate to let him in. So Peter stood outside knocking while the prayer group analyzed Rhoda's mental health and wondered who or what might be out there, since everybody knew Peter was in jail.

It wasn't funny to Herod or the guards when morning came and Peter was gone. Herod ordered the execution of the incompetent guard detail, and went to his lake house.

Peter wasn't the only one struck by an angel. Herod, arrayed in his royal finery and giving an oration from his throne, was struck down and died even as the audience proclaimed him to be a god. In a single contrasting sentence, Luke reminded his readers that the real word of the real God continued to increase and multiply. God was in control. No opponent could win; no one on the Lord's side could lose.

If you suffer for following Jesus, don't doubt that God is in control. Trust him. If you are imprisoned (literally or figuratively), don't doubt that God can get you out if he wants you out. Trust him. If you're praying in faith for what seems impossible, don't be so surprised when it happens. Trust him. Never confuse your own squeaky little voice (or anyone else's) with the mighty word of God. Trust him. And believe that one day all injustice will be rectified, and mysteries about why certain things happened as they did will evaporate. Trust him.

Day 102, Acts 13

As Barnabas and Saul went out on their mission from Antioch, their first stop was on the island of Cyprus, Barnabas' homeland. Some changes took place there that shaped the rest of the story in Acts. First, Saul became Paul in a single parenthetical phrase. And Barnabas and Saul became Paul and Barnabas. Barnabas will be mentioned first in the pairing another time or two, but Paul became the dominant figure, not only in his partnership with Barnabas, but across the rest of Luke's narrative. The story's emphasis shifted from Jews, Jerusalem and Peter to Gentiles, Antioch and Paul.

The core message of the preaching did not change. Paul's sermon at Antioch in Pisidia is essentially the same as Peter's at Jerusalem on Pentecost. A brief survey of the history, promises and prophecies fast forwards to Jesus. The Jews' rejection, the crucifixion, the resurrection, the promise of forgiveness and eternal life for those who respond in faith to the message—all the familiar elements are there. And just like in Jerusalem, the response was mixed. Some received it with joy; others rejected it and were filled with jealousy when the crowds began to swell.

Paul saw not only the elements of the story about Jesus, but also the acceptance or rejection by the audience as fulfillment of what God said. To Jews ("Men of Israel," "sons of the family of Abraham") and Gentiles ("you who fear God"), Paul said Jesus came, just as God promised he would. He said the Jewish leaders did not recognize Jesus or understand the prophecies, and they fulfilled the prophecies by condemning Jesus. His death was a matter of carrying out everything that was written. His resurrection was the fulfillment of the promises of God. Paul warned them not to fulfill Habakkuk's prophecy that many would reject the message when they heard it. When the unbelieving Jews started speaking against Paul, he said the Jews were judging themselves unworthy of eternal life, and that he and Barnabas would turn to the Gentiles as a matter of fulfilled prophecy.

Audiences were moved to trust God by hearing about the fulfillment of his word. That should still work the same way today. The messengers sensed (and still should) that the acceptance and rejection of the gospel is a matter of fulfilled prophecy more than a pride-fueling victory or a discouraging defeat.

Our faith is strengthened by seeing that God fulfills the prophecies in his word. Our confidence is bolstered by knowing God keeps his promises. As works in progress, it's good to know that God has promised to complete his work in us. As mortals living in a material world, it's comforting to trust what he's promised about the resurrection and eternal life. As guilty sinners, we find hope and peace in trusting God's promise to forgive us in Christ. All of this rests on the reliability of God's word. I hope you will be encouraged by his faithfulness.

Day 103, Acts 14

On the mission field, the gospel continued to do what Jesus said it would do—divide the hearers into receivers and rejecters. As the missionaries spoke and the Lord vouched for their message through miracles, many believed, but many others demonstrated their rejection through violent opposition.

When the pagans at Lystra saw a crippled man who had never walked up walking around, the deep desire to worship something greater expressed itself in an attempt to offer sacrifice to Barnabas and Paul, whom they had mistaken for Zeus and Hermes. The apostles stopped the sacrifice and told them about the real God who made everything and gave them all they had ever enjoyed. Paul's impassioned declaration of the true God contains one of the most lyrical sentences in the Bible: "Yet he did not leave himself without witness, for he did good by giving you rains from heaven and fruitful seasons, satisfying your hearts with food and gladness."

The public is fickle, and popular opinion is volatile. Paul's treatment at Lystra is a good example. The same crowd tried to worship

Paul, and then stone him to death. Some Jews who followed Paul and Barnabas from cities where they'd been came and persuaded the Lystrans to take up stones against Paul. Paul and Barnabas escaped at Iconium, but this time they got Paul, and thought they had killed him. Was he unconscious? Was he dead? I don't know, but I do know he got up and walked back into town. I might have booked my flight home after such treatment. But the next day Paul went on to Derbe, and then, incredibly, traced the journey back through Lystra where he had been stoned and back through the cities they'd already visited.

Paul and Barnabas went back to strengthen the young converts, to encourage and warn them about the adversity they would face as followers of Christ. I suspect a warning about persecution carries more weight when it comes from a bruised messenger. The apostles also appointed elders to lead the young churches, and committed the converts they left behind in each city to the Lord.

The whole church gathered to hear all God had done through the apostles (apostle means "sent one") when Paul and Barnabas returned. They told how God opened the door of faith to the Gentiles.

Have you ever thought about meeting brothers and sisters in heaven from those ancient cities where the missionaries preached? Those town names are just hard-to-pronounce words in our Bibles. But people who lived there then were saved when they heard and believed the same gospel you and I are saved by here and now, 2,000 years later on the other side of the world. Nobody gets in through the door of good works. Nobody goes through the door of self-righteousness. Through the righteousness of Jesus Christ and his redemptive work on the cross, God opened a door of faith for all who would enter.

Day 104, Acts 15

Conflict challenges the warmest fellowship and closest friendship. Differences of opinion are inevitable and feelings are at risk.

The growth of the church accelerated as more Gentiles came to Christ. Their integration sparked the first major doctrinal controversy among the disciples. Some Jews insisted that Gentiles had to be circumcised to be saved. Were Jesus' disciples required to bear the same distinction in their flesh as Abraham's descendants?

When this teaching reached Antioch, Paul and Barnabas debated with the Judean teachers. Paul and Barnabas saw that demanding Gentile circumcision was adding to the gospel. They went to the apostles and elders of the church at Jerusalem to settle the matter. The Jerusalem church welcomed them, and rejoiced about the Gentile converts. But some former Pharisees insisted Gentiles had to be circumcised and keep the Law of Moses. (Here's another example of what someone was before conversion affecting them afterward.) Their Pharisee heritage shaped their opinion about circumcising Gentiles.

Peter reminded everyone that Gentiles and Jews were equal in God's sight. The Holy Spirit settled that at Cornelius' house. Peter said all their hearts were cleansed by faith, and that Jews and Gentiles alike were saved by grace. He called the law an unbearable yoke, and asked why they would bind it on the Gentiles.

James quoted prophecy to show God's plan had always included Gentiles. He counseled against making it harder for Gentiles to come to Christ by adding the demands of the Law. He advised that Gentile converts should abstain from things associated with pagan worship to avoid unnecessary offense to the Jews. This solution considered the sensitivities of all parties. While it did not evaporate the ethnic struggles that would continue to challenge the church, it did set a pattern for maintaining unity. The meeting and the letter that came from it reiterated that salvation was in Christ alone.

In a twist of irony, Luke reported another conflict, this one personal instead of doctrinal. Paul proposed a trip to visit the converts from the first journey. Barnabas wanted to take John Mark again, but Paul refused. Unable to agree, Barnabas and his cousin sailed to Cyprus, while Paul took Silas and hit the road.

These conflicts were different. One was doctrinal and threatened the unity of the church. The other was a matter of opinion. Personal disagreements can disturb the peace in the church, but these men didn't let that happen. Neither of them quit working for the Lord. Neither launched a smear campaign against the other. Though they separated for a while, Paul would write warm, complimentary things about Barnabas and John Mark in epistles to come.

Some issues must be resolved. But it may be best to agree to disagree about other matters and go separate ways with mutual love and respect. May we be wise enough to know which is which, strong enough to contend honorably when necessary, and humble enough to submit to one another when we can.

Day 105, Acts 16

When should you give in to others, and when do you stand up for yourself? Is it hard to obey when God's plan differs from what you had in mind? When trouble comes, do you blame God or worship him?

As Paul and his company traveled across Gentile regions where churches had been planted, they brought the letter from Jerusalem about freedom from the Law of Moses. Encouraged by this news, those churches continued to grow.

At Lystra, Paul added Timothy to the team. Years later, the aging apostle would send Timothy on critical missions and hand responsibilities over to his trusted son in the faith. But the young man had to be discipled to be ready when the time came.

Paul decided to circumcise Timothy for practical, not doctrinal reasons. Timothy, the son of a Jewish woman and a Greek man, would enjoy wider acceptance and have greater influence among the Jews if he were circumcised. In contrast, Paul refused to circumcise Titus (a true Gentile) since his circumcision would serve no practical purpose, and could compromise the gospel.

The Holy Spirit directed the mission, vetoing some proposed routes, then leading the group to Troas, where Paul added another team member. Although he does not name himself, the pronoun "they" becomes "we" as Luke joined the entourage to be an almost constant companion for the rest of Paul's life.

Paul entered Europe after he saw a vision of a Macedonian asking for help. In Philippi, Paul's message was welcomed by some and violently opposed by others. The nucleus of the church at Philippi included a successful business woman named Lydia, who listened to Paul's teaching and was baptized along with her household.

After Paul cast a demon out of a slave girl, her owners who had used her for fortune-telling realized their income stream had been stopped. Through prejudice and lies, they had Paul and Silas beaten and imprisoned. In the most dramatic jailbreak in Acts, an earthquake set Paul and Silas free. The jailer, on the brink of suicide, became a believer and was baptized with his family the same night. He joyfully took his new brothers in Christ to his house and fed them.

After the magistrates learned they had beaten Roman citizens without a trial, they encouraged Paul to leave town. Paul insisted that the leaders come in person to escort them out of jail. The leaders came, apologized and asked them to go. Paul went back to Lydia's house to see the church, and moved on.

I need more of the wisdom Paul displayed. He knew when to concede and when to stand up for his rights. He was sensitive and submissive to God's guidance. His acted and spoke in the name of Jesus, not his own. And when adversity came and he was treated unjustly, he still worshiped God. If you also struggle in such situations, join me in learning from Paul how to deny self to follow Christ.

Day 106, Acts 17

Candidates used to give the same speech from memory at every stop on the campaign trail. Now they need teleprompters to read what their speech writers have written for today, since the 24-hour news networks have already reported every word they said yesterday.

Some well-known preachers deliver the same sermon many times in many places, reciting their material word-for-word. Paul's core message was always the same: "Jesus, crucified and raised from the dead, is the Christ." But Paul was a master of starting where the audience was, and bringing them to where he wanted them to be in their thinking. At the synagogue, the audience already believed in God and respected the Scriptures as God's word. So there, Paul reasoned, explained and proved that Jesus was the fulfillment of all the promises and prophecies about Messiah. But with a marketplace audience of polytheistic pagans, Paul rewound the story all the way to Genesis, telling how the one God they did not know was creator and sustainer of everything. Then he would get to the main theme. In synagogues and market places, the conclusion was always the same, always Jesus.

In one of his letters, Paul explained that he became all things to all people in order to win them to Christ. Paul started his campaigns in the Jewish synagogue in cities where there were enough Jews for one to exist. But he also interacted with the mainstream Gentile culture of the places he visited. His methods suggest some principles we should remember about obeying the Lord's command to make disciples.

When Paul addressed the philosophers in Athens, he had seen their city full of idols. He knew their reputation for curiosity. So when they brought him from the marketplace where they had met to the Areopagus to hear him speak, Paul knew where to begin.

He addressed them with courtesy, commenting on their proclivity for religion. Paul found inroads to their thinking in their contemporary culture. He noted the altar to the unknown god, and quoted their literature to illustrate how God knows and is near us. He explained the idea of one God to the polytheists, describing who God was and what God had done. As you would expect, Paul closed by talking about Jesus and the resurrection.

How about our outreach efforts? Do we ever go "outside" where "outsiders" might see or hear us? Are we interesting enough to get their attention? Are we courteous and respectful? Do we know enough about contemporary culture to connect with people in it by referring to it in our presentations? Do we have the courage of our convictions to stand for "the Way, the Truth and the Life" in a pluralistic society? Do listeners discern that our message is centered in Christ?

The results in Athens were mixed. Some people mocked the message. Some wanted to hear it again. Some became believers. We'll probably get the same responses from our efforts to share Christ in our culture.

Day 107, Acts 18

Do you find comfort or frustration in continuity? Does a routine give you peace, or make you long for variety? Discipleship is an every day calling. But the disciple's walk has some elements subject to change, and some that are constant.

Today's portion illustrates the "sometimes" elements of discipleship. Paul's ministry was usually itinerant. He went "from one place to the next through the region." But sometimes he stayed a while—a year and six months at Corinth.

Paul usually traveled with associates such as Silas and Timothy. Aquila and Priscilla were co-workers. But sometimes he sent his partners somewhere else, or left them behind to continue the work. Some life lessons are learned in solitude, but it's good to have people with whom you can share joys and sorrows.

Paul's tent-making suggests another variable: not everyone can serve full-time in ministry. It's sometimes necessary to support ourselves in secular work. Don't be discouraged if you want to serve the Lord, but have another job. Even the apostle Paul sometimes worked at his trade. God is able to use you and your desire to serve him in the workplace.

Also, your efforts to share Christ may sometimes be productive, and sometimes not. Some listeners will do as the Corinthians did—hear the gospel, believe and be baptized. But others may oppose you and your message. Our commission is not variable. We're supposed to go make disciples. But the results of our efforts will vary. We will be saved from pride (when it's going well) and despair (when it's not) if we will remember that.

For all the variables illustrated here, there are also some reliable constants in the disciple's walk. For instance, the core message never changes. Paul (and Apollos) had a constant theme: "The Christ is Jesus." Disciples are life-long learners, but the message we share with other about Jesus remains the same. Apollos was eloquent, competent and fervent; but he needed to know more. He was more effective as a preacher after being humble enough to learn from Aquila and Priscilla.

As Paul left Ephesus, he said he would return, "if God wills." Imagine the freedom from anxiety we could know if we learned to plan "if God wills." Remember Jesus praying in Gethsemane? He asked if the cup could pass and prayed, "Not my will, but yours be done." He prayed that way the night before the cross because he had lived his whole life that way, always speaking, doing, going as God willed.

There's another constant of following Christ in view here. When the Lord told Paul in a vision to not be afraid, he reminded him, "I am with you." He has promised he will never leave us or forsake us. Our courage should flourish and our excuses should melt as we trust the Lord's abiding presence. Whether circumstances are changing or staying the same, we can enjoy the calm confidence of knowing he is with us.

Day 108, Acts 19

Paul's adventures in Acts may make us think the apostles were larger-than-life super-heroes in a fictitious story. But the incredible episodes are laced with reminders of reality.

Apollos probably taught the disciples Paul found at Ephesus. Before meeting Aquila and Priscilla, Apollos had taught about Jesus at Ephesus, knowing only John's baptism. Later, Paul found disciples there who only knew about John's baptism. What's the point? A teacher can't take his students beyond his own knowledge. All who would teach or lead need to remember this. Continuing education, not necessarily of the formal variety, is a necessity for leaders and teachers.

The exorcists who invoked Jesus' name with a painful and embarrassing outcome remind us that it's useless to use Jesus' name without a genuine relationship with him. The exorcism failed, but the incident brought positive results. The name of Jesus was more revered, and many gave up the dark arts and burned their books in a bonfire where fifty thousand silver pieces' worth of occult books went up in smoke! In contrast, the word of God kept on increasing and prevailing.

The riot started by Demetrius reminds us that some people are opposed to the gospel because it impacts their finances. Demetrius claimed to be concerned about Artemis' honor, but he first mentioned that Paul's preaching was reducing the idol makers' income.

It's a reality of life in a material world that money is the reason why people do what they do.

It's also a reality that many who are vocal about some issue may know nothing about it. Luke said the Artemis pep rally was filled with people who had no idea why they were rioting. After they got tired (or maybe hoarse) from shouting for hours, the town clerk reminded them they lived under the shadow of Rome's imperial boot, and the Romans didn't like civil unrest. Some folks today may be audacious for a cause, yet understand very little about it.

A bold defense or reasoned argument may be ineffective in a hyper-emotional setting. Paul was no stranger to controversy. He wanted to go into the fray, but the disciples restrained him. When we're ready to take on all challengers with our reasoning and persuasive power, we should remember this occasion. Paul himself wasn't allowed to confront the widely-held convictions of the culture in an emotionally charged arena.

There's also a lesson for us in how the clerk described Paul and his company. He knew the disciples had done nothing sacrilegious or blasphemous against Artemis. If Paul had been caustic and arrogant in his preaching during the two years he had been in Ephesus, it's unlikely the clerk would have held such a high opinion of him. It's one thing to persuade; it's another to insult. In our passion and zeal for the cause, we would do well to remember the difference. It's not compromise to realize that discretion is, sometimes, the better part of valor.

Day 109, Acts 20

Who's been your most influential teacher or mentor? What set them apart from others you have known?

To Christians across the northeastern arc of the Mediterranean, Paul was the leading figure of the movement. Many of them heard the gospel from his own mouth, and others came to Christ in the churches he planted in city after city. Paul's description of his ministry paints a vivid portrait of an effective spiritual mentor.

Unjust arrest and incarceration, brutal mistreatment, assassination plots and forced departures were common in Paul's experience.

Paul explained how he kept going in his talk with the elders from Ephesus. He said he no longer counted his life precious. He wanted to testify to the gospel of God's grace wherever God's Spirit sent him. He cared more about the mission than his personal safety. His example convicts many of us who qualify our willingness to serve on convenience and comfort! Paul accomplished more for the Lord than any other worker we know, because he lost his sense of self (just as Jesus has told us all to do).

It must have been painful for Paul to describe the Jewish plots against him. Remember, Paul was a devout Jew himself. Decades after his conversion to Christ and hundreds of miles from Jerusalem, he was still marking time by the Jewish calendar. Luke described their departure from Philippi as "after the days of Unleavened Bread." Paul based his itinerary on getting to Jerusalem by Pentecost. No doubt many of the tears Paul shed as he served were out of love and concern for his fellow Israelites, who were rejecting their Messiah and the gospel of their salvation.

Paul said the Ephesian elders knew how he had lived among them during the three years he spent there. A spiritual mentor's example empowers and validates his teaching. A spiritual leader is foolish to think he can separate how he lives from what he says. Paul said he was a servant, working with his hands to provide for himself and others. People who are allergic to work and service are not likely to be strong spiritual leaders. Paul said he shed some tears during his ministry at Ephesus, showing his heart for the work and the souls of the people he taught. He said he was innocent of their blood because he never held back anything they needed to hear, and declared the whole counsel of God to them. It takes a great leader to say hard things in love that his people need to hear. He committed them into the hands of God and his word, the real source of his power as their mentor. We love our leaders and honor our mentors in the faith. But God's word is the real force behind the greatest teacher's words.

Paul's life is a powerful testimony to the amazing potential of a life surrendered to God's purpose. That qualifies him to be a mentor throughout the ages for us all.

Day 110, Acts 21

How do sincere, intelligent people disagree about a plain revelation from God? Many divisions among Jesus' followers are rooted in personality clashes and selective emphases. Like the Hatfields and McCoys, the current generations may have forgotten what started the feud. But people who agree about the core of the gospel sometimes disagree over direct statements from the Lord. It's simplistic and self-serving to claim that everyone who is sincere can understand it (like we do) if they would only be honest about it (like we are).

At several stops along the route to Jerusalem, the disciples warned Paul not to go there. Luke said the disciples at Tyre did so "through the Spirit." At Philip's house in Caesarea, the prophet Agabus bound himself with Paul's belt, saying, "Thus says the Holy Spirit," and then foretelling how the belt's owner would be bound and delivered to the Romans at Jerusalem. Did Paul rebel against the Spirit's guidance by continuing?

I think not. When the Spirit forbade them to preach in Asia and Bithynia, the missionaries obeyed and followed the guidance that led them to Philippi. If the messages the disciples were getting had been prohibitions, I think Paul would have listened.

These warnings and the disciples' fear remind me of how Peter reacted when Jesus started talking about the cross: "Far be it from you Lord! This shall never happen to you." Jesus rebuked him and told him he was thinking in human terms, not according to God's divine plan. I sense the same thing with the disciples and Paul. When the disciples learned what would happen to Paul when he reached Jerusalem, their emotional response was to plead with him not to go. Remember, the Spirit had already been testifying to him in every city that affliction and persecution awaited him, and that he was bound by the Spirit to continue. When Luke and the others begged Paul to change his plans, Paul asked why they were weeping and breaking his heart, since he was ready to be bound and to die for the name of the Lord Jesus. At last the disciples relented and said, "Let the will of the Lord be done."

After Paul got to Jerusalem, some Asiatic Jews caused an uproar based on a false charge. The mob would have beaten Paul to death if the Romans hadn't arrested him. Just like the Spirit said, Paul suffered persecution, affliction, and fell into the hands of the Gentiles.

The revelation was the same. The difference was in how it was received. Was everybody sincere? Of course. Was everybody honest? Yes. But based on their frame of reference (the disciples' affection for Paul, and Paul's selfless commitment to the mission), they were reaching different conclusions about the same Spirit-given word. As sincere followers of Jesus, let's avoid dogmatism about our interpretations and be less accusative of those who may reach different conclusions from our own. The difference may lie in our frame of reference.

Day 111, Acts 22

Suppose you've just been rescued from an angry mob trying to kill you. Given an opportunity to address them, what would you say? I fear I might be like James and John, who once wanted to call down fire from heaven to toast some Samaritans who didn't want Jesus to come through their town. But I'd like to grow enough to be like Paul in such a situation. His speech on the steps of the barracks shows his heart toward his own people who made themselves his enemy. It also displays his bold courage to proclaim Jesus as Lord to unbelievers, and his masterful skills at connecting with his audience.

Did Paul remember being Saul, standing among the angry Jews who murdered Stephen decades earlier? Like Stephen, Paul began by showing respect for and establishing common ground with his hostile audience. He built a bridge to them by explaining how Jewish he was, how he had been zealous for God just as they were, and how he had persecuted disciples of Jesus. He told them the amazing story of his conversion when the Lord Jesus appeared to him on the road to Damascus, and how he had been blinded by the experience. He stressed that the man who came to restore his sight and tell him to be baptized was a devout, law-keeping Jew with a good reputation among his fellow Jews. He said it was God who told him to get away from Jerusalem and the unbelieving Jews, and to take the gospel to the Gentiles.

That Paul's speech lasted as long as it did is testimony to the power of a story well-told. It kept the mob of would-be killers at bay

for a while. But when the stinging words about Stephen's death land-
ed on their conscience, and then when Paul said the "G-word"—talking about the Gentiles, they were done. The riot was on again. The
Roman official decided to torture Paul to find out why the Jews were
so mad at him. Paul escaped the flogging by showing his passport,
his Roman citizenship. As it had done before at Philippi, Paul's status as a Roman citizen made his captors nervous about how they had
already treated him, and helped them rethink their plans for dealing
with Paul.

Is there some word that signals the end of your willingness to
listen to the word of God? When the preacher gets to a certain subject, or you find a particularly convicting passage in your Bible reading, do you sometimes turn off your attention and turn on your anger? We need to be willing to identify what convicts us and provokes
us. Like a doctor pressing to find out where it hurts, the word of God
exposes our weaknesses and guilt. When we hear a word that makes
us defensive and want to tell God to mind his own business, that's
precisely where we need to repent and yield to him.

Day 112, Acts 23

Do you play chess? A smart player figures out his opponent's
strategy, and employs a counter-strategy to thwart his rival's plan.
The same strategic maneuvers that win in chess are used on athletic
fields and battlefields, in boardrooms and courtrooms.

For the second time in as many days, Claudius Lysias had to apply imperial force to extricate Paul from a bunch of angry Jews. The
second intervention was necessary after the Roman tribune called
the Sanhedrin together to find out why these people hated Paul so
much.

Paul began by telling the high court he had always lived in good
conscience before God. It's not a good sign your speech is going to be
well-received when your opening line gets you slapped in the mouth.
Paul returned verbal fire for the hypocritical and illegal insult, and
was inadvertently disrespectful to the Jewish high priest. Paul acknowledged it was not right to speak harshly against a leader. (That's

a lesson that politicians, media and the general public should remember here in America, too.)

"Divide and Conquer" is a time-honored strategy. Paul used it to split the Sanhedrin, turning their anger on one another instead of him. With political savvy, Paul claimed his Pharisee heritage, and said he was on trial over the resurrection, the main point of controversy between Pharisees and Sadducees. The ploy worked; the council split along party lines as the Pharisees suddenly found no fault with Paul after he waved the party banner. Paul's Roman guardians had to remove him by force from the ensuing violence.

After the Romans rescued him, 40 men vowed not to eat or drink until they had killed Paul. They either broke that vow or died of hunger or thirst, because 470 Roman soldiers formed a human shield and took Paul out of Jerusalem the same night. Soon Paul was at Caesarea before Felix, the governor. He was in Roman custody, but it was protective custody.

Paul's life was in God's hand. High priests and councils, tribunes and governors are God's pawns as he accomplishes his purpose. In the midst of all the violence and threats, the Lord stood by Paul in his cell and said, "Take courage, for as you have testified to the facts about me in Jerusalem, so you must testify also in Rome." God was in charge. Just as a Roman decree had unwittingly delivered Mary and Joseph to Bethlehem for Jesus to be born where the prophets predicted, now the Roman judicial system would be Paul's ticket to the imperial city. He didn't have to worry about whether or how he would get there. When God says you must testify in Rome, you're on your way.

A strategy is a good thing. Make plans, but remember you're in God's hands. In his sovereignty, he works through his people as well as their enemies to accomplish his purpose. This should ease our anxieties and give us confidence as we serve him.

Day 113, Acts 24

It's often tempting to be dishonest. Procrastination steals time and opportunity from almost everyone. It takes calm courage to defend ourselves without retaliating against accusers. Here are three lessons from three lives.

When the Jews came to accuse Paul before Felix, their spokesman was an orator named Tertullus. His presentation reeked of deceit. Tertullus' flattery may have been standard protocol for addressing Roman officials, but it was all a lie, and everybody present knew it. Jews had plenty of emotions toward the occupying Romans, but gratitude was not one of them. Yet Tertullus heaped praise on the governor and expressed appreciation for him. Then, every line of his so-called case betrayed their prejudice and bitterness against Paul. Like a spin doctor, Tertullus alluded to real events, but misconstrued Paul's actions in them. He resorted to name-calling ("plague," "ringleader of the sect of the Nazarenes") and recommended that Felix investigate the accusations. (The Romans usually investigated such things by torturing the suspect.) The spiritual leaders of Judaism affirmed all the lies.

Paul's candid defense was like an odor-removing disinfectant spray. With a nod to Felix's authority and experience, he stated facts and denied the false charges. He admitted he disrupted the Sanhedrin by crying out about the resurrection. This acknowledgment was masterful—it reminded the accusing Pharisees they had acquitted him less than a week ago. His conclusion asserted he was on trial for what he believed, not anything he had done.

If the Jews' tactic was deceit and Paul's was defense, Felix's specialty was delay. He postponed his decision until Lysias could come. Since the tribune had been involved, that seemed reasonable. During the delay, Paul was kept in custody, which was a mixed blessing. It kept Paul from his missionary travels, but it also kept him from being assassinated by the Jews. It did not keep him from preaching. Paul addressed the governor several times during his confinement. Once when Paul preached about righteousness, self-control and judgment, Felix was alarmed. Some versions say, "Felix trembled." But he delayed again, sending Paul away until he got "an opportunity." Felix may have rationalized the delay, thinking it helped everyone involved. It kept Paul from stirring up the Jews, and kept the Jews from killing Paul. But Luke unmasked Felix's real motives. One motive was to get a bribe from Paul. Then, as a political favor to the Jews (motive number two), Felix left Paul in jail when he moved out of the governor's mansion two years later. Bribery and political maneuvering are nothing new or modern; Felix was a product of his environment.

Which of these three tactics best characterizes your life? Are you honest, or are your words tinged with deceit? Is your life straightforward enough that you can defend yourself against accusations without becoming defensive? Do you miss opportunities because you delay taking action? These ancient Bible characters are very much like you and me. We can learn a lot from them.

Day 114, Acts 25

Porcius Festus had a common writer's problem—an assignment and no idea about what to write. It was a routine report to his boss. The quill was sharpened, the ink on hand. The parchment was waiting to soak up his words, if he only knew any words to write. Yes, Festus had writer's block.

Writers spend lots of time staring at an empty page or screen. Most of us don't know why we can't get started. But Festus' block came from a known issue: he could not make a decision because he was not guided by principle.

Festus inherited Paul's case when he became governor. The apostle had been incarcerated more than two years, but the previous governor, Felix, had never issued a judgment. The Jewish leaders asked a favor of the new administration—they wanted Paul transported to Jerusalem. Their animosity, like a bitter wine, had grown more potent over time. Their desire and their plan remained the same: get Paul out of protective custody, set up an ambush and kill him.

Festus refused their request, and told the Jews to come to Caesarea if they wanted to accuse Paul. When they came, their attack was tenacious, but still based on old, unprovable charges. Paul maintained his innocence. Festus, willing to make some concession to the Jewish leaders, suggested a change of venue. Paul protested that the case was already before the proper court. The charges would still be bogus and he would still be innocent anywhere they moved the trial.

He didn't mind dying if he deserved it, but he didn't want a lynch mob to decide his fate. To avoid falling into the Jews' hands, he used his Roman citizenship, appealing to Caesar. Festus granted the appeal.

When Agrippa and Bernice came to visit, Festus told them about Paul and explained his dilemma. He had granted an appeal, but had no charge to explain why Paul was a prisoner in the first place. Agrippa wanted to hear Paul, and Festus arranged the meeting, hoping to get some idea of what to put on Paul's paperwork. He sounded like a carnival barker introducing a circus oddity when he brought Paul before the royal guests.

Decisions should be made on principles, what we believe and know to be true. Festus knew Paul was innocent. But his desire for political clout with the Jews clouded the decision-making process.

Maybe you're struggling with a decision right now. Are your principles guiding your decision-making process? Maybe you, like Festus, inherited the problem at work. I hope you're not, like Paul's antagonists, nursing an old grudge that's keeping you from making the right choice. You may be like Paul, at a place where life seems to be on hold and you're waiting on the Lord. Let your principles, based on what is true and right, be your guide. It will be easier to explain why you did what you did, which will help if you're ever asked to put it in writing.

Day 115, Acts 26

Are you persuasive? Can you motivate people? Successful salespeople, politicians, coaches and preachers are persuaders. Their words and actions influence other people. Although this power is often used for selfish purposes, persuasion is a valuable skill for people who want what's best for others.

Paul was a persuader. Speaking to King Agrippa, he asked and answered his own question: "Do you believe the prophets? I know that you do believe." It's unclear whether Agrippa was really almost persuaded to become a Christian. He may have been mocking Paul, or asking if Paul intended to convert him. Translators choose how to cast the king's words, and many versions offer alternate marginal readings. Whatever Agrippa meant, he felt the tug of Paul's persuasiveness as he listened to the apostle's defense.

Paul wanted the king and everyone else listening to become just like him, except for the chains. He would later tell the Corinthians to imitate him as he imitated Christ, and the Philippians to do what they had learned, received, heard and seen from him. It takes confidence to tell people not only to listen to you, but to watch and follow your example.

Paul modeled some secrets of persuasiveness in his speech to Agrippa. First, he lived by convictions. Paul was intentional, not haphazard. When he was an enemy of Christ, his conviction fueled his raging fury against the disciples. He was convinced that persecuting Christians was what he ought to do. After the Lord appeared to him, he changed sides, driven by his new conviction that Jesus is Lord. Conviction is important because not everyone will agree with you. Some may persecute you instead of being persuaded. Others may mock and insult you. Conviction doesn't bend under the strain of persecution or wither in the face of ridicule.

Paul also lived with a strong sense of authority. He followed strict rules as a Pharisee. He arrested disciples under authority from the chief priests, and was traveling to Damascus by their authority when Jesus appointed him and sent him on a new mission. He was still under authority, but now that authority came from a different Master.

Paul's unwavering devotion was driven by hope. He said he was on trial for his hope in God's promise to the Jews. He saw the irony in Jews persecuting him for embracing their long-awaited hope. He told them Jesus was the fulfillment of all the promises and prophecies. But they rejected the message, and persecuted the messenger.

Paul wanted his hearers to be like him, except for his chains. Is there some exception about your life you would not want people to imitate? Is it something you need to surrender to Christ's lordship?

Could God use you to persuade people around you to follow Christ? It will require more than eloquence. Live by your convictions, submit to Christ's authority. Display the difference that hope makes in your life. Then you can be confident as you persuade people to be like you.

Day 116, Acts 27

You can be almost anywhere in the world tomorrow, thanks to today's transportation technology. We complain about a few hours' layover between flights. Imagine traveling with Paul and Luke, when the layover lasted all winter! Today, a massive snowstorm might shut down an airport for a day, but travel was suspended from fall to spring when Paul was headed to Rome.

Long distance travel was perilous in Bible times—a small craft on an open sea with no power but the wind and no guidance but the sun and stars. An unexpected storm gave plenty of propulsion, but took away steering and blinded the guidance system. That's where we find our heroes in today's action-packed adventure.

This was no modern cruise ship. There were no big engines, no sophisticated GPS system, no weather radar and no midnight buffet or 24-hour pizza shop. In rough seas, we might sense the gentle motion of the ship between the third and fourth course of our meal. Paul and company had not eaten for two weeks because of the violent storm that hijacked their ship.

The crew had thrown hope of a happy landing overboard along with the ship's cargo and tackle. As the storm raged, Paul told his shipmates they should have listened to him and not sailed from Crete. He also said they would all survive, but the ship would be lost. Like the four anchors the sailors threw out as they tried to keep the ship off the rocks, Paul's words reveal four anchors of his faith and confidence in God.

Paul had faith in God's presence. An angel of the Lord stood before him. We have been assured that God will never leave us or forsake us. He sees the worst threats, the deepest hurts and the most terrifying fears. His children never walk alone.

Paul had faith in God's promises. Paul knew things always turn out just as God said. Do we believe all God's promises? Do we trust him to meet our needs as we seek his kingdom? Do we believe God answers prayer? Do we trust him to raise us from the dead?

Paul had faith in God's plan for his life. Paul believed he would keep his appointment with Caesar, even when the little ship was in the big storm. God's purpose will prevail over all obstacles. You can face the storms with confidence when you trust God's sure plan.

Paul had faith in God's power. God was stronger than this storm. He knew the secret of David's victory over Goliath. He knew what the angel told Mary: "nothing will be impossible with God." He knew God was able to save every person on board when it appeared that all would be lost.

The storms are inevitable. Maybe you've already been through the storm. Maybe you're in one right now. Maybe your storm is on its way. If your faith is grounded by these anchor points, you will make it through the storm.

Day 117, Acts 28

Dearest wife, greetings from the capital. I am in good health, and hope you are as well. My present duty is neither dangerous nor demanding. I am in charge of Paul, a Jewish prisoner who is a Roman citizen. He has been in custody for several years, with no apparent reason for his confinement.

He came to Rome with a centurion named Julius and other prisoners who survived a shipwreck on Malta. While there, he was unharmed by a viper bite, which led the barbarians to think him first a murderer, then a god. Julius also said Paul healed sick people by touching them and praying to his God. When they resumed their journey in the spring, Paul was glad to meet people along the way he called his brothers and sisters. They were not his actual family, but were somehow connected through their belief about one named Jesus.

After arriving here, he met with local Jewish leaders. He claimed to be innocent, and said he had to appeal to Caesar to remain in protective custody after some conflict with Jews. He says he is in chains because of the hope of Israel. The Jews here knew nothing about the past conflicts, but had heard of Paul's sect, and were eager to hear his teaching.

Paul spent a full day teaching about a kingdom of God and Jesus being the Messiah predicted by Jewish Scriptures. Some of the Jews believed, but others didn't. Paul said a prophet had predicted their rejection. But he seems to have a great passion for the Jews, and is saddened by their unbelief.

His days are full. He is able to pay for a place to live, and I am his guard. He talks to all his guests about the kingdom of God and the lordship of Jesus. He even writes letters to others scattered across our great empire who share his faith about how they should live. One of his companions is his physician, a Greek who seems to be writing some historical account of the life of Jesus and the spread of this movement.

Wife, this man intrigues me. His body shows the scars of beatings, but there is an indomitable spirit within him, something no whipping or stoning or shipwreck can diminish. His wrists and ankles are calloused from his bonds, but his eyes show that something within him cannot be bound. Though he has been imprisoned without reason for a long time, he is full of joy and peace. My duty leaves me little choice but to listen, but I am secretly hungry to know what he knows and believe what he believes. Paul says this salvation he speaks of is for Gentiles like us as well as Jews, and that Gentiles are more receptive than Jews. I am a soldier in Caesar's army, but when I learn more about this king Jesus, I will share it with you. Until then, I remain your faithful husband. Farewell.

Romans

Day 118, Romans 1

You've heard the old routine, "I've got good news, and bad news." That's how Romans begins. Paul sounded the keynote of the gospel (good news) from the first line. At the midpoint of the chapter, he shifted to the bad news of how desperately wrong the human family has gone in turning away from God. Both the good news and the bad news are revealed by the same message.

It is not easy to appreciate how good the news of the gospel is without some understanding of how bad our situation is without it. We become much more interested in the flight attendant's instructions about the emergency exits when we realize the airplane is in trouble. The human family's plane is in a nose dive. When human beings suppress the obvious knowledge of God that is evident in creation, imagining themselves too wise for such "myths," they turn to unbelief and idolatry. Adrift without a moral compass, there is no limit to the perversity to which humans can and do descend. When the human family chose to exclude God from their thinking, three times Paul said "God gave them up" to the consequences of their choice. These people, made in the image of God, debased and dishonored themselves by refusing to acknowledge him.

The greatest tragedy in this awful picture is that the wrath of God is on such people. It's bad that their own lives and the lives of people around them are destroyed by their rebellion. But it is especially tragic to contemplate so many people facing the eternal wrath of God.

While humans are not and cannot of themselves be righteous, there is a righteousness of God from faith for faith revealed in the gospel. Those who trust the saving work of Christ are made righteous with God through him. Everything the prophets promised is realized in Jesus Christ. His resurrection stands as the certification that he is who he said he was, the son of David according to the flesh in which he came, but the Son of God according to the Spirit. The gospel calls Jews and Gentiles alike to belong to Jesus Christ, to be set apart and objects of God's special love and grace.

Paul was eager to get to Rome, to share this good news with people in the Roman capital as he had shared it across the empire. His sense of indebtedness for the grace shown to him made him eager to proclaim the gospel to everyone without reservation, because everyone needs the gospel, and everyone is invited to respond to it.

These words prompt some self-examination. Ask yourself, "Do I understand how much I need the gospel? Does any part of my life show that I have excluded God from my thinking? Have I trusted Jesus and responded to the gospel in obedient faith? Does my appreciation for God's grace compel me to share the good news with others who need to hear it?"

Day 119, Romans 2

Once upon a time, there was a judge who had two small children. On Saturday mornings, the children sometimes went with their father to his office in the courthouse. The children liked to play in the empty courtroom. One day, the little girl was brave enough to slip her father's robe off its hanger in his office and put it on. It was much too large, but she paraded into the courtroom pretending to be a real judge, just like her father. She stumbled over the pool of robe at her feet and mopped a path with the black fabric that trailed in her wake. Her brother went up the steps behind the judge's bench and climbed into his father's chair. His feet could not touch the floor and he could not see over the bench. So he stood in the chair and looked over the empty courtroom. He saw his robe-stealing sister, took his father's heavy gavel into his small hand and banged it down, crying "Guilty! Guilty!" He hit his finger with the gavel and cried out in pain. The old custodian came to investigate the disturbance and found the junior judges holding court. Suppressing his laughter, he marched them down the hall to their father. The real judge stifled a grin at the sight of his pint-sized jurists, and warned them about impersonating a judge.

You understand, don't you? Who do we think we are when we judge one another? We are not big enough to wear the robe, sit in the chair and hold the judge's gavel. We are not qualified to be the judge. In pronouncing sentence on our peers, we hurt them and condemn ourselves.

People who see themselves as religious or spiritual are sometimes quick to judge others, pronouncing sentence on lawbreakers who don't respect God's law. And in that moment of judgment, by the standard applied to others, the judge condemns himself. He, too, is a lawbreaker. He may not be guilty of the same transgressions he sees in others. But no imperfect human can afford to climb up in God's judgment seat and convict other lawbreakers.

The legalist knows what the law says and measures others by it. But when he finds them guilty, he condemns himself. Every person whose trust is in his affiliation with some group or obedience to some ritual faces this dilemma. God's impartial judgment will cut through every external layer of qualification and distinction to discern the heart of every person before him. He knows all our obedience is flawed. That's why Christ came. It's why he died. He will be looking for those who have trusted Christ and turned to him in loving faith and obedient surrender.

The gospel is good news for notorious and respectable sinners alike. Righteousness from God through faith in Christ is every sinner's only hope. Our Father will not be smiling if we have to account for impersonating the Judge when we stand before him.

Day 120, Romans 3

"NO" signs are everywhere, prohibiting some activity. Perhaps the most common ones are "No Smoking" and "No Parking." I've seen signs forbidding trespassing, swimming, singing, profanity, loitering and passing. Some commuter train stations have "No Kissing" signs, to keep traffic from being snarled by passionate goodbyes.

In the body of Christ, the church, there could be a "No Boasting" sign. The scheme of redemption excludes boasting by design. No sinner saved by grace has any room to brag. All the saved are justified by God's grace as a gift, through the redemption that is in Christ Jesus. Through Jesus' death on the cross, God can be just (requiring the debt for sin to be paid), and the justifier (the one who paid the debt himself) of those who trust in Christ. There is not one person, Jew or Gentile, who can rely on his or her own righteousness. No human being can be justified by works of the law.

"No Boasting" is also the rule about our service for God. Paul knew his work for the Lord was really the grace of God working in him. When he and Barnabas reported on their missionary journey, they told the church at Antioch all that God had done through them. When we're tempted to tell the Lord in prayer or others in conversation about all we've done for Christ, we need to remember it's his strength working in us. It's the same about our standing with God. We are kept by the same grace that saved us. We are not saved by grace and then put on a merit plan to stay that way.

None of this in any way overthrows God's law. It rather upholds it. The purpose of the law was to make us aware of our sin. Once transgressed, law has no saving power. When God saves us by grace, he has work for us to do. But he enables us to do it by his Spirit within us. As flawed human beings, we cannot secure our standing with God on our own anymore than we could attain it on our own. There's no room for boasting.

Why doesn't everyone rejoice in this? The main problem is our wounded pride. If we can't boast, we can't differentiate ourselves from the "less-deserving" ones. Our favorite math symbol must be the > (greater than) sign. As little children on the playground, we play the "my daddy's bigger, my mommy's prettier, my dog's smarter than yours" game. When we grow up, we keep playing—comparing paychecks, houses and even spirituality, trying to be greater. Righteousness from God by grace through faith won't let us play that game.

Every disciple needs a little sign with the international symbol of a circle with a slash through some word or picture reminding him that, in Christ, there is "No Boasting." Only when we're talking about what the Lord has done for us should we brag, and then on him, not ourselves.

Day 121, Romans 4

Do you ever watch those television programs about how things are made? I remember one I saw as a kid that showed how peanut butter was made. It explained the entire process, from harvesting the peanuts all the way to the jars of peanutty goodness leaving the factory. I was fascinated to see the process that produced something as mundane as the peanut butter on my daily sandwich.

If you like to take things apart to see how they work, or peer into a microscope to examine life processes on the cellular level, today's portion should interest you. Paul explains the process by which God makes us righteous. By emphasizing the chronological order of the facts of Abraham's life, Paul shows how guilty sinners are made righteous by grace through faith, and not by works.

To those who have violated it (and that's all of us), the law can only bring wrath, never righteousness. Our effort to attain righteousness by law-keeping is as impotent as childless old Abraham's body was when God promised he would be the father of many nations. Abraham believed God could give life to the dead (his aged body, Sarah's barren womb) and call into existence things that did not exist (nations of descendants). Because Abraham believed God and trusted his promise, God counted him righteous and gave him a son.

Paul said those things happened before Abraham received the sign of circumcision, long before the law was given. Abraham was declared righteous because of what he believed, not because of what he did. Paul said that made him the father of the uncircumcised believers as well as the father of those who are not merely circumcised, but who walk in the footsteps of Abraham's faith.

The promise came before circumcision and the law so it could be by grace through faith. This arrangement makes righteousness a gift instead of a wage, and gives all the glory for it to God. It focuses our trust, our hope and our boasting on the right person—God, not us, and on the right reason—grace, not works.

Do you see why Paul was so upset by the Jews who insisted that Gentiles had to be circumcised and keep the Law of Moses? Not only were they adding to the gospel, they were betraying their own misplaced trust. They were "merely circumcised." They had the external mark of the covenant, and were the physical descendants of Abraham. But they weren't walking in the footsteps of Abraham's faith.

Let's not make the same mistake. Jesus calls us to obedience, to hear his words and put them into practice. How can we claim to trust him if we don't obey him? But we must never believe our righteousness comes by our works of obedience. When our works, our understanding, our knowledge or our obedience becomes the basis of our confidence, then trust is misplaced, hope is hollow and God is robbed of the glory he is due.

Day 122, Romans 5

We're jaded. We want to believe, but experience tells us it's too good to be true. The bitter disappointments of life and the hollow promises of advertising have made us skeptics about "peace" and "free."

In the news, in relationships or in our own minds, peace is often a shadowy illusion, easy to shatter and hard to trust. But Paul says we have peace with God when we are justified by faith. Our lives and personal experiences certify that there is no peace in being justified by works. We can't undo the past. We never do enough. We know ourselves too well, and realize it's only a matter of time until we slip and fail. All of this is very unsettling, very anti-peace. When we learn to trust what Christ has done instead of what we do, we can find the peace we will never know as long as our standing with God is based on our own performance.

The peace that comes from standing in grace shapes our response to life. We find joy in the hope we now possess, even in the face of adversity. Trusting God allows us to see suffering as a forge in which we're shaped and strengthened for God's purposes and for our own good. It's the ongoing work of the amazing love that reached out to us when we were so unlovable. God allowed Christ to die for us, not because we were good, but because we weren't. Jesus endured the cross to reconcile us to God because we made ourselves his enemies.

Sometimes an item is truly free—no charge, no conditions, no strings attached. But most of the time we've learned that the cost is built into something else we're buying, or some stipulation attached to the gift keeps it from being truly free. Momma warned us about things that were too good to be true, and she's been right most of the time. The conditions of the deal are not printed in the same font size as the promise of what's free. It's understandable that we're leery of the promised free gift. But Paul says it's free five times in a single paragraph. Every sinful descendant of Adam has earned death. The amazing message of the gospel is that the righteousness and obedience of Christ brings justification and life. Through the sacrifice of Christ, God's grace is greater than all the guilt of our sinfulness. Grace isn't earned, merited, deserved or achieved. It is a free gift to be trusted and received.

These concepts turn the world's ideas about religion upside down. Religion is what people do, trying to get to God and find peace. The gospel is all about what God has done to bring us to himself and give us peace. It's not hard to understand why so many people struggle with these concepts. But it's worth the effort to think this through. God offers freely a peace that cannot be bought at any price.

Day 123, Romans 6

The beautiful doctrine of salvation by grace through faith has been ridiculed by legalists and abused by libertines for 2,000 years. Some modern day religionists echo the reaction of some who heard the gospel in Paul's day, saying, "That can't be true! You're saying people can go on living in sin and still be saved!" But other people misinterpret the message of grace to imply that saved people can indeed do as they please without consequence. Both perversions of grace are based on the same erroneous premise—that a person saved by grace can go on living the way he or she lived before they were saved.

Paul exposed the error of that premise with three illustrations. First, he said sin is a matter of life and death. When we come to Christ, we die to sin. Baptism depicts Jesus' death, burial and resurrection. So our identification with him in baptism should result in a death of our old sinful person, and a resurrection to a new way of life. He said we must count ourselves dead to sin and alive to God.

The second image is about slavery and freedom. Paul said those who come to Christ are no longer enslaved to sin. For many twenty-first century readers, slavery is a relic of history, but to many in Paul's original audience, servitude was a way of everyday life and freedom was a dream. Paul reasoned that a person is the slave of the master he obeys. Since we have been set free from sin, and sin no longer has dominion over us, it makes no sense to continue serving sin. We are supposed to be slaves of righteousness, not sin. We can serve only one master. It's impossible to claim one and serve another. Our conduct reveals our true master.

Finally, Paul contrasts the results of these two ways of living in terms of fruit-bearing. Paul said the fruit or result of serving sin was shame, and ultimately death. But those who have been freed from sin's dominion bear the fruit of holiness, and finally eternal life. It's the certain principle of sowing and reaping.

We're offered the free gift of eternal life in Jesus Christ. The alternative to accepting this gift is receiving the wages we are due from sin, which is death. Paul put this point in human terms because of his readers' natural limitations. I'm glad he did, because I can understand the difference in life and death, freedom and slavery, and being set apart for God's glory versus living with the shame of my sinful conduct.

Jesus promised the truth would set us free. There's a huge difference in serving because you're free, and thinking that your good works will somehow earn your freedom. One is the appropriate response of loving gratitude for salvation. The other is living by the lie posted over the gates of the Nazi concentration camps: *Arbeit Macht Frei*—Work will make you free!"

Day 124, Romans 7

Do you remember my remark about the human family's favorite math symbol? It was the "greater than" sign. What's the master communicator's favorite punctuation mark? I'm no master communicator, but I do admire (and imitate) their methods. That's why this and many other essays in this book begin with questions. The question mark is the effective teacher's best friend. What do scientists in the lab, researchers in the library, detectives at the scene of a crime and good communicators all have in common? They use questions to guide their thinking. Why is this powerful little squiggle so helpful to teachers? A teacher has the additional responsibility of bringing others along on the journey. Can you see how a question mark looks like a hook? It also acts like one, snagging your attention and pulling you along. A good teacher asks question to engage and influence the audience.

That little Q&A was somewhat heavy-handed, but not much more than Paul's use of questions in Romans. How many questions can you find in the chapters we've covered? Paul introduces new subjects, makes complex arguments and answers anticipated objections, all with questions. In today's portion, he shows his readers how they're free from the law by asking them about marriage. He explains how the law that promises life brings death when it arouses desire within our flesh. He takes us deep inside the conflicted thinking process of a person who knows, but doesn't always do what is right. And he guides us along this challenging itinerary by posing questions.

When Paul asks, "Don't you know...I am speaking to those that know the law," he starts where his readers are, using what they know to build a bridge to where he wants them to go. If they understand that death ends a marriage and the survivor is free to remarry, they can understand how when they died with Christ in baptism, they were freed from the law when they were raised with him. The law (holy and good in itself) makes us aware of sin, and appeals to our desire to do wrong. The conflict comes from our dual nature—our flesh wants what it wants, and our spirit wants to do right. Paul called it a war, with one side fighting to capture and dominate the other. Commentators disagree about whether Paul is confessing this about himself, or just explaining how it works. Either way, we understand, because it's going on in our own lives.

Paul poses one final question to ease the tension and point from wretchedness to blessedness: "Who will deliver me from this body of death?" And he points to the ultimate answer: "Thanks be to God through Jesus Christ our Lord!" Over all the questions, Paul proclaims Jesus as the answer. How do we win this conflict? It is not through knowing all the answers to all the questions. We find victory in knowing the one who is the answer. Do you know him?

Day 125, Romans 8

Would you prefer a death sentence or paid-up life insurance? Since you are, in fact, faced with those alternatives, let's explore them today.

The flesh-controlled life leads to fear, slavery and death. It's ironic that many who live like this think they are fearless, free and really living. The focus of the flesh-controlled life is self—gratifying all desires and rebelling against God's will. All who live this way are under a death sentence. At the end of living in the flesh, there is only death and condemnation.

The alternative to living according to the flesh is living according to the Spirit of God within you. If you live in Christ under the control of God's Spirit, you are guaranteed life and no condemnation. There is peace in trusting what God has done in sending Christ to die for our sins. Under his guidance, we submit to God and please him, grateful for what he has done for us in Christ. Living in the Spirit is obviously better in the end, when you get life instead of death. But it's also better all along the way.

In Christ, you exchange slavery under the law of sin and death for freedom and life. Hope and expectation replace dread and fear. No one is granted immunity from suffering in this fallen world. But in Christ you have the assurance of God's help as you endure suffering, and the promise that the glory to come will far outweigh the suffering. Your redemption is part of God's plan to redeem the entire fallen creation. Everything that happens to you is not good, but you know that as a chosen object of God's love, he is able to make whatever happens work for your good. He uses the adversities of life to fulfill his ultimate purpose of making you like his Son.

Because you are his beloved child and heir, his Spirit lives within you, giving you help when you are weak, victory when you face opposition and the guarantee of life when you face death. You can be confident of all this because he has already given his Son! Won't he also graciously give you whatever else you may need? This is your inheritance in Christ. This is the result of living under the control of his Spirit. This is the guarantee for your life.

There are only two ways to live. We can live in the flesh and be condemned to death under the righteous law of a holy God. Or, we can live under the direction of his gracious Spirit within us, be heirs instead of enemies, have hope instead of despair, and live instead of die.

This alternative is brought to you by Jesus, who fulfilled the righteous requirement of the law and condemned sin, so that we might share in his righteousness and live with him forever. That's the good news of the gospel. It is my fervent prayer that you will receive it, and live.

Day 126, Romans 9

It's in a missionary whose heart for the lost compels him to take the gospel to people in a distant land. It's in a woman so devoted to a ministry that she pours her heart into whatever she does. And sometimes on the printed page, an author's words convey the passion in his heart.

Paul had a heart-broken passion about Israel's rejection of Jesus as Messiah. He said he could wish himself accursed and cut off from Christ for their sake! Perhaps to soothe his own broken heart as well as to enlighten ours, Paul explained how God knew and foretold Israel's rejection of the Christ.

We know from Acts that Paul had little success and lots of hostility from Jews in the cities he visited across the empire. Some Jews did believe when Paul and his traveling companions would visit their synagogues and preach Jesus as Christ. But the uproar created by unbelieving Jews was often the catalyst that caused Paul to leave town. The bitter resistance among his Jewish brothers and sisters drove him to a fruitful ministry God said he would have among Gentiles. Jewish persecution eventually drove him into Roman custody to protect him from the very people for whom he had such passion.

Paul cited the privileges and blessings Israel had enjoyed in their covenant relationship with God, culminating in Christ's Jewish ancestry. How could they not recognize and receive him? He quoted Moses and the Hebrew prophets to show that God was not taken by surprise when Israel rejected Jesus as the Christ.

Beginning when the nation was only a family, Paul illustrated from their history that not all who descended from Israel actually belong to Israel. Not all of Abraham's children after the flesh, but only the children of promise are really his offspring. Not even all of them are elect; God chose Jacob over Esau before they were born. Paul said God is sovereign in his decisions about his creation—no creature can question his Creator's choice. As God the potter, he prepares some vessels for honor and others for dishonor, some for destruction to contrast with the vessels who are shown mercy, and some from among the Gentiles as he said through his prophets he would do. God foretold that not all Israel, but only a remnant would be saved, and that many would stumble and be offended by Messiah.

Here's the essence: By God's sovereign choice and according to his sure promise, his true people attain righteousness through faith in Christ, not through physical descent from Abraham or works of the law. The Jews' problem with Paul's gospel was the very core of the message. So while Paul was frustrated by the situation, he could not compromise. He understood the Jews' position perfectly; he had opposed Jesus and the gospel himself before his conversion. Paul found peace about Israel's rejection through trusting God's faithfulness and foreknowledge. But his heart still ached for Israelites who stumbled in their unbelief.

Day 127, Romans 10

What inspires a mentor to give so much of himself to his protégé? Why is a mother so devoted to her child's development through the difficult passages of adolescence? Perhaps the tutors see something of themselves in their pupils. That may be why Paul was so intent on bringing his fellow Israelites to faith in Christ. He had been where they were.

As a Pharisee, Paul's reputation for righteousness based on works of the law had been blameless. He knew about having zeal for God, but not according to knowledge, because he had lived it before coming to Christ. When he met Jesus, his quest for works righteousness ended. There was no sense of pride or merit as he obeyed Ananias' instructions to get up and be baptized, calling on the name of the Lord.

Remember the rich young ruler who came with such enthusiasm, respect and moral excellence to Jesus? He wanted to know what he could do to inherit eternal life. When Jesus called him, the young man sorrowfully walked away from the one thing he lacked: a right standing with God through faith in Christ. Maybe you are reminded of someone you know—a committed, energetic, sincere adherent of some religion that promises righteousness through law-keeping. It's possible that you've been there (are there?) yourself.

Paul longed to reach Israelites who were trying to establish their own righteousness. He contrasted living by doing with living by faith in Christ. Remember, he had tried it both ways, and learned one was impossible and the other was God's intention all along.

Paul reversed the process to show how Christ-rejecters were without excuse. They could not call on one in whom they hadn't believed. They couldn't believe in one of whom they had not heard. They couldn't hear unless someone preached to them, and they wouldn't hear unless the preacher was sent. But his life and work was evidence that all those prerequisites had been met. He had been sent! He had preached! They had heard! But they would not believe or call on Christ for salvation.

Imagine Paul's passion for this subject and these people. He was living out the prophecies and the process he described! The Lord had sent him, and by his own voice the Israelites had been called to believe in Christ. He witnessed the Jews' jealousy that Moses prophesied as Gentiles came to God through Christ. He felt the pain as misguided people rejected God's appeal.

The great apostle to the Gentiles brought thousands to Christ by his preaching during his lifetime and millions to faith by his writing through the ages. But his heart was heavy and his prayers were fervent for a stubborn group of kinfolks he could not persuade. If there are people who have resisted your efforts to share your faith, take heart and don't stop praying about it. Know that the apostle Paul lived with the same situation, and would understand exactly how you feel.

Day 128, Romans 11

In today's portion, Paul asked and answered the question that looms above Israel's rejection of the gospel and salvation by grace through faith. If the Jews are rejecting the gospel of Christ, and Gentiles who accept it are being called God's people, has God in his sovereignty rejected his people Israel? Paul's emphatic answer is "No!" Paul explained that God elected a remnant of Israel who will be saved by grace as surely as the Gentiles, and on the same basis. He made his argument by asking rhetorical questions, citing Israel's history, applying principles from psychology and botany and quoting prophecy.

Paul used questions again to draw his readers to the place where they could grasp and accept his arguments. He asked five or six questions and quoted a couple of others posed by Isaiah. Some of Paul's questions remind the readers of what they already know. Others synthesize what they know and what he's telling them to build understanding. We get the doctrinal lesson, along with another demonstration of this master teacher's technique.

Paul reminded us the Jews' current rejection of the gospel was not the only time they had been at odds with God's will. In the days of Elijah, the nation had forsaken God and was consumed with idolatry. But even then, God reminded Elijah there was a remnant that had not bowed before Baal.

Jealousy is a powerful motivator. We usually think of it in its negative, destructive form. But Paul said God included Gentiles in his plan to provoke the Jews to jealousy, and spur them to accept Christ. He balanced that with a warning to the included Gentiles: "Do not become proud, but stand in awe." As the true Master Gardener, God had cut off the natural olive branches (Israel) to graft in the wild shoots (Gentiles). He reminded them that faith, not merit, was the basis of their inclusion. The comedian Bill Cosby used to warn his kids, "I brought you into this word, and I can take you out!" He was being funny, but Paul was being serious. God can bring in those who believe and remove those who do not continue in faith. No branch can boast!

We've already seen how much Israel's hard-hearted rejection of the gospel bothered Paul. I suspect Paul's own spirit was soothed by Isaiah's prophecy that Jacob's (Israel's) sins would be taken away when the Deliverer came. By God's own design, the Jews' hardening opened the door for the Gentiles, and the Gentiles' inclusion would bring Israel back.

Let's not be alarmed if we lack perfect clarity about this deep teaching. After the explanation, Paul exclaimed, "Oh, the depth of the wisdom and knowledge of God! How unsearchable are his judgments and how inscrutable his ways!" I still have questions. I'm going to keep studying and pondering. But I am grateful that our standing with God in Christ is neither attained nor secured by full understanding, but rather by trusting faith.

Day 129, Romans 12

If you have children, access any media, or have contact with other people in the course of your day, you encounter and practice the art of persuasion. It may be simple and straightforward ("Mommy, can I please..."). It may be subtle and sophisticated (like advertising). But we're all targets of people attempting to influence our behavior. We do it, too, with family, friends and co-workers. Sometimes it's manipulative—the persuader will benefit if we do it. Occasionally it's altruistic—we're asked to do something for our own good, or for the good of someone besides the person asking. It may come from an authoritative voice, or a pitiful cry for help. But we're all transceivers of persuasion. We send it out, and it returns to us every day.

Maybe you've heard people say, "I'm not going to lower myself by begging you." Paul wasn't concerned about that. He had full authority as an apostle to command, but he often chose instead to beseech his readers to obey the Lord. His motives were pure and transparent. Paul wasn't trying to sell them something or get their vote. He had no devious hidden agenda. He wanted them to obey for their own good and God's glory. He warned his readers about other powerful influences: "Do not be conformed to this world, but be transformed by the renewing of your mind...." That's a reprise of "walk not according to the flesh, but according to the Spirit" from a few pages back.

Paul wasn't afraid to ask for the big things. He wanted the Romans and you and me to lay down our lives as sacrifices to God. In

some contexts, that has been a call to martyrdom. But it's really an appeal for living sacrifices, not bloody, dead ones. It is surrendering self to God's will. It is using what we have received by grace to bless other members of the body of Christ. It is showing consideration for others and treating them better than they deserve. It is thinking, speaking and acting in ways that authenticate our love for God and neighbor. It is refusing to be overcome by evil, and choosing to overcome evil with good.

What's the rationale behind such big requests? Why should we give up self and self-interests? Why share? Why show kindness or honor? Paul says we should do it because we have received mercy from God. Are the people around us undeserving? So are we. Will people take advantage of us? Maybe, but you'll be happier not lugging around all that negative emotional baggage.

This compacted list of behaviors and attitudes that should characterize our lives is a call for non-conformity to the ways of the world. To live this kind of life, we must be transformed, changed from the inside out. Paul begs us to present our bodies and yield to God's transforming power. He promises when we do so we will prove to ourselves that God's way is best.

Day 130, Romans 13
This section of Romans is not popular with people who believe salvation and a relationship with God are abstract concepts. Paul's description of what it means to live in Christ brings these matters out of the ethereal haze of how we feel, and into the concrete reality of what we do.

Paul said we show respect for God's authority over us by submitting to the authorities God places over us. The context is about civil obedience as citizens, but the principle also applies wherever an authority structure exists—at home, at church or at work. All authority is ultimately from God. Are some governments godless and evil? These words were written under a Roman government that went from indifference to antagonism toward Christianity in Paul's lifetime. Still, he told Christians to submit to authority. The official who enforces the law is God's servant (Paul used the word for deacon) to avenge wrongdoing. Those who do what is right need not fear the authority. So Paul said, "Pay what you owe—taxes, revenue, respect, honor."

Paul used the idea of paying what is owed to transition to the next tangible demonstration of obedience in a Christian's life—loving your neighbor. Jesus said this command was second only to loving God supremely. Paul said all the other commands are summed up in this one, because love keeps you from doing wrong toward a neighbor. We fulfill the law when we love our neighbors.

Paul also called on those who belong to Christ to walk in the bright daylight of salvation instead of the shadowy darkness of self-indulgent disobedience. It's the familiar theme of living by God's direction instead of following the misguided desires of our flesh. We're not surprised to find fleshly stuff like orgies, drunkenness, sexual immorality and sensuality in this list. But don't miss the other items Paul mentioned here—quarreling and jealousy. These more respectable indulgences of the flesh are also forbidden to those who have put on Christ. Paul went beyond just telling us to resist these temptations. He said, "Make no provision for the flesh, to gratify its desires." I realize that response to temptation can sometimes be like a reflex. But many of us can shamefully admit it sometimes takes a plan, a scheme to do the wrong thing. We must not harbor and nurture thoughts that would lead to actions of indulging the flesh.

It's possible to have a romanticized, impractical view of what it means to "put on Christ." One of the most convenient heresies ever perpetrated is that being saved need not have any effect on how one lives. That cannot be squared with what Paul, the champion of salvation by grace through faith, has written here. Obeying authority, loving your neighbor and walking in the light can't save you, but such conduct is evidence and fruit of salvation. You don't do those things to be saved; you do them because you are saved.

Day 131, Romans 14

A leader must qualify what constitutes "the win" for a group working together. We want success and progress. But without a clear objective, the most enthusiastic team member may be working against the group's goals.

In the body of Christ, the win is not getting your way or prevailing in some controversy. Differences of opinion are to be expected. We have varied backgrounds, unique personalities and different levels of spiritual maturity. All these factors color our perceptions and convictions. We should not be anxious when differences arise. We should know what to do (and not to do) when diversity disturbs the peace among believers. Internal conflict turns our focus inward and makes us forget the real mission of making disciples and seeking and saving the lost.

When Paul wrote Romans, the hot issues were diet and days. It's easy to see why. Local churches across the Roman Empire were melting pots, where people from long-segregated cultures came together because of their mutual faith in Christ. Religious rules about dietary restrictions and holy days were deeply ingrained in these people, and they brought their cultural conditioning with them into the church. Dietary rules and holiday observances would be public enough issues to make the differences obvious. We do the same things, but many of us have been insulated in homogeneous culture for so long we think everyone is just like us.

The issues have changed through the centuries and around the world, but the principles for dealing with diversity remain the same. We are not in the body to quarrel about issues or to judge those with a different opinion. Although we enjoy great freedom in Christ, we are never free to do as we please without regard for others. My liberty is no license to pressure you to violate your conscience.

Paul reminded us we are all God's servants, and the master is the one who will judge his servants. He doesn't need our help to adjudicate our fellow servants. Paul knew people on both sides of a dispute may be sincere in their attempt to honor God by their actions. He insisted that we replace our tendency to police others with policing ourselves so we do not cause others to stumble.

Love should characterize all we do. It's unloving to show callous disregard for the consciences of our brothers and sisters. When we pursue peace instead of division, and build people up instead of tearing them down, we'll be more on task. Our kingdom agenda is righteousness, joy and peace—not dietary or calendar rules made into tests of orthodoxy. The win is loving one another, not controlling one another. The win is living with joy in the kingdom of God, not fighting over preference or tradition. Whose kingdom is it, anyway?

Much shameful division in the body of Christ has come from confusion about what constitutes the win. Ugly sectarianism could be avoided and healed if we would practice what Paul preached.

Day 132, Romans 15

A baby or spoiled child cares nothing about the comfort or convenience of others. The little one wants what he wants when he wants it. He advises everyone, "It's my way, or the cry way." We tolerate it in babies, but it's irritating with people who are old enough to have a broader view of life than "The World, starring Me, featuring the rest of you as bit players in the supporting cast of my story."

I hope you're not tempted to interpret Paul's words about showing consideration for others as permission to insist on having your way. If you do, you are accepting the role of the weak and immature believer by demanding such consideration—the spiritual equivalent of a pouting child. Most of the people I've who known like this see themselves as the mature and strong ones. They're going to guide the rest of us out of our dark ignorance into the blissful light of doing everything exactly as they like it. But Paul made it clear—such people are the weak ones.

Remember our purpose as maturing disciples is to become more like Jesus. The immature want to hold the rest of the church hostage, demanding their way. Those who are becoming more like Jesus follow his example of not pleasing himself. The Bible writers say he gave himself up, emptied himself, made himself nothing and became a servant—all to glorify God and accomplish the Father's long-established purpose.

By fulfilling the prophecies written centuries before he came instead of pleasing himself, Jesus encourages us to live in harmony with one another, even with those brothers and sisters who are sometimes difficult. Jesus did what he did to show the faithfulness of God.

Through Jesus, God kept all the promises made to Abraham and Israel, and fulfilled all the prophecies about including the Gentiles in the covenant. (Here's a subtle clue that the threat of division over days and diet was along the racial/cultural line between Gentiles and Jews.)

Paul cast the vision of all believers gathered together in one great, unified group that can, "with one voice glorify the God and Father of our Lord Jesus Christ." The goal of unity goes far beyond just getting along; it's so God can be glorified by his people in unison. When we accept or welcome each other in the body of Christ, it is to the glory of God.

Look at the big word Paul uses to describe how we should welcome one another: "as" (as in "as Christ has welcomed you"). How did Christ welcome you? Were you welcomed because you thought and acted just like him? No. Were you welcomed because you were worthy of his fellowship? No. Were you welcomed because you were right about all the essential points of doctrine? No. But he accepted you anyway. And that's how we're supposed to accept one another, as Christ has accepted us, for the glory of God.

Day 133, Romans 16

If you've ever participated in a mission trip, you probably understand the common sentiment among missionaries that a part of their heart stays with the people on the mission field. The joy of seeing new believers come to Christ, the encouragement given and received working side by side with local believers and the shared burdens of challenging ministry create a bond that time or distance cannot dissolve.

If missionaries leave a part of their heart wherever they serve, it's a good thing Paul had such a great heart. His converts, fellow workers and helpers were scattered across the breadth of the Roman Empire. Do you have maps in your Bible? Those lines that chart Paul's missionary journeys represent and connect not only places, but people, thousands of people, along Paul's route. A list of names such as the one in today's portion reminds us of how many lives were impacted for all eternity by Paul's zealous service.

Some of the names among the greetings we recognize from other places in the text—Timothy, Prisca and Aquila. These men and women are dear to his heart and vital to his ministry. Others named here would have been lost in antiquity if not for Paul's mention of them—Phoebe, Urbanus, Staychs, Tryphena, Tryphosa and all the others. Don't allow the difficulty of pronouncing the names make you skip over Paul's descriptions of these people: beloved, kinsman, fellow worker, fellow prisoner, servant, mother, brother, sister, saints, holy. He says these people worked hard, were his patrons, his hosts, had risked their necks for his life and were all in the Lord. The sweet and precious bond of this loving family that was both widespread and close-knit is conveyed in every line. Have you ever made a list and expressed your appreciation for cherished fellow believers?

Against that background of loving fellowship, Paul issued a strong warning and a pointed reminder to bring this letter to a close. He warned his readers to watch out for people who would divide this unity. He told them to avoid those who put obstacles in the way of others who would come to Christ through the simplicity of the gospel. He accused such people of serving themselves instead of the Lord. Because these divisive people prey on the naive, Paul wanted his readers to be wise about good and innocent about evil. Although it is discouraging to see Satan's helpers at work, disrupting harmony among Christians, Paul assured the believers the God of peace would crush Satan under the feet of the saints. The accuser and adversary will not win.

Finally, Paul reminded us that God gets all the glory. Our strength comes from God. God has revealed the secret of the gospel to all nations, replacing a system of convicting law with a gospel of saving grace. Our obedience is rooted in faith and love, not fear and despair. For those reasons and more, the glory is all his.

1 Corinthians

Day 134, 1 Corinthians 1

You're at a committee meeting, sifting demographics, study-ing research, choosing your group's next church-planting mission. A committee member suggests the most ludicrous idea you've ever heard: "How about _____?" (In this blank, please insert the name of the most wicked city you know—a place so corrupt, so im-moral, so crawling with vice and perversity you wouldn't think of planting a church there.) The suggestion provokes groans of disap-proval. You say the seekers there aren't looking for what we're trying to help them find.

I doubt Paul went to many committee meetings to plan his mis-sions. But in his day, the city in the blank could have been Corinth—a city located on a lucrative ancient trade route, teeming with diver-sity and perversity. When Paul went there and preached, many of the Corinthians heard the gospel, believed it and were baptized. Paul stayed there a year and a half before moving on, leaving a church in one of the most unlikely places on earth.

Paul wrote to the young Corinthian believers, saying they were called by God to be saints and to have fellowship in Christ. They had been given grace and spiritual gifts. But like all of us who are trophies of grace, the Corinthians still needed instruction and improvement.

Quarreling factions claiming allegiance to different teachers had disrupted the church's unity. To those who had denominated themselves by their favorite teacher, Paul posed some questions: "Is Christ divided? Was Paul crucified for you? Or were you baptized in the name of Paul?" (Answer key: No, No and No.) It was not who baptized them, but into whom they had been baptized that mat-tered. Paul's ministry was centered in Jesus, not himself. He preached Christ crucified. This offended Jews who refused to hear the words

"Christ" (Messiah) and "crucified" in the same sentence. The message about a Jew executed by Romans being the Son of God and the Savior sounded foolish to the pagans. But Paul said this "foolishness" was the wisdom of God, who used things despised by the world to save people in a way that gave the saved no room to boast.

What's the takeaway for us, many years and miles removed? Never doubt the gospel's power to change you or others. If the Corinthians could be saved and sanctified by grace, don't count anyone beyond hope. We must resist the temptation to make our standing with God about us: who taught us, how smart or how good we are. Christ is the source of our life. God made him our wisdom, righteousness, sanctification and redemption. We can brag only about what a fabulous Savior we have. Think how much shameful division this single principle could heal. The solution to fractured unity does not lie in making treaties or holding unity summits. (That's still about us and what we've done.) When individual disciples make Jesus and what he's done the basis for unity, we'll be closer to what Paul urged the Corinthians to be.

Day 135, 1 Corinthians 2

Would you listen to my confession today? I've made my living since I was a teenager as a communicator. I've been a radio disc jockey, a teacher, and for the past three decades a preacher. I admire masters of the craft of public speaking. I appreciate the art of a well-delivered message. I admit it: I enjoy hearing people say they enjoyed listening to what I had to say.

Paul's description of his preaching is a direct challenge to my flesh, my pride, my self. There's a precarious balance between the boldness needed to communicate with passionate conviction, and the humility required to be the delivery vessel for the message without taking glory for oneself. I have sometimes been too anxious about the human skill and technical details of presentations. My motives were pure—I wanted to communicate the gospel with persuasive clarity. But sometimes it's been too much about me, and not enough about the message.

Paul never worried about how the video looked on the screen. He was never distracted by a sound system glitch. But Corinth was as almost as famous for eloquent oratory as it was for immorality. Comparisons between Paul and those famous orators were inevitable. He knew the only thing that would save his listeners was Christ crucified, and he stuck to the subject. Their faith had to be in Christ, not him as a preacher of Christ. He cared more about winning souls than oratorical contests, and that priority shaped his message.

The gospel requires trusting what God has done instead of what we do. It's important that the message also be communicated in a way that takes pride out of the picture. The gospel is wisdom beyond human ability to originate or even comprehend without divine intervention. If God had not revealed it by his Spirit, we could never know it. Preachers use the verse about eyes not seeing, ears not hearing and hearts not imagining what God has prepared for us to talk about heaven. That's true, but it's not the context. The context is that the saving gospel cannot be known apart from God's gracious revelation. You can't pick up an FM station on an AM radio, regardless of long you try or how carefully you tune. Just so, human minds would never get the message from the mind of God unless the Spirit of God revealed it.

Have you ever gone to hear a best-selling author speak, and been disappointed with the oral presentation? Did the words, so vivid and persuasive on the page, not come across as well on the stage? Some gifted writers aren't dynamic public speakers. We know Paul as a prolific and persuasive writer. Luke's accounts of his preaching suggest that he was a stronger preacher than Paul's modest descriptions imply. But Paul knew it was the message, not the messenger that mattered. When you and I have any opportunity to share the gospel, we need to remember that.

Day 136, 1 Corinthians 3

Imagine your favorite meal. See the table in your mind. Is the main course steak or seafood? Maybe you'd prefer peas and cornbread. Whatever you like is fine. How about a nice soup or salad for an appetizer? How about both? Then, what delightful dessert would you select? Would you like coffee with that? Sounds tempting, doesn't it? Now see yourself—a toothless baby still getting all your nourishment from Mother's breast or a bottle! So you want some turkey, or ham? Sorry, you're not even ready for that runny baby cereal yet.

Paul told the feuding Corinthians they were still milk babies when it came to spiritual food. Whatever rich, deep spiritual teaching he had for them would be useless and inappropriate in their present state of development. It must have been a stinging rebuke, being called fleshly and foolish when they imagined themselves spiritual and wise.

A disciple of Jesus is supposed to grow toward maturity. Spiritual maturity is measured more by what controls you than by how much you know. Does God direct more and more of your thoughts, words and actions, or is your flesh still controlling you? Paul warned that quarreling, jealousy, turf wars and preoccupation with division are all evidence of flesh control and spiritual immaturity.

When we denominate ourselves over human teachers or leaders, Paul said we're missing the point of who the teachers are, and whose we are. The teachers are only servants—field hands who plant and water the crops. It is God who makes us grow and bear fruit, not the workers. God gets the glory, not the field hands. We're God's farm. We belong to him. The teacher is a builder, erecting a building on the foundation of Jesus Christ. The human teacher is not the foundation. We are not the human teacher's building; we are God's building. If we divide the building by aligning ourselves with one of the builders, we are destroying God's temple, and God won't tolerate that. It is serious business to fracture the unity of the church, to injure and insult the holy oneness we have in Christ.

Have you heard a well-meant but misguided application of this text about destroying God's temple? Some use this passage to argue that God will judge us if we do things that harm our bodies. We could add gluttony and sedentary lifestyles to the usual warnings about tobacco, alcohol and other drugs. But let's not use this passage as our proof text. The context is about disrupting the unity of the temple of God, the church in which God dwells. The "you" is plural. There is a passage in this letter that teaches us not to dishonor our bodies because God dwells in us, but this is not the one. This is a warning to stop glorying in humans, and an exhortation to grow up in Christ. There's plenty of conviction in what it really means; there's no need to go beyond the context.

Day 137, 1 Corinthians 4

Why are we attracted to celebrities? In countries where monarchy still exists, people are fascinated with the royal family. In America, stars are the royal class. Adoring fans pay athletes and entertainers lots of money and attention. Could it be a misguided remnant of our impulse to worship? One of the most popular recent television shows in the world was a singing competition, where millions of people voted by phone each week to determine a winner. Maybe it's no coincidence that the show had the word "Idol" in its title.

Paul told the hero-worshipping Corinthians who were divided as they aligned themselves with their favorite preachers that those celebrities were really only servants and stewards. This is a sobering assessment for preaches and followers alike. As servants, they would be judged by their master. No other opinion mattered. As stewards, they weren't owners or creators; they only managed someone else's resources. Paul warned them not to be puffed up with pride for one or against another. Neither they nor their celebrated preachers had anything they had not received. There was no room for boasting, and no basis for elitism.

Do you detect some gentle sarcasm in Paul's description of the Corinthians' riches, royalty, wisdom, strength and honor? He contrasted their lofty opinion of themselves with the humble state of the apostles, who were suffering abuse and dishonor without retaliating. He was not shaming them, but calling them back to his example of humility. He warned there would be a showdown with those who persisted in arrogant boasting.

Every parent can identify with Paul's question to his spiritual children: "Shall I come to you with a rod?" It's a very early version of "Do you want to do this the easy way, or the hard way? It's up to you." They needed a course correction. Paul wanted to do it gently, but he told them it was going to be done one way or the other.

It's a blessing to have a gifted spiritual teacher and mentor, but that blessing turns into a curse when we think too highly of the person. They are due honor and respect, even imitation. But we dishonor them and ourselves when we divide the body of Christ over unhealthy allegiance to our guides. Jesus is Lord; the very best spiritual teacher in the world is only a servant and a steward.

Remember, it's better to learn from gentle rebuke than the stinging rod. It's a lot less traumatic for everyone involved when the low impact method of discipline is allowed to work. As a child, I doubted the line, "This is going to hurt me more than it hurts you." As a parent, I found out it was true. Imagine the great loving heart of God, wanting what is best for us, sacrificing so much on our behalf! How it must grieve the Lord when we persist in our stubbornness and leave him no choice but to be rough with his beloved child!

Day 138, 1 Corinthians 5

It's known by different names: "withdrawing fellowship," "shunning" or "church discipline." But have you ever seen it practiced? Even where it is practiced, it is often not done in the right way for the right reasons.

Ancient Corinth was notorious for immorality. Lewdness was commonplace. So when Paul pointed to immorality in the church that the pagan neighbors would not tolerate, it was really perverse—a man was living with his father's wife. Paul shamed the Christians for being arrogant instead of broken-hearted about it, and told them to remove the immoral man from their fellowship. Had they misunderstood their liberty in Christ? Or were they so wrapped up in division and judging that they ignored the flagrant immorality? For whatever reason, they had not addressed the situation, and Paul insisted that they do so.

The instructions are steeped in allusions to the Law of Moses and Israel's history. The phrase "purge the evil from your midst" is like a chorus in Deuteronomy, calling Israel to shun (or even execute) false prophets, idolaters, rebels against authority, incorrigible adult children and the sexually immoral. The ostracism from family and society spurred offenders to repentance and restoration. Paul also borrowed imagery from Exodus, calling Christ our Passover lamb, and commanding the redeemed to purge the old leaven of malice and evil to live as the unleavened bread of sincerity and truth. Evil influence would spread throughout the church unless it was identified and removed. God calls his people to live holy, redeemed lives as a testimony to outsiders. Flagrant sin in the church compromises that testimony.

It is sober business when a church member has to be disciplined by the body, but it is sometimes necessary. Discipline must never be abused as a tool for settling personal grievances, or for a leader to impose some private conviction on others. It is not done by individuals, but by the collective body. It is not excommunication. The goal is not to banish the sinner for life, but to restore him to his place among God's people.

Paul was not calling Christians to monastic withdrawal. He had already written about not associating with certain people in a letter we don't have (a hint that Paul was even more prolific than we know). But here he made it clear: the church is not to tolerate immoral conduct among its members.

Perhaps the abuse of the practice has contributed to its decline among churches that claim to follow the Bible, but resist this instruction. Lawsuits against churches who tried to discipline their members have probably discouraged the practice as well. But the guilty brother needs to be restored, the spread of his influence within the church must be stopped and the church's testimony to the world must be strong. For all the right reasons, churches committed to following the Lord will learn to discipline their members by the right authority (in the name of the Lord Jesus) and in the right way.

Day 139, 1 Corinthians 6

Are you discouraged about the state of civilization, about our society and the way people live today? It's been like this a long time, but Jesus' disciples are called to live in stark contrast to the world.

Paul's instruction about not taking one another to court is counter-cultural in today's litigious society. People are quick to sue over real or imagined wrongs. The advice to suffer wrong rather than go to court sounds foolish to people obsessed with their rights. Paul said it was shameful for members of God's family to take disputes over minor matters to the public courts. Whether they won or lost the case, Paul said they were already defeated if they went to court. Someone among our spiritual siblings should be wise enough to address internal grievances.

Could an unscrupulous swindler, posing as a Christian, defraud a fellow Christian and get away with it? Paul said they weren't going to get away with anything. Those brash enough to cheat and hide behind this paragraph need to read the next one. Paul said swindlers, as well as other rebels, would not inherit the kingdom of God. We have sins in our past that make us unclean, profane and unfit for God's presence. But the amazing power of the name of Jesus and the Sprit of the Lord will cleanse us, set us apart and redeem us. After the list, Paul said "And such were some of you," (past tense). Grace frees us to live a godly life. It does not grant a license for ungodliness.

There's a higher purpose in life than gratifying desires. Our bodies were created to glorify God, not to be enslaved by fleshly appetites. Is sexual temptation the most dangerous kind? Sometimes we are counseled to resist, or stand or fight against Satan's schemes—but against this powerful seduction, Paul's recommended strategy is "Flee from sexual immorality." The stakes are too high to misjudge your power to resist; so run away. God invented sexuality and made it a blessing for husbands and wives to share. Outside of marriage, the blessing is perverted into a curse. A Christian is united with Christ as a member of his body. It is unthinkable to join one in the body of Christ to another in an illicit sexual union. A Christian at Corinth who had sexual relations with an idol temple prostitute dishonored the body of Christ and his own body. We need to hear this in a culture that denies there is any shame or sin in promiscuous behavior.

In this personal matter, we may resist, saying, "It's nobody's business what I do with my body." Perhaps you've said it, or heard others say it. Paul closed this call to purity with a reminder that it is God's business what a Christian does with his or her body. His spirit dwells in us. We do not belong to ourselves; we have been bought at the high price of the blood of Jesus Christ.

Day 140, 1 Corinthians 7

Churches today are asking questions about marriage similar to the ones Paul addressed two thousand years ago. Marriage situations are still complicated after many generations have been influenced by this teaching. Imagine how unfamiliar all this must have been to new believers living in a pagan context from which they had only recently been delivered.

We don't have the Corinthians' questions, just Paul's answers. We infer their queries from Paul's replies. That's probably fine, but beware of dogmatism on this or any issue based on inference.

Paul defended and validated a life of chaste singleness in a world where marriage is the norm, calling singleness a gift from God that not all people are given. Much of what we do as the church is geared toward families and couples, the mainstream context of life for most people. But single people need to be included and encouraged, too.

Paul prescribed monogamous marriage as the means for fulfilling sexual desires, and a defense against temptation. Sex in a healthy context of mutual consent strengthens a marriage. The general rule of marriage is that it is for life, and that couples should stay together. If they separate, the goal is reconciliation if possible.

Many new Christians at Corinth were likely married to unbelievers, and wondered about those marriages. Paul said such marriages are valid, and the Christian mate in a sense sanctifies the family. If the unbeliever is willing to stay, the Christian should stay married. If the unbeliever is unwilling to live with a Christian spouse, the Christian can't make the unbeliever stay, and is not enslaved to that person.

Paul stated the general rule: Lead the life to which God has called you. Becoming a Christian doesn't dissolve all commitments and situations. Paul illustrated this with two big first-century issues. He said it doesn't matter if you are circumcised or not when you come to Christ; you don't have to change that. He said whether you are a slave or free doesn't matter in Christ. Be free if you can be, but glorify God in your service if you're a slave. Likewise, the issue isn't whether you're married or not in Christ. The issue is devotion to the Lord.

Because of the persecution that characterized first-century discipleship, Paul said it might be better for unmarried people and widows to stay single and avoid some anxieties of family life. But he quickly asserted it was also fine to be married. Whatever we do about such matters is to be done "in the Lord," in harmony with God's will and our relationship to Christ.

Some teachers feel compelled to solve all marriage dilemmas, based on their understanding of these principles. It seems to me that Paul himself gave general guidelines and not specific instructions about these matters. Let's be careful to examine and order our own lives by what we learn from this passage. Let's show others the courtesy of allowing them to do the same.

Day 141, 1 Corinthians 8

What if fast food places that dot our urban landscapes and cluster at interstate highway exits were idol temples? What if all the food sold there had been sacrificed to the burger god or the pizza god before it was offered for sale? At one time, you worshipped those gods, and you also spent some time at the fried chicken god's temple, too. But now you know better. You heard and believed the message about the one true God who gave his Son to save you. You turned from idols to worship the Lord. Could you, as a Christian, believing in the one true God and the Lord Jesus Christ, eat at the temples? Could you get it to go, or maybe at least go through the drive-through?

Paul's answer is yes, and maybe no, too. Knowing that an idol is not a real god, and knowing that eating certain foods makes us neither better nor worse in our standing with God, we could eat a barbecue sandwich or have an ice cream cone from the idol temple without doing anything wrong. But as we indulge, puffed up with all that sophisticated knowledge about our rights and privileges in Christ, we also need to know that some fellow believers might still be struggling with the concept. We could offend their weak conscience by eating the questionable food, and might lead them to violate their conscience if they ate with us. What we "know" and are free to do without hurting ourselves could destroy a brother or sister for whom Jesus died! By insisting on our rights and exercising our liberty without considering our influence on others, we could sin against them and Christ who died for them by disregarding their conscience. So

Paul said he would never eat meat that he was free to eat, if doing so would make his brother stumble.

In our time and place, there's not much confusion about the religious significance of food offered for sale to the public. But there's a portable principle here that goes beyond the context. When we do what we do with a haughty assurance based on our advanced knowledge, we may be puffed up, but it's unlikely we'll be building up the people around us. When I assert and exercise my right to do a questionable thing without loving regard for my brother and sister, I jeopardize their well-being by tempting them to violate their conscience. How dare I claim to be a disciple of the Lord who taught us to deny ourselves and follow him when I stubbornly cling to my rights? Jesus laid down his life for you and me. We should be willing to lay down our privileges in humble consideration of others, who may not yet know or understand all that we've been blessed to learn.

Day 142, 1 Corinthians 9

Social and political movements have worked to establish and secure the rights of certain groups throughout our history. Indeed, one of the founding principles of our nation was that we were endowed by our Creator with certain unalienable rights. In a land that treasures freedom, champions equality, and upholds liberty and justice for all, it's not surprising to find a strong emphasis on individual rights.

Have we become far more concerned and vocal about our rights than our responsibilities—finding insult in every remark, and offense in every action? Jesus calls us to deny self to follow him. Yet many Christians campaign for their "rights," even in the church. American culture (or maybe just human flesh) teaches us to demand on our way and fight for our rights. But Paul taught believers to resist the urge to insist on always getting their way.

Paul talked about liberties and privileges he was free to enjoy. But he refused his rights, if exercising them might put an obstacle in the gospel's path. If taking support for preaching the gospel hindered or diminished his effectiveness, he refused the support. He had a right to be married, and to be supported as a preacher. But he chose not to exercise those rights. Scripture gives clear authority and example for those who minister being supported by the people they serve. The Lord authorized paying ministers of the gospel. But Paul found a reward in refusing the support to present the gospel free of charge.

We sometimes seem to have it backward about crossing cultural divides to reach people. We discuss outreach to different ethnic or social groups. But too often our practice has been, "We're open for business and we invite you to come. Learn our habits, songs and encoded jargon, and you can be one of us." Paul was willing to be the one to leave his comfort zone to go wherever people were to share Christ with them. He was willing to become all things to all people to win them to Christ. He wanted them to share in the blessings of the gospel.

Paul cited athletic training as an example of self-denial. Like their modern counterparts in the Olympics, ancient athletes trained and dieted to tune their bodies to compete at the highest level in world-wide competition. The athletes learned endurance by pushing themselves. Their effort was not futile exertion; the goal was to win, to be the best, to be the one who clinched the evergreen garland of victory. Paul said a far greater crown of victory awaited not just one runner, but all those who learned to submit to Christ. So he disciplined his body and made it his slave. An undisciplined body will be the master of an uncommitted will.

Self-denial and self-control are key components of a disciple's walk. Let's imitate Paul (and Jesus) by being less concerned with our rights and more concerned with God's glory.

Day 143, 1 Corinthians 10
Winston Churchill said, "Those that cannot learn from history are doomed to repeat it." A few decades before him, George Santayana, put it this way: "Those who cannot remember the past are condemned to repeat it." About 55 A.D., Paul wrote the same message: "Now these things took place as examples for us, that we might not desire evil as they did."

All Israel was redeemed from Egypt and led out by Moses. But most of them died in the wilderness, because of idolatry and immorality. They accused Moses and God of bringing them out to kill them in the wilderness. Because of their grumbling and complaints, God destroyed many of the Israelites he had delivered from slavery. Paul used their example to warn the redeemed to be careful about falling into sin through similar temptations. With the warning came a precious promise—God will not permit temptation greater than our ability to withstand, and will always provide the way of escape from it. Everyone is tempted, but Christians have God's faithful word that they can endure and escape it.

We usually make a wider application of these words, but they were first applied to the Corinthians' quandary about eating food offered to idols in the ubiquitous idol temples of their city. Paul used the Lord's Supper to show that all who partake of the one bread are one body. He said the Israelites who ate the sacrificed offerings were participants in the offering. That, Paul told the Corinthians, was the problem with going to the idol temples to eat. It was not that the food or the idol to which it had been offered were anything, but by eating what had been offered to demons, they became participants. We put ourselves in danger of falling into the sins that destroyed the Israelites when we think we can handle the temptation. Our jealous God does not want his people who eat the bread of forgiveness and drink the wine of redemption at his table to also sit at the table where demons are revered.

Beyond personal jeopardy, there was also the matter of influencing others. Paul said there was no need to fret about every bite of food at a dinner or from the market. The issue was not the food. But if they were warned that the food had been sacrificed to an idol, Paul said not to eat it, for the sake of the one who warned them. When God's glory means more to us than our liberty, and the salvation of the people around us means more to us than satisfying our appetites, it will be easier to avoid needless offense.

Day 144, 1 Corinthians 11

The epistles show how becoming a Christian influenced the early followers of Jesus, and how those changed lives intersected with the culture around them. The letters were continuing education courses. The believers had started a journey by turning to Christ, but they needed direction, instruction and correction along the way. Each epistle addressed some problem in that church or responded to questions they had asked. That is pointedly the case in 1 Corinthians.

Sometimes the issues were big-picture doctrinal ones that would cross every cultural barrier around the world and through the centuries. At other times, the problems and the solutions seemed to be culture-specific. In those cases, we look for the abiding principle to apply in our lives instead of trying to apply the specific direction to a culture where it doesn't fit.

There may be both universal and specific guidance in the passage about the head covering. Customs and cultures assign different meanings to head coverings. A modern western man removes his hat in church as a sign of respect. But an ancient Jew would never remove his yarmulke in the synagogue, because it was a symbol of respect for God above him. Head coverings or their absence have indicated one's status as free or slave, whether one was a prostitute or not, and whether one was in a position of submission or authority. So it's not always easy to sort out the universal principle from its cultural trappings.

The words about hair length for men and women lie within the discussion about head covering. It is related to nature, to the creation order and to male and female cultural roles. It is sadly ironic that people have been judged and driven away over the length of their hair, and churches have divided over the meaning and nature of the head covering Paul described here. It's sad because the context is unity; yet these words have been made the basis for division. It's ironic because the paragraph ends with a disclaimer about contention. Paul said the churches of God have no such practice as contention about these things; yet many have been contentious over these issues, making laws and enforcing them on others.

The trouble surrounding the Lord's Supper at Corinth reminds us of how a beautiful channel of blessing can be perverted into a harmful curse. Remembering the body and blood of Jesus when we gather to eat the Lord's Supper should give us spiritual strength and bind us together as one body, each member redeemed by the same Savior. But instead of remembering the Lord's sacrifice and celebrating their oneness, the Corinthians selfishly indulged themselves without regard for one another. We are taught to remember Jesus, remember the body of Christ and to examine ourselves when we eat the Lord's Supper. It's a time for self-judging, course-correction and renewed love in the shadow of Jesus' cross. It's a shame when selfishness steals the memorial supper's meaning and effectiveness.

Day 145, 1 Corinthians 12

Once upon a time there were two brothers in the same church. Ed was a talented, dynamic speaker who enjoyed being in front of people. His charisma attracted people to listen and agree with his words. Folks called him a natural leader. His brother Don seemed to lack all that Ed possessed. Don was shy and reserved. He seldom initiated a conversation, almost never spoke up in Bible class, and never stood before the congregation to read the Scriptures or lead a prayer. Don's skills lay in other areas. With quiet patience, he could work through an intricate process that would quickly frustrate his brother. He understood mechanical things that mystified his outspoken sibling. Although he could repair almost anything, Don felt that Ed was the one who got all the talent. Ed felt dumb and inadequate when his mechanical ineptitude once again forced him to call his brother to ask for help.

God's plan for the body of Christ supplies what both those brothers need. In his wisdom, God designed the body so each member finds both humility and dignity in his God-given role.

Paul told the Corinthians they had always been led. As pagans, they had been led to worship idols that were not gods. Now they called Jesus Lord as they were led to do so by the Holy Spirit. There are no free agents or independent contractors when it comes to membership in the body of Christ. All who are in it were led to it.

Paul said every member of the body has a gift. But the gifts are not all the same, even though they have been given by the same God. The gifts aren't given for the individual's benefit, but for the common good of the body. The members are all gifted and enabled by the same power source, who decided what gift each member should receive. Look at the verbs about what God did—he willed, appointed, chose, apportioned, gave, empowered. This is humbling to those who know they're gifted, and might be tempted to think they're the power and source of their gift.

It's both humbling and dignifying to realize our gift was given for the benefit of others. We're conduits, not just receptacles of God's blessings. We pass them along to other members of the body. It humbles us to realize we are what we are so others will be blessed. But it also gives dignity and significance to every member to realize God gifted him, and put him exactly where he wanted him for the good of the body.

Equality and unity comes from having a common power source. Our interconnectedness gives us a healthy dependency upon and sympathy with one another. Our diversity brings both responsibility and dignity to our gift and place in the body. It is an ingenious design! Let's celebrate instead of criticize our various gifts, and cherish our membership in the body of Christ.

Day 146, 1 Corinthians 13

It's printed on coffee mugs and bookmarks. It's written in calligraphy on parchment, cross-stitched into fabric and woven into wedding ceremonies. It's memorized and recited almost as much as Psalm 23 or John 3:16. But few people realize Paul's best known chapter was originally written in the context of a long discussion about spiritual gifts. The unity of the body at Corinth was threatened by quarreling over who had the best spiritual gift. Paul taught them a better way to live by showing them the power, performance and permanence of love.

Corinth was, as we noted earlier, the home of many of the ancient world's finest orators. From the context in which this description of love is found, we learn that the Corinthians were particularly enamored with the gift of tongues—the ability God gave certain disciples to speak in languages they had not studied. Paul told them the highest language was devoid of meaning without love. In the infancy of the church when there was as yet no such thing as the written New Testament, the spiritual gifts of prophecy and knowledge were essential to the growth and health of the church. While those gifts were desirable and those who possessed them were no doubt esteemed, Paul said they were "nothing" without love. He also said the greatest acts of sacrifice and expressions of self-denial were of no value when such behavior was not motivated by love. Love empowers and gives significance to all that is worthwhile.

When I read this detailed description of love, I am convicted as I realize my thoughts, words and actions are frequently not expressions of love. I am sometimes impatient and unkind. Jealousy and pride too often taint my actions. I do want my way, and I am sometimes irritable. Must I go on? Don't we understand that we don't always match this description? Think of the relationships that have been destroyed because people were unwilling to love like this. Think of the broken marriages and fractured friendships that could be mended if all parties were willing to adopt this as their code of conduct.

If we've grown accustomed to instant things in our modern time, we've also gotten used to how quickly valuable items become obsolete. In the wake of technology's rapid advance, today's new and improved model is tomorrow's antique. All we know in this material world grows old and wears out, but Paul said that love never ends. It is not a passing fancy. It is not a temporary state. It outlasts and overcomes everything else we know.

Love gives life meaning. Far from being an abstract concept, its presence (or absence) is demonstrated in tangible, observable ways. Love is undiminished by the passing of time; it never goes out of style or loses its potency. It speaks more eloquently, knows more deeply and gives more sacrificially than anything else in the world. No wonder "the greatest of these is love."

Day 147, 1 Corinthians 14

Here's a riddle: When is 5 more than 10,000? Paul said the answer is when five understood words are better than ten thousand words that no one understands. Allow me to illustrate. Which do you prefer? <a> *A proclivity for compendious and perspicuous conveyance of requisite data is preferable;* or <b> *When communicating important information, brief and clear is better.*

Here's another one: <a> *A propensity for verbosity precludes the un-ambiguous promulgation of imperative intelligence*; versus <b> *Using too many big words keeps people from getting the important message*. Can you tell I'm having fun with my new thesaurus?

Paul encouraged the Corinthians to behave in love and desire spiritual gifts, especially prophecy (inspired teaching). Gifts were given to build up to body, not to show off. They were to be used in a manner consistent with their purpose. Tongue-speaking (talking in a language they had not learned) was impressive. But it did not serve the highest purpose of building up the body through clearly understood teaching. So Paul regulated how to use the gifts in the assembly: no more than two or three, one at a time, when another starts the first should stop, the wives should ask their prophesying husbands questions at home, no tongues without interpreters present. The rules were to promote peace and prevent confusion.

I suspect a first-century assembly would surprise us. I doubt there was an "order of worship" printed in the bulletin, dictating what was done when. But Paul said it was all to be done decently and in order to facilitate understanding.

"Decently and in order" isn't a code word for our comfort zone, what we're used to or how we like it. This phrase comes up whenever a church changes something in its meetings. If we confuse tradition with command, we'll call any variation from our experience indecent and out of order. In context, Paul was describing how to use the gifts to build people up and promote understanding. No building, encouraging or consoling takes place without understanding. If the goal is showing how much we know, then pile on the obtuse verbiage. If we want people to feel uncomfortable and distant, obscure the meaning in unfamiliar language. But to reach people and change lives, brief and clear is better.

This is true about teaching people inside the church, and reaching people outside the church. The longer we've been in, the harder it is to hear how we sound to outsiders. We know the jargon; we're fluent in Churchese. It's not just the words we use—it's also the channels through which we speak. Guess what? Most post-moderns do not know church vocabulary, and they don't get formal sermons based on a centuries-old communication model. It's like broadcasting on a frequency they're not monitoring in a language they don't speak. The goal is understanding. If we're serious about bringing people to Christ and building them up in Christ, we'll make it brief and clear.

Day 148, 1 Corinthians 15

We're who and where we are today as the culmination of everything that's happened in the past. Choices and events that seemed mundane or insignificant in daily life become defining moments as we look back over our lives. While everything has affected us, sometimes we can point to one single thing that gave our lives context and direction.

For Paul, it was meeting the resurrected Jesus. The persecutor became the preacher after his Damascus road encounter with the risen Christ. The gospel message of Jesus' death for our sins, his burial and resurrection, all according to the Scriptures, was the keynote of his preaching. The gospel of grace changed him, motivated him and humbled him.

Paul's whole life and career was built on the validity of the resurrection. When someone suggested there was no such thing as the resurrection of the dead, it was an attack on the core of Paul's life. Paul rejected the suggestion that his life was based on a fable. The fact of the resurrection was not some whimsical item in a curio collection to be examined; it was not an intellectual badminton shuttlecock to be batted back and forth. It was the foundation of all the confidence, hope and purpose that Paul knew and shared with others.

When the Corinthians were influenced by some false teachers to doubt the resurrection, Paul showed them the implications of that doctrine. If there was no resurrection, then: Jesus was not alive and was not who he claimed to be. Paul's preaching and the Corinthians' faith was empty. They were still lost in sin. The dead were lost without any hope, and the living had no hope of anything beyond this life. Whatever intellectual exercise led them to doubt the resurrection also robbed them of all the peace, joy, hope and meaning they had come to know in Christ.

Against that dismal prospect, Paul reaffirmed the resurrection of Jesus. All that went wrong in Adam was set right in Christ. Living for Jesus and suffering for him only makes sense in light of the resurrection. Skeptical questions about how it will happen and what kind of body the resurrected will have do not change the fact that it is real. Paul gave examples from the natural world to illustrate. The plant that comes from a sown seed doesn't look like the seed. We see different kinds of bodies in the animal kingdom and the objects in the sky. Paul said our present flesh bodies were not suited for eternity, and that God would change everyone's body immediately when Jesus came and the dead were raised.

From an earthly point of view, death is final. No one escapes its grasp. The grave wins every time. But Paul said the resurrection was our assurance of victory over death. In that promised victory, we should find strong incentive to hold onto our faith with unwavering determination. We should serve the Lord faithfully, trusting that our service is not an exercise in futility.

Day 149, 1 Corinthians 16

"Life coaching" is a popular form of personal counseling. Clients pay their life coach to help them form and follow a plan to maximize performance and reach goals.

The apostle Paul wore many hats in his career. He was an evangelist, a missionary and a master theologian. But much of his writing was application-oriented, filled with the kind of guidance a wise life coach might give clients to help them succeed.

In this exclusive interview with *The Abiding Companion* (OK, I got it from today's portion), Paul shares inspired wisdom about a variety of life topics.

Abiding Companion: Paul, could you share some pointers about handling money wisely, especially other people's money?

Paul: Obey the law of accumulation. Put a little aside each week to accumulate a nest egg. Each contribution doesn't seem like much, but it gradually becomes far more than you'd have at any one time. Unfortunately, the law of accumulation also works for debt. When you spend a little more than you make each pay period, those little sips of the credit card kool-aid add up to a staggering amount of indebtedness.

When handling other people's money, obey the law of accountability. Be honest and open about every penny. Involve the givers in the administration of the funds. Let the contributors select a representative to share the responsibility.

AC: You have accomplished so much. How about some tips for getting things done?

Paul: Always have a plan. Under the umbrella of God's will, write down your intentions, and act on the plan. I always have an itinerary.

Invest in your people by spending time with them, and helping them reach their goals. Show respect for them and recognize their accomplishments.

Do what needs to be done today. Planning for the future is fine and necessary; it does not replace doing today's work today. Seize present opportunities with optimism. Be realistic about obstacles in the way of success, and meet them head on.

AC: Can you summarize a life plan for maturing disciples, maybe just a "bullet list"?

Paul: Sure. I do that when I'm closing a letter and still have so much to tell the people. Here's a good check list for a disciple's life: Be alert and on guard at all times. Be well-grounded in what you believe. Keep trusting the Lord. Grow up! Overcome immaturity in your thinking, talking and actions. Act from strength, but remember the strength comes from the Lord. Do everything in love; it's the highest and best motive.

AC: Let's close with a comment about the motivational factors that work best for you and the disciples you're mentoring.

Paul: Look forward to Jesus' promised return; that will clarify your priorities and keep you on track. Rejoice in the grace you've been shown, and remember to share it with others. Love each other; cherish and honor your relationships.

AC: Thanks, Paul.

Paul: It's my pleasure. Send my greetings to your readers, until I can hug them in heaven.

2 Corinthians

Day 150, 2 Corinthians 1

The heat is oppressive. He's gotten used to the sandy grit and the blinding glare. He is in danger, but he's more concerned for the folks back home than for himself. He misses his wife and children. He missed the baby's first birthday last month, and next week he'll miss celebrating his fifth wedding anniversary. There's plenty to eat, but it's not like Momma's table during the holidays. Thanks to technology, he's in touch by e-mail every day, on the phone regularly and sometimes face-to-face (sort of) via video conference. He's glad to do his duty and honored to serve his country. But he's lonely for home.

When the package arrives, the heat, grit, glare, danger and even the loneliness lose some of their oppressive power for awhile. He cuts through the tape and peers into the box. Some of his favorite comfort foods are there, accompanied by travel-sized containers of body powder, portable packs of handi-wipes, mouthwash and other little personal comfort items—luxuries in this inhospitable place so far from home. The practical gifts sent by thoughtful loved ones comfort him. And he does what perhaps only those who've been in a similar situation can understand—he shares the little treats and goodies from home with others in his unit. The comforted one becomes the comforter as the blessings are shared.

In the normal adversity that is part of life, our Father is "the God of all comfort, who comforts us in all our afflictions." And like Paul, we are blessed to be able to bless those around us with the comfort we've received. We are not vaccinated against trouble when we become Christians. But we do know the source of real comfort, and we can share in his great ministry of comfort by passing it on to others.

God is also the source of deliverance in affliction. When Paul thought he was going to die, he learned to rely on God who raises the dead. When we are pressed to the limit and hardship is at its worst, we learn to trust him to deliver us when we cannot save ourselves. In such dire straits we learn to appreciate the prayers offered for us, and God's faithful response to those prayers.

God is also our source of certainty in an uncertain world. When your confidence has been shaken by unpredictable and uncontrollable circumstances, it's good to know God is not a God of doublespeak. His "Yes" means "Yes" and his "No" means "No." Experts say parents raising children need to be consistent and keep their promises. Father God is ultimately faithful. Through Jesus, every promise God ever made is going to be kept. His spirit within us guarantees his faithfulness.

Plans and agendas may change; we may not know what God is doing, or why he's waiting so long. But we may rest assured that our source of soothing comfort, sure deliverance and certain confidence is faithful.

Day 151, 2 Corinthians 2

Holding his newborn daughter fills him with a sense of awe. His cheeks are wet with tears of joy. He feels deep love for this little one he's just met, for his wife who's endured so much to bring this baby into the world, and for God, who has blessed him with such a rich gift. He feels responsible for the child's well-being and training. Has anything prepared him for this awesome task? (Autobiographical? Yes, indeed.)

She has worked hard, and savors the achievement of her college graduation. The interviews come next. She has some anxiety, but she is well-prepared and unintimidated. Then the call: she got the job! After the elation comes the realization that this is a big job with grown-up responsibilities. And she wonders, after all the training and hard work, "Am I competent to do this?"

Maybe you've felt responsibility as a parent, or with a new position or promotion. Have you felt it as a disciple of Jesus? Have you realized he gave you a gift as a member of the body of Christ, and responsibility to use that gift to bless other people?

The apostle Paul felt it. When he contemplated his place in God's scheme, knowing his preaching would be the catalyst that would turn some to life and others to death, he asked, "Who is sufficient for these things?" He was not peddling the word of God for profit; his zeal and suffering proved his sincerity. He reminded the Corinthians (and maybe himself) of three components of his competency for ministry.

Paul knew he was sent by God. That first meeting on the Damascus road and subsequent messages from the risen Lord convinced him he was doing the work God commissioned him to do. Knowing we're serving God and trusting that he equips those he commissions helps us bear the responsibility of serving him.

Paul also knew he was working in the sight of God. Throughout his epistles, he called God as his witness and reminded his readers that God is watching us. God sees every effort and knows every motive. No sacrifice for Christ goes unnoticed. Knowing he's watching builds my courage and confidence, and deflates all my excuses for not obeying him.

And Paul knew he was speaking in Christ. It was Christ's gospel he proclaimed. So Paul labored with the love and compassion of his Master, who came to seek and save the lost. It wasn't what he accomplished, but what Christ accomplished through him. When correction was necessary, Paul did it with tears, not with delight. When discipline was required, Paul reminded the church that the goal was forgiveness and restoration, so God's plan (not Satan's) would be fulfilled.

When you remember that you are commissioned by God, that he sees all you do, and when you speak and act as Jesus would do, you can have confidence as you serve him.

Day 152, 2 Corinthians 3

Counselors teach clients to use a two-columned list as a decision-making tool. You've probably done it when faced with some choice. In one column you write the positive things about something you're considering, and in the other column you write the negative consequences or implications. A list helps us compare options, writing the features or costs in columns. Maybe it's the one you have versus the new model. Which is better quality? How long will each last? Does the difference in performance justify the expense? Do I really want to do this?

Today's portion is like a two-columned list. In one column we have the Law, given by God to Moses at Sinai, the old covenant. On the other side we have the gospel of Christ, the new covenant. (You may have to put aside 2,000 years of pre-conditioning to understand why such an analysis was necessary back when Paul wrote this.) Most of the epistles contain teaching to counteract Jewish teachers who wanted to bind the Law of Moses on Gentile converts. Paul had to show that the freedom of the new covenant in Christ was superior to the yoke of the old law. He contrasted the two to show the weakness and failure of the old covenant.

The old was written with ink, or originally carved into stone tablets. The new is written by the Spirit of God on tablets of human hearts. The old killed and condemned; the new gives life and justifies. (That seems like a clincher to me, but Paul goes on.) The old was glorious, so much so that Moses had to wear a veil to cover his face that glowed with the glory of God when he came down from the mountain. But the new is so glorious that the glory of the old one fades away in comparison, just as the glow faded from Moses' face. The old put a veil between God and those who would draw near him. The new reveals the unveiled glory of God and transforms those who gaze on it into the same image of glory, making us like him. In every way, the new is superior to the old.

Paul said God's grace made him a competent minister of this new covenant, and the Corinthians' transformed lives were evidence—like letters from Christ, delivered by Paul, verifying his apostleship. He did not need the Corinthians to issue or check his credentials; they themselves were his credentials.

You may not be tempted to swap your relationship with God in Christ for the types and shadows of the Old Testament. The temptation today would be to exchange the new covenant for an even newer idea claiming to make you complete and give richer meaning to your life. You will likely be tempted to swap your allegiance to Jesus Christ for some temporary worldly gain or momentary gratification of the flesh. Do the comparison. Make the smart choice. Stay with Jesus.

Day 153, 2 Corinthians 4

"It's all in how you look at it." Have you heard that expression before? Perspective is our viewpoint or attitude about the people, things and events around us. The difficulties you encounter because of your decision to follow Jesus may be discouraging. Not everyone will share your faith in Christ. When your values clash with the world's values, you might wonder if you made the right choice. Perspective helps overcome these obstacles.

Paul saw his ministry as a gift he received by God's mercy. That perspective shaped his attitude toward serving the Lord. When people reject the message, it's good to remember you're privileged to know and share it because of God's mercy. When circumstances discourage us, remember we're only able to do this because God, in his mercy, chose us for this ministry. This perspective keeps us encouraged in trouble and disappointment. I suspect more disciples are knocked out of service by smothering discouragement than fierce persecution. We need this viewpoint to stay on task when it would be easier to quit.

Paul saw himself as a servant of Christ and his people. The spiritual father of these Corinthians, the author of thirteen books of the New Testament, the greatest missionary of all time saw himself not as a master, but as a servant. This viewpoint vaccinates us against another deadly threat to faithful discipleship—our own pride. How many have failed to follow and serve because their feelings were hurt? How often have we taken it personally when people rejected our efforts to share the gospel? Pride makes us vulnerable in those situations. Paul saw himself as a jar of clay—formed by the hand of another, fragile and imperfect. But he had treasure inside his jar! The gospel, the knowledge of the glory of God in the face of Jesus Christ, was inside him. His significance was in that treasure, not in himself. His life was a medium for showing Jesus to others. This perspective kept the focus (and the glory) in the right place. It kept Paul humble. We need that, too.

Paul saw the resurrection and eternity as reality. Afflictions and persecutions were not overwhelming in light of eternity. Death itself was not so threatening to one with steadfast confidence in the resurrection. Paul looked past the shame and suffering he endured all the way to heaven, and saw himself and the people who had been saved by Christ through his ministry rejoicing around the throne of God. He endured so they could join in the thanksgiving, so God would get more glory. With this viewpoint, Paul's suffering here seemed slight and momentary.

Are you in the "we" of this perspective? Paul said "we" don't lose heart because we have received our ministry by mercy. "We" are servants and jars of clay. "We" look beyond the things that are seen and temporary to the unseen and enduring reality. Is Paul's perspective yours? Remember, it's all in how you look at it.

Day 154, 2 Corinthians 5

"She is not a happy camper." Have you ever heard that colloquial expression about someone who was upset? I would never say that. I never liked that saying, perhaps because I never liked camping. Well, maybe I did as a boy, but not now. So, to me, there's no such logical thing as a happy camper. (I'm sorry if that's your favorite phrase or if camping is your favorite activity. I'm happy for you. Go camping. Be happy. I just don't want to go with you, to sleep on the hard ground with snakes slithering around and bears clawing at the tent trying to get my trail mix and who knows what else. But I digress.)

Paul said living in this body is like camping, staying in a tent. Dying and going to heaven is like going to the house after being out in the tent. We groan in the tent, not to lose the tent's shelter, but to gain the security and comfort of the house. Death isn't losing life; it's being swallowed up by life. God has something far better for his people than the flesh tents we live in here. God has prepared a house for us in heaven, where we can be with him forever. He gave us his Spirit as a guarantee, and lets us see our home with him by faith.

Paul's aim, whether here in the tent or at his permanent address in heaven, was to please the Lord. The ultimate win in Paul's life strategy was to stand before the judgment seat of Christ and be approved. Paul was controlled by the love of Christ. That love compelled him to tell everyone how Jesus died for them, and to persuade everyone to live for Christ. After God reconciled sinners to himself through Jesus' death, he made Paul and the other apostles messengers of that good news.

As you reflect on these words, may I ask a few personal questions? What's the aim of your life? Is it wealth or possessions or some achievement? If your aim is anything less than pleasing the Lord in everything you do, I encourage you to raise your aim.

What controls you? Are you driven by the love of Christ? Aren't we sometimes driven by less noble compulsions? Think of how our thoughts, words and actions would be changed if Christ's love controlled us.

And finally, do you really like camping? I don't mean the tent in the woods. I mean like Paul described it—living in a flesh tent in this world. These tents are remarkable creations, but I'm sure you've noticed how they do wear out. They are not intended to be permanent residences. Trust that there's much more and better waiting for those who are reconciled to God in Christ.

So enjoy the camp-out. Be a happy camper, if you insist. But don't get too cozy in the temporary housing. Don't settle for a tent when God has a house for you.

Day 155, 2 Corinthians 6

Paul worked hard to bring the good news of God's grace to people everywhere. He wanted them to know about and respond to God's amazing grace, to be saved and to be sustained by it throughout their lives. He warned people not to receive grace in vain, but to respond in a timely way to God's gracious offer to save them in Christ.

The great apostle was serious about his influence. Paul took care to avoid causing anyone to stumble. He didn't want anything he said or did to become an obstacle in anyone's spiritual path.

On one hand this meant enduring some hardships. Paul suffered a lot for the cause of Christ—this passage alone lists afflictions, hardships, calamities, beatings, imprisonments, riots, labors, sleepless nights and hunger. For many of us, just one of those rough spots on the journey might have made us quit, claiming life wasn't fair and the cost of following Jesus was too great.

On the other hand, Paul modeled the character and conduct that should be found in every believer, but must be present in godly leaders. Purity, knowledge, patience, kindness, the Holy Spirit, genuine love, truthful speech and the power of God were on display in Paul's life. Between resisting the discouraging bad things and living out the encouraging positive ones, Paul deployed both defensive and offensive weapons in his fight against Satan. As soldiers use both shield and sword to survive and win the battle, so Christians need the full armor, too.

Not everyone who looks at your life is going to be kind, supportive and encouraging about your attempt to live for Jesus. The events of life are not always fair. Still, we should persevere as Paul did. We must not allow people and circumstances around us to define who we are or diminish what we have in Christ.

It seems strange that Paul, the Corinthians' father in the gospel, should have to plead with them to receive him and his words. But haven't we at some time resisted the wholesome and embraced something harmful? All who would enjoy God's holy fellowship must turn away from evil. A holy God cannot live among compromised, polluted people. God provides the cleansing and then the strength to separate ourselves from the world. Our Father expects his sons and daughters to live holy lives that reflect his image. There should be a distinct difference between believers and unbelievers—for God's glory, our holiness and a visible testimony to the world.

The message of God's grace is universal in its invitation, but the reception is individual. God has shown remarkable patience in dealing with the world and with each of us, but his patience has a defined limit. It's better to respond to the gospel right away for the sake of your own salvation and well-being, as well as for your influence on others.

Day 156, 2 Corinthians 7

He's old enough to test Momma's restraint. So, looking right at her, he defies her and does what she's warned him not to do. Mom can't afford to lose this contest of the wills. Her words are sharp; her grip is strong. The punishment is measured and swift. His defiance crumbles, his lip trembles, the tears flow. He is sorry he disobeyed. Her reassuring expressions of love comfort them both in the aftermath. She loves her son, and wants what is best for him. He needs correction for his own good. And somewhere, behind the tears, he appreciates it.

Every loving parent can understand Paul's mixed feelings about correcting the Corinthians and making them sad. He regretted it was necessary, but he rejoiced at the outcome. His rebuke hurt their feelings, but helped them make a needed change.

The Corinthians were Paul's "children," having come to faith in Christ under his teaching. Paul found it rewarding to watch his children grow, and painful to correct them when it was necessary. The parenting dynamics were somewhat different because these "children" were adults. That made the correction harder, and the outcome more uncertain than doing the same thing with a small child.

Has your heart ever been broken by a correction from the word of God? Maybe it came right off the page, or through a faithful teacher who loved you enough to tell you the truth. If so, you can understand the Corinthians' sorrow. It reminds me of David, stricken by grief and regret when Nathan convicted him of his sin with Bathsheba. This grief is not being sorry for getting caught, or for the consequences we've brought on ourselves. This sorrow comes from realizing we have done wrong. We have broken God's law, insulted his love and offended his holiness. The tears are genuine. We truly regret our disobedience.

What Paul calls "godly grief" leads to a good outcome—it produces a change we do not regret. The Bible word for that change is repentance. Instead of self-destructive behavior or angry retaliation, repentance leads to restoration and reconciliation. The Corinthians were earnest about doing what was right and indignant about having done wrong. With renewed zeal and a holy respect for God, they longed for his approval. This positive outcome pleased Paul, and made the unpleasant rebuke worthwhile.

Here's a pattern for both sides of such a situation. When we're the parent figure, we should speak and act with the desired outcome (repentance) in mind. We don't correct to vent our anger or to destroy the person we're correcting. And when we're the disobedient child who needs correction, we should be humble enough to hear and have our hearts broken by the rebuke. Then we need to show by our actions that the godly grief has produced a positive change in us. When we can respond with genuine gratitude and not malice toward those who lovingly correct us, we'll know we're on our way to maturity.

Day 157, 2 Corinthians 8

You've seen the commercials and received the mail. The pictures stir our hearts for the plight of people living in unimaginable poverty. The charities appeal to your compassion and conscience through two main avenues. They make you aware of the need, and give examples of how some famous person or maybe someone like you made a difference. They tell you how pennies a day could alleviate some of the suffering. Call the number on the screen. Have your credit card ready. Operators are standing by. And thank you.

Some organizations that raise money this way are very efficient, delivering a high percentage of revenues received to the intended recipients. We applaud their efforts. Unfortunately, other groups have been exposed as bloated, self-serving, fraudulent scam artists who exploit the hardship of some to steal from the goodwill of others. It's wise to get the facts.

Paul didn't have video, still pictures, credit cards or toll-free numbers to raise money for needy Christians in Judea. But he used the same appeal model employed by modern charities—after telling about the need, he used an example to spur them to action.

The Macedonians' demographics didn't suggest that they would be good prospects to give. But they gave beyond their means, despite their own poverty and suffering. They weren't begged to participate; they begged to participate. They didn't think they were doing others a favor; it was a favor to be included. They surprised Paul with their generous, free-will gift. Paul said they gave by grace (which is, ultimately, the source of all we have and the inclination to share). He said they first gave themselves to the Lord. When you've given yourself, your stuff isn't a problem.

Giving is more about one's readiness than resources. The Macedonians had more joy in their hearts than money in their pockets. But like the widow who gave her last two coins, the Macedonians were willing to give. That, Paul said, is what makes the gift acceptable.

Generous giving expresses trust in leaders who handle the funds. Paul explained who would administer the gift and established their trustworthiness. Open, honest accounting is the key to credibility among organizations that collect and distribute money, from local churches to international charities. Donors are saying, "We trust you to do the right thing with this money." (It's wicked to betray that trust.)

Above all, giving proved their love. Paul called it an opportunity to show their love was genuine. By sharing what they had, they would be like the early Jerusalem church, where selfless sharing met the needs of every member. Like the ancient Israelites' manna, none had too much or too little. Best of all, they would be like Jesus, who gave up everything for our sake.

The Macedonians teach us how to give. Paul and his associates teach us how to raise funds with integrity. In a world with a sharp distinction between the "haves" and "have nots," we need both lessons.

Day 158, 2 Corinthians 9

During the year in which I wrote this book, many farmers across our region lost their crops due to severe drought. In our own yard, many of our young shrubs and trees died despite our efforts to water them. One lone survivor of the drought in our back yard was a stalk of sunflowers, which grew in a large flower pot where my wife thought she had planted zinnias. (No zinnias ever appeared.) This tall green stalk sprouted from a single seed and produced flowers, each bearing hundreds of seeds. I'm no botanist or gardener, but I think I can have lots of sunflowers next year by planting those seeds.

I will save them, plant them, and when I'm looking at a sea of sun-flowers, I'll remember the law of sowing and reaping.

Paul cited the law of sowing and reaping to encourage the Corinthians to be generous and keep their year-old promise to give. He had used them as an example to motivate others; now it was time for them to give. It's good to have enthusiasm, and it's great to have a plan. But emotions and preparations must become actions for benefits to be realized.

The old-as-the-world law of sowing and reaping applies to more fields than farming. It helps us see giving as an investment, not a tax or expense. A farmer can sabotage his crop by stingy sowing or increase the yield by generous sowing. Just so our efforts are limited or enhanced by how much we're willing to put into a project. This explains many situations of life. It explains why families fall apart when all the energy and time is invested in work or other pursuits instead of making family a priority. It also explains why some people complain that they never get anything out of Bible study or worship. The poor yield may indicate a paltry investment of time and effort.

Generous giving produces great benefits. The giver is enriched by the experience. Paul wanted the Corinthians to be generous so they would learn that God (who gave them what they had to begin with) could be trusted to give them more. The recipients are blessed, too, as needs are met. And God gets more praise and thanksgiving from the chain-reaction of positive results.

Cheerful giving testifies to the lordship of Christ and the work of grace in our lives. When we trust what the Lord says and give liberally, we're controlled by his will, not our own selfishness. When we're conscious of how much God has given us by his grace, we'll rejoice in the opportunity to imitate his generosity. All our gifts are put into perspective when compared to God's inexpressible gift to us in Christ.

Do you want to be enthusiastic and faithful about your giving? Read this encouragement from Paul again and again. If we want the blessings of the harvest, we must be willing to plant the seeds.

Day 159, 2 Corinthians 10

Conflict seems to be inevitable among people who interact with one another about significant matters over time. Families have feuds, and churches do, too. It's because we're flawed people living in a fallen world. Weakness colors our very best behavior; flesh is always seeking opportunity to rebel against the lordship of Christ in our lives. Don't you sometimes do less than your best? When we think, speak or behave in less than ideal ways, we bring tension into our relationships, even among fellow believers. Let's look at Paul's example as he dealt with people who discounted his ministry and authority. We can find a model in his method to resolve tensions in our own relationships.

Paul was meek and gentle as he entreated the Corinthians. He defended himself without being defensive (which often turns into being offensive). Meekness is not weakness; it is strength under control. We are imitating Christ himself when we deal gently with people in conflict whenever possible. Our flesh wants to raise its voice and throw its weight around. Long ago, Solomon observed that a soft answer turns away wrath, but a harsh word stirs up anger. Paul knew how to be firm and stand his ground. He would use apostolic authority if necessary. But his first approach was gentle entreaty. If we'd make it ours, we might resolve differences before they erupt into major confrontations.

When Paul fought, he did not wage war according to the flesh. Instead, he employed weapons of divine destruction when tensions threatened his life and ministry. He did not resort to fleshly tactics, and neither should we. In conflict, it's tempting to reflect others' actions and attitudes back at them, but that's not the best strategy. Conflict does not have to be carnal. Godly people use godly means to meet ungodly opposition.

Paul never forgot the source or purpose of his apostolic authority. He knew his authority was from God, to build people up, not tear them down. Every leader in a church, a family or any organization should remember that leaders can have authority without being authoritarian. We chafe at the abuse of power. Being an authority-wielding bully may appear to be a shortcut to defusing tension, but it really only makes it worse.

Also remember it is pointless and unwise to measure and compare ourselves with one another. Seeking approval and commendation, we may judge ourselves to be more faithful, more effective, more disciplined, more loving, more spiritual, more fruitful than someone else. But Paul said people who make such comparisons lack understanding. When we commend ourselves, we're only boasting. The only approval that counts for anything is the Lord's approval. So why irritate and agitate one another by making pointless comparisons?

Perhaps you feel the same shame I do as I read these words. I don't always deal with tension and conflict in wholesome, holy ways. But I'm glad to have Paul's example to teach and encourage me to do better.

Day 160, 2 Corinthians 11

I hope you're not the type, but I'm sure you know the type—the person who is his own favorite subject. Conversation is easy—he does all the talking, and it's all about him. Nobody else has done so much so well. Like they used to sing about Flipper, the dolphin on TV, "No one you see is smarter than he!"

It's a common character flaw, even among Christians. We sometimes excuse such behavior, saying, "That's just their personality." But Paul labeled boasting as "foolishness." As he wrote about what he had endured for the sake of Christ and those he had won to Christ, he said he was speaking as a fool and as a madman. He did it to respond to the false apostles who had discredited him at Corinth. Paul not only taught the credo, "Let the one who boasts, boast in the Lord;" he lived by it. Since he was uncomfortable telling about himself, he boasted about things that showed his weakness. That's unusual boasting!

This passage reveals some information about Paul we sometimes forget. We usually say he accomplished more than any other person for the gospel of Christ. These words remind us he may also have suffered more for the gospel than any other person—far more imprisonments, countless beatings, often near death. He was whipped, beaten, stoned, shipwrecked, in constant danger and desperate need—sometimes even of food, clothing and shelter. I don't want to sit down in heaven and swap stories with Paul about suffering for Christ, do you? "Hey, Paul, that's bad. But you're not the only one who's had it rough. One time the air conditioning was off at church. It was so hot in there! We really suffered that day. This other time, a visitor was in my seat and I had to sit somewhere else. That really hurt. But this was the toughest one—somebody once made fun of me for being a Christian. That was hard, but I didn't quit!"

One of the finest men I ever knew did not enjoy being introduced before he spoke. People who meant to honor him would praise him, and he would shake his head and say "No" quietly to himself during the accolades. He told me that such introductions actually hurt the presentation, since no one could live up to the expectations created by such a build-up. He wanted God to get the glory. I'd like to be more like him, more like Paul and much more like Jesus, whose greatest glory was total submission to his Father's will. Wouldn't we boast less if we were more concerned with God's glory and less concerned about our own? Maybe our desire not to look foolish will trump our desire to boast.

Day 161, 2 Corinthians 12

What if Paul had a publicist to get good media exposure and present him in the best possible light? Let's imagine a conversation between the apostle and his publicist. Since he's imaginary, we can name him anything we like. How about Bob?

Bob: OK, Paul. We're getting close to the end of this letter. I know you're reluctant to talk about your successes, but our polls in Corinth say you need to enhance your credibility. Why not tell about that mystical out of body experience you had a while back? That's impressive. The Corinthians will like that!

Paul: No. That was fourteen years ago. There's not much to say, really. I can't even talk about what I do remember seeing and hearing. Let's tell them more about my weaknesses, so the Lord gets glory instead of me.

Bob: You don't understand! Your approval rating is way down! You're trailing the guys who went in and discredited you. It's time to accentuate the positive, the big successes.

Paul: I think I'll tell them about my thorn in the flesh.

Bob: What? Are you out of your mind? You're going to admit you have an embarrassing, debilitating problem? If you open up that box, it will look like you're not even well-connected enough to get your prayers answered!

Paul: They were answered. The answer was no. I asked the Lord three times to take away this aggravating physical problem. He said no. He promised his grace was sufficient, that his strength would shine through in my weakness. God's design is greater than my desires.

Bob: You've got to come across as strong!

Paul: That's exactly why I boast about the weaknesses and hardships. In those negative situations, I have plenty of strength, and it's obviously from him, not from me. That's how I learned to be content despite the calamities and persecutions. He's in control. Anyway, they know I'm an apostle. They saw the miracles. The only difference in them and any other church is that I didn't take any support from them.

Bob: Right. They owe you! It's time for them to ante up, to show you some respect.

Paul: They're my children. A father ought to give to his children, not the other way around. I want to give to them, not take from them. Nobody in our organization has taken anything from them— not Titus, not Timothy.

Bob: You've got to defend yourself!

Paul: That's not the point. We're writing this to build them up, not to defend ourselves. You know, I dread going there if we have to be rough with the ones who haven't listened to my warnings about changing their ungodly lives.

Bob: I don't know, Paul. It doesn't make sense to me. This boasting about your weaknesses and giving instead of taking—that's just not how it's done in this old world.

Paul: I know, Bob. It's OK. We're not doing it like it's done in this world. Let's finish the letter.

Day 162, 2 Corinthians 13

Most people who go to church have heard the last words of 2 Corinthians at the end of a service: "The grace of the Lord Jesus Christ and the love of God and the fellowship of the Holy Spirit be with you all." Often called "The Benediction," these rich words should influence our lives after the "amen." Today's portion not only contains the benediction; it also illustrates the effect of the blessing on the blessed.

The grace of the Lord Jesus Christ is the foundation of every redeemed person's hope. We rejoice in the forgiveness of our sins by his grace. But living with that grace does not mean we are soft, weak and tolerant about sin. Paul had been patient, but time was up for the impenitent among the Corinthians. They had been warned, and if they still refused to repent, he would be strong against them when he arrived. That strength would not come from his own flesh or power. Instead he would discipline the impenitent ones with the power of the risen Christ.

The love of God should color every thought, word and deed of our lives. Do we behave in love? Do we examine ourselves before and maybe instead of critically evaluating others? When our love mirrors God's great love for us, we want the best for the ones he loves. There is no greater love or greater authority than God's. When we use authority, do we use it in love as God intended? Do those under our authority understand that we use it to build them up, not tear them down?

We are not called to be soloists in God's great choir. The fellowship of the Holy Spirit is much, much broader than your relationship with him. We have individual responsibility toward God, and mutual responsibility toward one another. Shared joy is deeper and sweeter than solitary joy. We're called both to experience God's comfort and show it to others. Fellowship means you don't always get your way. We know more than we do about living in peace, because it takes mature restraint to show genuine consideration for others. All our talk about fellowship is meaningless without pure, holy expressions of it.

It would be bad if we missed the meaning of these ancient words because we're distracted by gathering up our stuff, getting jackets on the kids or plotting our escape route from the church's parking lot. Maybe our familiarity with the frequently repeated blessing dilutes its significance to us. As bad as that would be, it's even worse when our lives don't reflect the fact that grace, love and fellowship are supposed to be gifts from God shared in relationship with one another. These blessings are not just given to us, but through us as well. The words of the benediction are more than a sanctified "The End;" they're a blessing. But the blessing is realized only when the blessed live out the words in their daily lives.

Galatians

Day 163, Galatians 1

Do people ever change? We know change is swift and unavoidable in the world around us. But we're sometimes skeptical about people changing. We've been jaded by repeated disappointments. It's a cycle—someone does wrong, the perpetrator admits it, seeks forgiveness with tears and pledges to change. Tender hearts believe the emotional promises and once again extend trust, only to be hurt again when the person does the same thing, completing the circle of frustration. Maybe our skepticism about change comes from looking in the mirror. We've know we've broken our word about what we would always or never do again.

Paul, by his name, is a testimony to the possibility and reality of dramatic, lasting change. Saul, the arch persecutor of Christians became Paul the apostle of Christ, employing the same tenacious spirit in spreading the gospel he once applied to stopping it. He described how the Judean Christians heard about him after his conversion: "He who used to persecute us is now preaching the faith he once tried to destroy."

Although personal experience may suggest otherwise, change is real and possible. Today's portion suggests some key factors in producing changed lives.

A person finds power to make radical change by accepting God's call on his life. From the opening words of this letter, Paul stressed that he was sent (the meaning of the word "apostle") on this mission. He realized God had set him apart for the mission of preaching the gospel to the Gentiles before he was born. Believing God has a purpose for our lives and that he can accomplish it through us is powerful motivation to get in line and stay in line with that purpose.

Awareness and appreciation for the price God paid to redeem us is another incentive to change. Jesus had to die to deliver us from evil. Shouldn't that motivate us to change? What a callous insult to divine love and grace to keep living the old way after Jesus gave himself to get us out of it! The core message of the gospel should convince us of the wickedness of willful disobedience. It was no light thing Jesus did at the cross. But a so-called disciple whose life is not changed takes for granted what Jesus did on his behalf.

Another powerful catalyst for a new life is choosing whose approval we seek. Peer pressure melts in the bright light of having God's approval. Pleasing ourselves loses its appeal when pleasing God means more to us. That is genuine self-denial. We serve the one we seek to please. When God's approval means more to us than pleasing others or ourselves, we will be changed for the better and for good.

When willpower and guilt have failed, if you doubt it's possible to change, remember Paul and the remarkable change in his life. The same factors that changed him can change you, too.

Day 164, Galatians 2

There is an irritating gap in my life, and probably in yours, too. It's the gap between what I know and believe, and what I do. Ideally, conduct would match conviction at all times. Honesty compels us to admit the ideal is seldom achieved.

When Paul met with Peter and the Jews at Jerusalem, everyone approved Paul's evangelism among the Gentiles. Everyone understood that Gentiles enjoyed equal standing in Christ. When Peter came to Antioch, he ate with the Gentiles until some Jews from Jerusalem came. Then, feeling the pressure from his Jewish brothers, he segregated himself from the Gentile Christians, even taking Barnabas and others along with him. See? There's the gap. Theologically, they knew better. Practically, their fear of what others would think controlled their conduct.

Peter's error is a warning for us. Are you sure you're immune to peer pressure? We warn teenagers, but adults are vulnerable, too. In Sunday School, we know the right answers about moral purity. Does our conduct on a date reflect that knowledge? Most people at AA or

NA meetings believe the principles that are taught there. But later, under stress, at some old playground with old playmates, the commitment falters. It threatens our pride to concede we are influenced by our peers. But if the apostle Peter stumbled under peer pressure, who am I to say it doesn't bother me?

As a matter of fact, the whole discussion of justification by grace and not by works threatens our pride. For many of us, it's the gap again. Theologically, we know that Christ died for us because we could not save ourselves. But still we're tempted to make our performance the standard by which we approve ourselves and condemn others. When a godly person dies, we hear about how they will surely be in heaven because they were so good, and if they're not going, nobody else has a chance. But don't you see? That contradicts the gospel! The gospel says that person is going to heaven because of their trust in Christ, not their own good conduct.

So Paul, who wrote so much about submitting to one another, refused to submit to the Jews who wanted Gentiles to be circumcised and keep the Law of Moses. He could not let Peter's hypocrisy at Antioch pass without rebuke. He would not compromise the core of the gospel. If we trust law-keeping, we nullify the gospel of grace and make the death of Christ meaningless.

I admit there's a gap in my life sometimes. I want to narrow that gap and be more of what God calls me to be as I grow in Christ. But as my conduct becomes more consistent with my convictions, I must never think my progress has earned my standing with God. As Paul said, by works of the law no one will be justified. We must live by faith in Christ because we will not make it on our own.

Day 165, Galatians 3

The pouring rain made it hard to see as we returned from a spring beach vacation shortened by bad weather. After creeping along for two hours, we were near the interstate that would take us home. Just north of Bay Minette, Alabama, I saw a drenched man standing in the road, waving his arms. I stopped, and rolled down my window. He shouted above the pelting rain, "You can't make it this way! The bridge is out!" I told him I was only going to the interstate. He shook his head, "No! You have to turn around. You can't get to the interstate. The bridge is gone!" So we backtracked, and took another route toward home.

My young family and I were traveling through the most intense rainfall our region had seen in decades. The following day, Saturday, March 17, 1990, the Pea River broke through the levee at Elba, Alabama, almost destroying the town. I remember the stranger who saved us from tragedy that day, warning us that the way I was trying to go was impossible. I wish I knew his name to thank him.

These words from Paul remind me of our rain-soaked messenger. To people trying to be justified by law keeping, Paul shouted, "You can't make it that way!" He contrasted two ways to righteousness. One way (trusting Christ) is blessed and connected to the promise God gave Abraham. The other way (relying on law keeping) is cursed—impossible and impassible. The problem with the law route is that our sins have washed the bridge away. I can't make it that way, and neither can you. The law was never intended to be the way, but to point us to Christ, the way. Paul said the law was not against the promise, and if a life-giving law could have been given, it would have been done. But we're all guilty under the law so the promise can be given to those who trust Christ for righteousness.

Do we get it about being saved, but miss it about living saved? After trusting grace to save us, do we despair when we can't live a godly life by our own strength? Or do we claim to be saved by trusting, but prove by our disobedience we don't really trust him at all? Paul laced the prophets' promises together and tied them with Habakkuk's familiar line, "The righteous shall live by faith." He reminded his readers the standard of law is: "Cursed be everyone who does not abide by all things written in the Book of the Law, and do them."

Jesus took our curse by dying on the cross. The way of life and blessing is through trusting him. The way of death and cursing is to trust your own law-keeping. If we're trying to do enough or be good enough to make it, Paul is waving his arms, telling us the bridge is out. We can't make it that way.

Day 166, Galatians 4

Ah, the joys and anxieties of parenthood! We agree with the psalmist that children are gifts from God. Our love and sense of responsibility for them produces natural anxiety about their well-being. They grow up and make their own choices, but we still want to offer parental advice.

Paul witnessed the "birth" of his "children" in Galatia. He had fond memories of their first steps as disciples. But the Galatians were making a choice that upset him. Influenced by teachers who wanted to bind the Law of Moses on Jesus' followers, they were being led away from what Paul taught them. Paul pressed the consequences of that decision, and begged them to avoid the bondage of legalism.

Paul's main question was, "Why would anybody choose slavery over freedom?" He reasoned from two examples—one about rules of inheritance, the other from Scripture.

In a family, Paul asked, would you rather be a slave or a child who is heir of the estate? He compared Jews under the law before Christ came to minor heirs, who were not really different from the servants. But when those young heirs reach their majority, they enjoy full privileges as heirs. Paul said when Christ came, the difference between the heirs and the slaves became reality. Why would anybody choose slavery instead of living as a free heir?

Paul then referred to the story about Abraham, Sarah and Hagar from the Scripture. He said Hagar's son Ishmael was born according to the flesh, not according to God's promise. He was not the rightful heir, but the son of a slave. But Isaac was the son of promise, born of Sarah, just as God had said. Christians are Abraham's heirs through faith. They are children of the promise, like Isaac. Trusting the law takes one out of the inheritance and puts him into the slave quarters. Paul assured the Galatians they were born under the promise and free. Why would they forfeit their inheritance?

When we think we're old enough to choose for ourselves, we don't always welcome our parents' input. Paul reminded them of how they loved him when they first received the gospel, and asked if he was now their enemy because he was telling them the truth. He exposed the dishonorable motives of the Jewish teachers who were mis-leading them, and told them he was anxious about their decision.

Beyond the validation of normal parental anxiety that echoes in Paul's words, we need to hear his warning if we're tempted to trust something other than Christ for justification. It doesn't have to be a Jewish teacher binding circumcision. It can be a new "enlightened" teacher offering fulfillment through some other path. The disguise may change, but the underlying intent of our adversary stays the same—to get us to trust ourselves or something other than God. Like a good parent, Paul warns us, "Don't fall for it. Don't give up your freedom and your inheritance." That's still good advice.

Day 167, Galatians 5

The young woman, giddy with anticipation, walks through the pharmacy. She has a doctor's appointment, but she can't wait. She finds the right aisle, and scans the shelves. She's never bought such a thing. There it is. Clear results in five minutes. She buys the kit, takes it home. She shows the result to her husband. They embrace in joy. The home testing kit says she's pregnant. The baby they've waited and prayed for is on the way.

Self-exams and home testing kits can be important first alerts and early warnings. They can't replace professional medical treat-ment, but they serve a useful purpose.

There's a spiritual do-it-yourself test in today's portion. The question of control lies at the heart of daily living and spiritual well-being. It might seem too complicated an issue to ascertain on our own, but Paul gave the Galatians a self-testing kit, consisting of two lists. It only takes a few minutes and some honest introspection to determine whether we're controlled by the flesh or by the Spirit. Tak-ing the test doesn't make you the judge, but it does point out who or what controls you.

Does the idea of being controlled offend you? Do you imagine you're in charge? We're all under someone's control. Christ freed us from the bondage and slavery of sin for expressions of love and ser-vice, not for self-indulgence. Freed from the cruel and impossible yoke of the law, we express our trust in the Lord by living under the

Spirit's control. We are free in Christ to bless the people around us, not to run over, hurt or use them.

Which of these lists describes your attitudes and actions? Do your conversations show the works of the flesh in your life? Are your relationships marked by the fruit of the Spirit?

The results of this exam have strong implications. People who practice the works of the flesh cannot inherit the kingdom of God. The apostle of grace warned that living like the first list shows we are not really God's people, and we're not headed for eternity with him. On the other hand, people who live like the second list are Christ's. They walk by his Spirit, not their own fleshly desires.

There's no law against the fruit of the Spirit, but there are plenty of laws against the works of the flesh. Grace enables us to live by the Spirit's guidance. Relying on the law severs you from Christ's sacrifice and shuts the door on grace. The law is all-or-nothing; there's no cafeteria plan to choose which commands to obey. Its demand for perfection and our imperfection are not a good match.

So, who's in control of your life? You can read the lists and find out for yourself, in a few minutes, in the privacy of your own home. Be honest with yourself, and remember the evidence is probably already clear to the people around you.

Day 168, Galatians 6

One of life's simple pleasures is a juicy, ripe, home-grown tomato. My tomato crop is going to be a dismal failure again this year. I'm always at the mercy of generous friends who share their tomatoes with me, or I go to the store or a fruit stand to buy tomatoes. Ah, the indignity of it! Charity tomatoes! Store-bought produce! Why has this happened to me again?

It's probably because I didn't plant any tomatoes. The age-old law of sowing and reaping has caught up with me yet another year. Since the day God established the plant kingdom, sowing seed and reaping a harvest has been the natural order. We reap what we sow beyond the garden, too. Seed produces after its kind. The harvest is greater than what was sown. Drought or other factors may sometimes alter the general rules of crop production, but in life only God's mercy and grace can save us from the bitter harvest that comes from unwise sowing.

Paul advised the Galatians to remember this principle as he closed his letter. He encouraged them to keep doing the right things so the desired harvest would come. Let's see how this broad principle affects some specific matters.

We are sowing seed by supporting those who preach the gospel, investing in the harvest their labors will produce. We share in the joy when souls are saved and lives are strengthened. The return on the investment in faithful teachers is secure, better than the FDIC. These deposits are insured by GINM—"God is not mocked." He will enforce the law of sowing and reaping.

When someone in our fellowship sins, spiritual members are supposed to restore them gently, not humiliate or excommunicate them. Paul used the same word for "restore" that his companion Dr. Luke would use for setting a broken bone or mending a torn net. It's getting a person back in their rightful place. That's sowing to the Spirit.

We each have personal responsibility to God that no one can bear for us. But many of life's heavy burdens can and should be shared. Paul said we fulfill the law of Christ when we help one another. It's another way to sow to the Spirit.

Finally, Paul returned to the false teachers who wanted to force the Galatians to be circumcised. He reiterated that being a new person in Christ was what mattered, not circumcision. Paul's boasting was in the Lord, not in imposing the fleshly sign of an old covenant on people to whom it was never addressed. Ritualistic law-keeping is sowing to the flesh; becoming a new creation in Christ is sowing to the Spirit.

If your spiritual harvest is going to be greater than my tomato crop this year, you'd better pay attention to what you're sowing. The sowing (or lack of it) is inevitably tied to the reaping (or lack of it). I pray your harvest will be rich and rewarding in the Spirit.

Ephesians

Day 169, Ephesians 1

I've seen it in the movies, but not often in real life. It surely hasn't happened to me. A letter arrives from an attorney. You've inherited a vast fortune from a distant relative. Your first reaction is that this is too good to be true. You begin looking at the terms under which you will inherit the wealth. Could it really be your modest lifestyle is about to be infused with a tremendous amount of cash? Are you about to gain the power that comes with tremendous wealth, simply by being designated as the heir in a rich aunt's will?

You've receive sweepstakes offers built on the same desirable circumstance—you've been selected to receive a big prize! But a letter about an inheritance or a monetary prize falls short of the inheritance Paul described to the Ephesians.

He addressed them as "the saints in Ephesus and the faithful in Christ Jesus." It was not their physical address that brought the blessing he was about to describe, but their spiritual location. They were "in Christ." Today's portion is infused with 20 or more references to Jesus, either by name or pronoun. It is his blood that redeemed them, his resurrection that assured them of God's sufficient power, and his authority that subjected everything to him. Everything about the Ephesians' inheritance is tied to the fact they are in Christ, members of his body, the church. In Christ, they are predestined by God's will to be heirs of the riches of God's grace. His purpose and plan to bless, enrich and empower his chosen ones in Christ encompasses all time and eternity, earth and heaven.

Paul's prayers for his fellow believers are rich tutorials about how to pray for others. Those prayers describe a disciple's progress and mark the path of spiritual development. He wanted the Ephesians to see the hope, know the riches and experience the power of

God in their lives. Imagine the transforming effect of such aware-ness! No obstacle or circumstance could drive us to despair with the confident assurance of hope. No enticing trinket offered by the world could draw us away from the real treasure of our inheritance in Christ. We would not collapse in surrender or defeat if we had a deep, real understanding of the power of God at work within us.

When our hope, riches and power are all from the Lord Jesus and in him, all the glory is his as well. We are chosen and adopted in Christ, but it is to his praise, not ours. God has given us every spiri-tual blessing in Jesus, so all the glory belongs to him.

You may never get a letter informing you of a rich inheritance. The celebrity prize presenter may never knock on your door with an over-sized sweepstakes check. But this letter reminds you of greater riches, and the Lord himself knocks on the door of your heart, invit-ing you to enjoy the things he has provided for you.

Day 170, Ephesians 2

With all due respect, I have noticed the dead are quite help-less. They are powerless, incapable of doing for themselves. It's odd that so many people are afraid of the dead. Of all people you might encounter, the dead are the least likely to do anything that could hurt you. They're dead. They can't do anything at all.

It is significant that Paul said we were dead in our trespasses and sins. Sin did not wound us, or make us sick. It killed us. We were dead. The path of disobedience, rebellion and worldliness leads to a dead end, in the truest sense of that term. In this single word—*dead,* Paul exposes the fallacy of any self-help, do-it-yourself brand of reli-gion and spirituality. If anyone has life, hope and power, it is because of what God did for us. When we were dead, his mercy was rich to-ward us. Because of his great love for us, he made us alive in Christ. With grace that cannot be measured, God has raised us to new life and usefulness in Christ. This is the good news of the gospel: You were dead in sin, but God made you alive in Christ.

Understanding we were dead deflates our pride. The debate about meritorious works is conceded at this word. It takes away all boasting about how we saved ourselves by anything we did. We were dead, and the dead don't do.

Realizing we were dead focuses our praise. He deserves all the glory and praise for what he did for us. He created us to do good works, but all the praise for the good works belongs to God. If you've ever seen someone steal credit for a good idea or a successful project at work, you know how unsavory such hypocritical boasting can be. That's how every person who boasts about his standing with God looks to the one who actually did the work.

Also, by giving his life for us, Jesus established peace between us and God. His sacrifice removed our alienation from God and the hopelessness that resulted from it. His blood closed the gap our sin had opened. When he drew us to himself in Christ, we were reconciled to one another since we're all added to the same group. Division and quarreling among God's people is an insult to his grace and the cross by which we were reconciled.

How ironic that an instrument of violent death and cruel torture should be the means by which we are given life and peace! But that's what the cross of Jesus did for us. How can we thank him? How can we show our appreciation for new life and a new relationship with God? We can be thankful for the mercy and grace we've received, give him all the glory, do the works he prepared for us to do and be peacemakers among his people. Isn't it good to be alive?

Day 171, Ephesians 3

Do you enjoy a mystery? Some of the most popular books and movies ever made are representatives of this enduring genre.

Mystery stories have been favorites of readers in different cultures around the world for centuries. In the most common form, a first person narrator takes you along as he solves the mystery, or an omniscient narrator unfolds the unknown little by little until at last the mystery is solved. When the story is finished, the mystery becomes knowledge.

God hinted at the mystery of Christ through promises and prophecies spanning centuries. Israel's prophets were given clues and details to pass along to the people, but not even the angels knew what

God would do. Finally through Spirit-guided apostles and prophets, the plan for redeeming the fallen race was revealed. It was no longer a mystery, but good news to be shared: Gentiles were fellow heirs with Jews, all members of the same body, both groups partakers of the promise in Christ!

This may seem like old news to those of us who've heard it all our lives, but it was an astounding mystery to Paul's contemporaries, who saw a distinct line of separation between Jews and Gentiles. Jews, who had known about God and his covenant with them for centuries, had developed a haughty sense of exclusivism. Gentile believers in God, outside the covenant looking in, had been, at best, second class citizens in Jewish culture. When Paul and others began stressing the absolute equality of Jews and Gentiles in Christ, the information was a mystery revealed.

Paul's prayer for the Ephesians is a good pattern for our own prayers. You and I still need the specific things Paul sought for these young believers. He asked that they might be fortified with God's power in their inner being. He prayed that Christ would dwell in their hearts by faith. He sought the stability and security that would come from being firmly grounded in God's love. He wanted them to know the awesome dimensions of God's love that extended beyond their ability to comprehend.

Paul's requests were specific and bold. Have you considered the incredible privilege of making such requests before the throne of God who is able to do far more than you can ask or imagine? Too often, our prayers must sound like the man who brought his demon-possessed son to Jesus: "If you can do anything about it...." He can! The unlimited power of a sovereign God is at work in our lives. That fact prompted Paul to ascribe all the glory possible throughout time and eternity to God.

If you're in Christ, you're in on the mystery and you have access to God. Don't let familiarity rob you of the wonder of being included in Christ. And do not allow faithlessness to keep you from asking for what your heart desires, trusting God's good will for you and relying on his power to give you the very best.

Day 172, Ephesians 4

The stream flowed past, fluid yet solid. On one side, the people waited, their gaze fixed on a single point above the heads of the people waiting on the other side. At the appointed moment, the swift flow of the stream stopped and the path appeared. On cue from the sign, the people stepped out and crossed over, passing strangers from the other side. As the time for the crossing ran out, the last stragglers climbed out of the channel seconds before the deadly flow resumed.

Did you guess the image? What did you see? Perhaps the children of Israel crossing the Jordan? No, this phenomenon is repeated thousands of times a day in cities around the world. The traffic stops, the pedestrians cross the streets, following the instructions of the Walk/Don't Walk signs. This portion reminds me of those flashing electric signs, with the little animated walkers, the countdown clocks, but especially the ones I remember from my childhood, with the green "Walk" and the red "Don't Walk" instructions.

Paul told the Ephesians not when, but how to "Walk" and "Don't Walk." The revealed mystery of the gospel and the privileges it brings to Jews and Gentiles alike call all the members of the body to "Walk" with humility, gentleness and in unity, using their gifts to build up the body. Paul also said "Don't Walk" the way we used to, before coming to Christ. He said to "Walk" with a mind renewed by the knowledge of God and imitating his great love, and "Don't Walk" in the dark futility of a disobedient, alienated life. He told them to "Walk" in telling the truth, respecting others' property rights, controlling their anger and their tongues, and "Don't Walk" in a way marred by the corruption and impurity of the old life. See what I mean?

Here's more clear evidence that a changed life will accompany a confession of Jesus as Lord. It's the old self versus the new self, the way they used to walk contrasted with the way in which they were now supposed to walk. Other passages talk about dying to the old self and walking in newness of life, or putting off the old deeds of the flesh and putting on Christ, like a change of clothing. We're called to be renewed, to be changed, and to become more and more like Christ.

It's dangerous to walk when the "Don't Walk" light is flashing. That river of steel, chrome and glass is hazardous to those who try to cross at the wrong time. In the same way, it is perilous and costly to walk where the Lord has said, "Don't Walk." God's redeemed people should walk just as he calls us to "Walk." Paul's directives are for our good and God's glory. The wise listen to warnings and appreciate them. Would you warn a fellow pedestrian? Would you appreciate a warning?

Day 173, Ephesians 5

Is anybody an original? Young people often wear a particular style of clothing or style their hair in some way to make a statement about their individuality. Influenced by entertainment figures or sports stars, they dress and talk like their heroes. These efforts to express themselves as individuals are almost comical since they're imitating someone else and joining multitudes of other kids wearing the same fashion and talking the same way.

Adults are imitators, too. We may not pick our clothing based on what our favorite singer wears, but most of us have some sense of fashion rooted in admiration of some person or ideal. I've gone through seasons of oxford cloth button downs and khakis, dressing in all black and wearing Hawaiian shirts everywhere. (I liked that last one. People smile at you more often when you're wearing an outrageous shirt, and it feels like you're wearing your pajamas all the time.)

Paul called believers "children of light," and called them to imitate God instead of the surrounding vulgar culture. The "Walk/Don't Walk" motif crosses the chapter division, as Paul made more specific application of what it means to be a new person in Christ. A man or woman who has been called to new life in Christ walks in love and wisdom. Christians are supposed to walk in light, not in the moral darkness that characterizes the world.

In a clever play on words, Paul contrasted being under the influence of wine to being filled with the Holy Spirit. Instead of engaging in rowdy, uninhibited debauchery, the children of light sing to one another and to the Lord with all their hearts. God's children give their Father thanks, and selfishness is replaced with mutual submission.

The imitation impacts every part of life. When a woman honors her husband and a husband loves his wife in a conscious imitation of the relationship between Christ and the church, their marriage honors God's design and blesses the partners. When lack of respect or lack of love casts a shadow across a marriage, the relationship is weakened and blessings are diminished or forfeited. In the cruel irony that accompanies most rebellion, a self-seeking marriage partner actually hurts himself by failing to honor his mate. Thinking we know better than God is as old as the garden of Eden, and forfeited blessings have been the price of our selfish declarations of independence.

If you're married, or ever hope to be, please believe you can do the most and best for your marriage by listening to God's counsel. Husband, love your wife sacrificially. Put her best interest ahead of your own. Wife, you can do more for your marriage by showing respect for your husband than by dishonoring him. Husbands and wives help their mates, their marriages and themselves by modeling the relationship after the union of Christ and his church. Whether you're married, single, male or female, imitating God is the most blessed and holy way to live.

Day 174, Ephesians 6

Isn't "One Size Fits All" an absurd idea for clothing? Something in your closet probably has that optimistic promise on the tag instead of a specific size. It's loose-fitting, has some elastic, or can be adjusted. But it's more like "One Size Fits Some Profoundly Average Person Somewhere." A casual look around at the mall will tell you that, like Goldilocks, most people are going to find the item in question too big or too small, and only a few will think it's just right.

Could the gospel be "One Size Fits All"? With all the personalities and situations of life, could a single message fit every person, meet their needs and apply to their lives?

Today's portion says the answer is "Yes." Child or parent, slave or master, God's will for you will bless you and others around you. Whether your position is under authority or in authority, everyone answers to the highest authority. God is glorified, regardless of your situation, when you obey his will.

Remember when David was about to fight Goliath, the Philistine giant? King Saul offered his armor and weapons to the brave young shepherd, but David chose not to wear the king's armor or use the king's sword because he was unfamiliar with them. They were not his size. David's trusty slingshot, powered by faith in God, brought down the trash-talking enemy.

Goliath was big, but he was human. Our opponent is not human. Remember Martin Luther's line from the old hymn: "On earth is not his equal." Every child of God needs the armor of God to stand against a formidable enemy. We cannot win this fight on our own. So Paul prescribed the whole armor of God for every Christian soldier. This belt, this breastplate, these boots will fit. With the armor, the shield of faith and the sword of the Spirit, you will be equipped to fight and win. The word of God has been tested and found effective against this enemy. As you pray about everything all the time and rely on God's strength instead of your own, the victory is yours through him.

Despite our diversity, we have a common need for salvation by grace through the sacrifice of Jesus for our sins. It's "One Size Fits All" because all have sinned and he died for all. It's "One Size Fits All" because we will all answer to God in judgment, regardless of status or position in life. It's "One Size Fits All" because the same malevolent opponent is trying to destroy us all, and God's power is the only way to win.

Perhaps you're accustomed to the luxury of custom tailoring. But most of us buy our clothes "off the rack." We're blessed to live in a time when modern technology has made well-fitting clothing and shoes affordable. Whoever you are and whatever your circumstances, I am confident the gospel of Christ will fit you perfectly. It really is "One Size Fits All."

Philippians

Day 175, Philippians 1

Do you know a sports fan who drinks his morning coffee from a mug emblazoned with his team's colors? He always wears at least one item that bears the team logo. The license plate on his car declares his allegiance to his team. He checks the team's website and scans the paper for news every day. His home decor may lack taste, but not team loyalty, from the special collector's edition soft drink bottles on the mantle to the sheets and pillowcases on his bed. He's the kind of fan who reminds us of where the word *fan* came from—an abbreviated form of *fanatic*.

With others, it may be their work, their hobby, their health, or their grandchildren. Every situation and conversation is going to come around, usually sooner than later, to their particular focus. The setting may change, but the subject will stay the same.

Most readers who know about Philippians associate the word *joy* with it, and Paul did write a lot about joy in this short epistle. But he wrote so much about joy because he wrote far more about his main subject—Christ. Paul said, "For to me to live is Christ," and the number of times the name of Christ appears in this portion helps us understand just how true that statement was. Paul saw himself as a servant of Christ. He saw his readers as saints in Christ. The grace and peace of his greeting came from Christ. He loved the Philippians with the affection of Christ. The approaching day of Christ was on his mind. The maturing fruit of a disciple's life came through Christ. Even though he was in prison for Christ, he rejoiced when Christ was preached, even by some with ulterior motives. Paul intended to honor Christ by his life or by his death. He had a great desire to be with Christ. He wanted all their conduct to glorify Christ, even their suffering as believers in Christ. See what I mean?

The joy, servant-heartedness, righteousness and contentment Paul wrote about in Philippians all center in Jesus Christ. We admire these traits in Paul and want to have them in our lives, too. Paul's secret and ours to this kind of living is making Christ our passion. That single-mindedness grows out of loving the Lord with all our heart, soul and mind. It comes from seeking the kingdom of God first. It is the natural result of forsaking all, even dying to self, to follow him.

What would an observer detect as your focus, your passion? What if every word you said today was audited and every action was reviewed? Here's a frightening one—what if your thoughts could be monitored? Would a sold out devotion and life-dominating allegiance to Jesus be clear in your daily thinking, speaking and acting? How will knowing him influence your life today? Who will hear his voice in your words, and see his love in your actions today?

Day 176, Philippians 2

The ugly details of "too good to be true offers" are usually buried in tiny print on the promotional piece. The radio equivalent of fine print is the fast talking at the beginning or end of a commercial. What seems like such a good deal usually isn't after the fine print or fast talk.

Jesus didn't hide the deal-breaking details of discipleship in fine print, or wait until potential followers were on board before revealing the demands of following him. He announced it to the crowds: "If anyone would come after me, let him deny himself and take up his cross daily and follow me." A demand for self-denial is the last message most people want to hear. But Jesus put it right up front, without adornment or apology.

Difficult concepts are often simplified by examples. In today's portion, Paul asked the Philippians to deny self by counting others more significant than themselves, and by looking out for others' interest as well as their own. He then gave four examples to show what this looked like in real life.

He told them he was willing to be poured out as a drink offering on the sacrificial offering of their faith, saying he would rejoice if such a thing happened. He told the Corinthians he died daily, serving the Lord and the church. He told the Romans he could wish himself accursed to win unbelieving Israel to Christ. Paul was willing to sacrifice himself for the spiritual benefit of others. Self-denial and putting others first wasn't just rhetoric for Paul. He modeled what he taught others to do.

Paul's next example was Timothy, whom he was sending to Philippi because of his genuine concern for them. The young man had proven himself alongside Paul in their work for the Lord. Not only would Timothy do a good job on Paul's behalf, the Philippians would learn from his unselfish example.

Then Paul wrote about Epaphroditus, who had come to Paul from the Philippians. They had been concerned about his health when they heard he was sick. This man was so others-oriented it distressed him for them to know about his illness. He risked his health, in fact almost died, to serve Jesus and his people. Paul bragged on him, and said he wanted to send Epaphroditus back for their good.

But the greatest example of self-denial is Jesus. The one equal with God emptied himself and became a servant. He humbled himself to do the will of God, even dying on a cross. God raised Jesus and exalted him. One day every one will bow and confess before him. But the point Paul made about Jesus in the context is how willing Jesus was to do, in the most unimaginable extreme, the very thing he called his disciples to do—to deny themselves. That's the attitude Paul wanted us to have about being selfless servants of others for Jesus' sake.

Day 177, Philippians 3

He's lied too many times, and she no longer trusts anything he says. Down the street, a kid has been abused by people who should have protected him, and now he's encased himself in an impenetrable shell of distrust. Across town, a young couple is jaded about spiritual things after a painful encounter with a manipulative group. They believe in God, but are leery about getting involved with church again.

After we've grown up and faced a few adult issues, we know the pain of violated trust. We're cautious at the first hint of vulnerability. Despite the risk, we have to trust someone or something to make meaning of life and to engage in relationships. This is especially true about spiritual matters. Trust is the essence of a relationship with God and a spiritual perspective on life.

Paul trusted there was much more to life than here and now. In today's portion, he discussed the ground of his confidence, his commitment to his goal and our need for godly mentors to lead us where we ought to go.

Paul's confidence was in God, not Paul. He claimed if anyone could have confidence in human performance, he could have it. He cited his pedigree, credentials and reputation as a Pharisee, and then said he counted it all as loss to gain Christ. It was no small matter for someone raised in legalistic righteousness to denounce his blameless performance to embrace a righteousness from God that comes through faith in Christ. But Paul staked his trust in Jesus, and was willing to share in his suffering and death to share his resurrection.

Paul trusted God to develop him and his converts into full maturity in Christ. That requires acknowledging we're not there yet. Trust prevents us from developing a prideful spirit, and calls for a forward-moving, goal-oriented focus. As we maintain the maturity we have attained, we continue to trust God, not ourselves.

Paul also said we should choose our mentors carefully. We need to make sure the ones we choose to follow are headed where we want to go. Some would-be mentors are themselves headed for destruction. We need someone like Paul, whose heavenly citizenship secured his future while he waited for the Lord's return.

Our confidence in the resurrection, the return of Christ and the waiting reward are all trust issues. *Trust* is the most common word for *faith* in the Old Testament. From the patriarchs who received God's promises to the prophets who told the chosen people about things to come, it was a matter of trusting God for things not yet visible. We're blessed with much more information and more pieces of the puzzle than Old Testament saints enjoyed. You and I should be eager to do his will instead of ours, not to earn God's favor, but to show our trust. Is faith risky business? It may seem so to some, but it's far more secure than any alternative I've found.

Day 178, Philippians 4

Jesus often said that blessings come from hearing and doing. The epistles also recommend applying what we know to daily living.

One of those appeals to do and be blessed is here: "What you have learned and received and heard and seen in me—practice these things, and the God of peace will be with you." We can enrich life by doing what Paul said to do. The instructions in this brief portion alone would make a significant difference if we'd let them shape our conduct. I challenge you to look at the list and examine your own life (not your spouse, not your neighbor) and find places to make application. (Warning: that means you'll have to change.)

Get along with one another. Be a peace-maker instead of a trouble-maker. Since we've got reservations to spend eternity together, let's practice getting along while we're here.

Choose to rejoice. It's not what happens to you; it how you respond to it. This little letter overflows with Paul's joy and thanksgiving while he was a prisoner. Remember the one who's telling us to rejoice endured traumatic hardships in his work for the Lord, but he still radiated joy.

Avoid extremes. It's easy to see how this one relates to the previous two. How many times has your peace been disturbed and your joy diminished by going to an extreme about something? The versions translate this instruction as reasonableness, moderation, gentleness or consideration—none of which are possible out on the fringe.

Worry less and pray more. When some threat to your peace and well-being comes along, is your reflexive response hand-wringing or knee-bending? These responses are polar opposites. Anxiety depletes your emotional energy and accomplishes nothing. Prayer increases your emotional energy and gets your request before the one who can do something about it by his power.

Control what you think. I doubt there's any better way to program your life for joy. If you are troubled by undesirable thoughts that come to you when you're trying to think with wholesome purity, remember Martin Luther's counsel: "I cannot prevent birds from flying over my head, but I can keep them from building a nest in my hair."

Learn to be content. Isn't it good to know we can learn what we lack? It's a blessing to know how the peace and strength of Christ overcomes our fleshly discontent.

Share what God has given you with those who are in need and those who are teaching the Word. God will give you more to meet your needs, and you'll get credit in heaven for supporting the work of God here on earth.

See? If we do what Paul says, it will make a dramatic difference. Resisting and refusing to obey robs God of the glory he is due from your life, and robs you of the joy and peace he wants you to have. Which of these directions could you put into practice today?

Colossians

Day 179, Colossians 1

God's plan centers in and consists of Christ. He is not a way, but the way. He's not part of it; he is it. In Colossians, Paul presents Jesus Christ as God, the creator and sustainer of all that is. He has the pre-eminence in everything. The fullness of God is in him. People alienated by sin can be reconciled and find peace with God only through Christ.

Christ is the only hope of a fallen world. No message is clearer in Scripture. The apostles told Jews that their hope and confidence could not be in their law keeping or being Abraham's descendants. Their only hope was in Christ. Gentiles who did not know the true God were told that Christ was God and the way to God.

That message bore fruit wherever it was preached and believed. Sins were forgiven and sinners were reconciled in Christ. Jews and Gentiles were delivered from darkness and transferred into the kingdom of Christ. Redeemed and forgiven, they became heirs of God's promises and members of Christ's body.

The fruit showed up in the lives of the people who came to Christ. Evil deeds were replaced with good works. Hostility was transformed into holiness. They endured adversity with joy. They were stable in their faith and steadfast in their hope. They were energized by power from Christ himself.

What are the implications for us? First, there is no good news or hope apart from Christ. Was Paul narrow and intolerant for insisting that Jesus is the only way to God? That is the essence of the gospel. The point of the cross is that there was no other way for sinners to be reconciled except through the sacrifice of Jesus. We should be kind and considerate toward everyone, but we can't compromise the core of the gospel. It's inclusive in the sense that all are invited to come to God through Christ. It's exclusive in that there is no other way to come.

Also, we're not redeemed to continue in our sinful ways. Our conduct should reflect the change in our standing with God. The redeemed are supposed to live holy, blameless lives. It is a process of growth. Let's be patient with one another, but never use the concept of growing in Christ as an excuse to persist in sin.

All the good we do and progress we make is by his power at work in our lives. The same grace that redeems us enables us to serve the Lord and live in a way that pleases him. Paul's prayer wasn't just that they would do the right things, but that they would be strengthened with God's power to do them. He knew his own hard work was accomplished by Christ's energy within him.

At every step of the process, it's about Christ. All the glory belongs to him. God designed it that way to put our hope on a solid foundation and keep us from deadly pride.

Day 180, Colossians 2

The advertising industry exists to create desire. The ads are designed to make us dissatisfied with what we already have, and want whatever they're selling. Then, spurred to action by our discontent, we spend money to acquire whatever it is. You know how it works. You're not even hungry until the pizza commercial comes on, and the next thing you know, the delivery person is at the door. Your car was fine until you saw the new model zipping down the winding coastal highway in the ad. And now that the good-looking guy in the commercial brought it up, your teeth are looking a little yellow, and probably do need a whitening treatment.

Contentment is the antidote to the venom of desire. A healthy appreciation for what you have lessens the magnetic attraction of what someone is trying to sell you. It works the same way in the spiritual marketplace. Paul used strong words to describe what people were doing to the young Christians at Colossae. He counseled them, "Don't let anyone delude you, take you captive, pass judgment on you or disqualify you." We overcome the efforts of people who want to "sell" us something more than we have in Christ by fully appreciating what we already have in him.

If we know and believe that our spiritual understanding, wisdom and knowledge is full and complete in Christ, we won't be led away by some scheme promising more and deeper meaning. Philosophy and tradition enslave more than they enlighten. Observing the rituals of law (circumcision, festivals and days) cannot add to the life and forgiveness that are ours in Christ. No one who already knows the Lord Jesus should be judged by those obsessed with the shadows of him in the law. You are not inferior to or disqualified by people who claim to have special revelations. You don't need their visions to grow to maturity in Christ.

So Paul advised his readers to be content with the wonderful fullness they have in Christ. Our appreciation and understanding of our blessings in him should grow, but we need not look beyond Christ for more meaning or fulfillment. Self-made religion and asceticism may seem to be spiritual, but Paul said they were really powerless even to control the desires of the flesh.

We express our faith in Christ by being buried and raised with Jesus in baptism. God makes us alive and forgives us, canceling the debt of our sin by nailing it to the cross of Christ. No one can add to that. No one can pass judgment on you or disqualify you when you're in Christ. So in spite of all the appeals to do something or believe something else, stand firm in the Lord. Grow up in him. Hold to your faith, and be very thankful for what you have in him. When you realize what you have in Christ, the other offers you'll receive lose their appeal.

Day 181, Colossians 3

You may not need this message. Maybe no one in your family ever hurts anyone's feelings and all your neighbors, co-workers and fellow church members are always kind and considerate. So, do you need this? I thought you might.

"Bearing with one another" is easy to understand, but difficult to obey. There are some challenging people in our lives. We love God and want to obey him. We want to honor Christ and please him. But these impossible people God put in our lives are about to get on our last nerve. How do we bear with them? Let's see three pictures from this text, three pantomimes to help you remember.

Imagine someone has offended you (again). It's the last straw. Before you blast them with a hot barrage of words, please do three things.

First, hold your hand up as if your palm is a mirror and look at yourself. The first key to bearing with others is seeing yourself clearly. You are God's chosen one, holy and beloved. You must remember this before you stop bearing with someone. I'm sure they don't deserve your forbearance. Did you deserve God's? He chose you, set you apart and loved you when you didn't deserve it. You need to know that before you go.

Next, choose what you'll wear to the confrontation. Will you put on the wardrobe Jesus provides—the compassion, kindness, humility, meekness and patience with which we're supposed to be clothed? Or, will you go out to the trash can and dig out the old, filthy clothes of anger, wrath, malice, slander and obscene talk? You took them off and threw them away when you started following Jesus. You have legitimate complaints against others. Choose to love and forgive as the Lord has forgiven you. The old you died with Christ; the new you was raised with him. You are destined to share his glory. Don't go back to the old rags. Wear your new clothes.

Then write the name "Jesus" on one of those peel-and-stick name tags, and put it on your chest. Blasphemy, you say? Not at all! We're supposed to do everything in the name of the Lord Jesus. His peace is supposed to rule in our hearts. His word is supposed to dwell in us. We should be Jesus to the people around us, especially to those who are not kind and loving to us.

So when you can't bear with an annoying person any longer, follow this simple strategy to find strength beyond yourself. *Look in the mirror.* See yourself clearly—you were chosen, set apart and beloved of God, when you didn't deserve it. *Put on the right clothes.* Put on your best, not those filthy rags you discarded when you came to Christ. *Remember your name tag.* Be Jesus to the people around you. Show them his compassion. Demonstrate his love.

Imagine how our homes, churches and communities would be changed if we would bear with one another!

Day 182, Colossians 4

We are individuals with personal accountability. But we're also responsible for how our actions affect other people.

If you have authority over others, remember your authority is delegated by one who has authority over you. The master/slave relationship that was common in Paul's century is not part of many cultures today. But this principle should guide how we treat people we supervise at home, at work or in the church. Your conduct as a leader shapes a subordinate's understanding of authority, which may affect his whole life and eternal destiny. Also, how many of us would want to be treated by our Master in heaven the same way we treat the people under our authority?

Intercessory prayer is a dynamic element of community life. Paul was serious about praying for others and requesting their prayers. From prison, he asked his brothers and sisters to pray that God would open doors for him to preach the gospel. Prayer acknowledges God as sovereign over all our circumstances. He gives both the opportunities and the ability to respond to the opportunities. We should never say we can do nothing about a brother or sister's difficulty. We can always pray for them!

Influence is also powerful factor in community. How much of what we do can be attributed to the training and influence we receive from others—our parents, teachers, mentors and peers? Wise Christians weigh their words and actions, conscious of their effect on others. Jesus said we are supposed to be the salt of the earth and the light of the world. We must make conscious effort to have the right influence on the people we know outside the church if we ever want to see them in it.

In a discouraging world, it's important to participate in the mutual encouragement that's supposed to be part of life in Christ. Encouragement can come through many channels. No doubt Paul found great encouragement through the years in Luke's constant companionship. Paul had earlier declined to take John Mark on a mission trip, but here he called him a fellow worker and a comfort. Mark's progress must have encouraged them both. Paul's words of commendation and recognition for his fellow workers remind us that partners should encourage one another. Networking is the current buzzword in business, but being connected to other like-minded people has been an important part of Christian encouragement for 2,000 years.

All these matters grow out of living unselfishly—caring enough about one another to use authority properly, pray faithfully and be careful about our influence. Appreciating our community will make us bold enough to give and humble enough to receive needed encouragement. Perhaps all this is reflected in Paul's request to remember his chains. Imagine the links scraping across the parchment as he wrote the closing lines of this letter. We cannot take these matters lightly when we remember how much they meant to him.

1 Thessalonians

Day 183, 1 Thessalonians 1

Has the word of God affected you? If you claim to be a disciple of Jesus, and particularly if you made that decision as an adult, would people who know you notice a difference in you since you started following him?

It's not easy to make a direct comparison of our experience to that of the Thessalonians. I can't remember a time when I didn't know about the Lord. I have not always behaved as if I knew him, but I was blessed to grow up in a home and in a church where I was taught the word of God from my youngest days. But I have been to places where people who were raised in what I call circumstantial atheism heard the gospel of Jesus for the first time as adults, like the Thessalonians. The most "first century" experience I've ever known was seeing adults come to faith who had not previously believed in God or known Jesus as his Son. The visible effect of the gospel in their lives was quite dramatic.

Paul worked in Gentile cities among atheists and polytheists. When he declared the one God and told them the gospel, those who received it were transformed. He did not stay long in Thessalonica before being forced out of town by jealous Jews. But he left with fond memories of the Greeks there who responded to his preaching. When he prayed for them, he remembered three things—their work of faith, labor of love and patience of hope. Instead of telling people in Macedonia and Achaia about the Thessalonians, they told him about three effects the gospel had on them. They said the Thessalonians had "turned to God from idols to serve the living and true God, and to wait for his Son from heaven."

I think the triad of Paul's memories about these people is related to the three-point testimony Paul heard about them. What is the "work of faith" but the dramatic turn from idols to believing in God? How better to describe their zealous devotion and service to the Lord than a "labor of love"? Their "steadfastness of hope" kept them turned to God and busy in serving him as they waited for the return of Christ.

Even though our situation may not be exactly parallel to theirs, these triads should be evident in our lives, too. Would Paul see and remember your work of faith, labor of love and steadfastness of hope? Would the neighbors testify about the differences in your life, your service for the Lord and your anticipation of his return? If we really believe the gospel, it will make a discernible difference in our lives.

Day 184, 1 Thessalonians 2

A good detective looks for the motive that drove a suspect to commit a crime. Whether we're inspired or disturbed by someone's behavior, we try to understand the motive behind their conduct. Since we admire the apostle Paul so much for his zeal and effectiveness as a servant of Christ, it might help us imitate him if we understood not only what he did, but why he did it. There are some clues in today's portion.

Three of the seven times the unusual phrase "gospel of God" occurs in the New Testament are found in this passage. What Paul did with that gospel and the reasons why he did it are here for those willing to look.

Paul wanted to please God so much that he was bold to declare the gospel of God despite mistreatment and conflict. If Paul had been trying to deceive his listeners or if he had been preaching to please people, it would not have been worth the pain and shame he experienced as an apostle of Christ. But he was driven by deeper, purer motives than greed or personal glory.

Paul loved the people he taught so much that he was ready to share not only the gospel of God with them, but himself as well. He described his tender feelings for his converts by comparing his gentleness with them to a mother's care for her own children. Mothers exhibit sacrificial, unselfish love for their children, and Paul had just that sort of affection for the people he taught. He wanted what was best for them, and was willing to sacrifice for them to have it. His converts were his hope, joy and crown as he anticipated the return of Jesus and standing before him in judgment.

Paul sought the glory of God in everything. That's why he proclaimed the gospel like a father guiding his children. With just the right blend of encouragement and exhortation, he charged them to live in a way that reflected the glory of their call into God's kingdom.

Paul's intense loyalty to God, his love for others and his pursuit of God's glory produced authentic preaching that moved his hearers to accept the message as the word of God, not just Paul's words.

Paul looked beyond the present material world to the spiritual reality. He saw Satan's hand in the hindrances he encountered as he made and matured disciples of Jesus. Such formidable opposition requires the very best effort, backed by the highest, most noble motives.

Would you agree with me that we sometimes need to check our motives for doing what we do as servants of Christ? When our efforts lack enthusiasm or if we ever wonder why we're trying to serve him, we need to make sure we truly want to please God more than anything. We need to gauge our love for the people around us, and make sure we want all the glory to be God's.

Day 185, 1 Thessalonians 3

Adversity is an unavoidable part of life. Living in a flesh body in a fallen world filled with imperfect people, it is impossible to escape trouble. As Longfellow put it, "Into each life some rain must fall, some days must be dark and dreary." Following Jesus does not vaccinate us against trouble. In fact, living for Jesus may attract some troubles that the world would not inflict on its own.

Affliction had been a way of life for the Thessalonian Christians since Paul came to town and taught them the gospel. Was he still bruised or limping from the beating he received in Philippi when he arrived? Within three weeks, the local Jews had started trouble, saying that Paul and Silas were turning the world upside down and accusing them of acting against the decrees of Caesar. Paul and Silas left town under cover of darkness, leaving behind a little group of new believers in a troubled environment. He warned them that trouble was coming, and it came.

Paul sent Timothy back to Thessalonica to establish and exhort the young Christians in their faith. He wanted to know about their faith, and he rejoiced when Timothy brought back a good report about their faith. He was eager to get back to them to supply what was lacking in their faith. Why all the concern about their faith? It's not because faith is a spiritual mosquito net, keeping the buzzing troubles away from us. Instead, faith is the lens through which we view trouble, and the weapon by which we overcome adversity.

Faith enables us to see two forces at work, both with a purpose in mind for the troubles that come to us in life. Satan wants to destroy us. The tempter will use trouble to suggest that God is not good and cannot be trusted. Satan's goal is to break down our faith through discouraging circumstances. On the other hand, God's purpose for trouble is to develop us into the people he wants us to be. He builds our character and develops our reliance on him through our experience of adversity. Trusting God through affliction connects us to his power to endure it. Like a precious metal purified by intense heat, we are tempered by the negative experiences of life. If we are to be strengthened instead of weakened by adversity, we need faith in what God has promised and confidence in his faithfulness.

Habakkuk said it in the Old Testament and it is echoed in the New: "the just shall live by faith." That's true about every part of life. It's especially true when we cannot see or understand why God allows suffering and trouble to come into our lives. Our faith gives us peace in the midst of pain, calmness in the face of calamity. When we trust God completely, we will believe that he can and will bring what's best for us out of what seems to be the worst.

Day 186, 1 Thessalonians 4

Have you heard that the Bible is outdated and irrelevant? Some critics say it has no message for our enlightened times since it was written so long ago to primitive people in ancient cultures. Some may not want to hear it, but that doesn't mean the Bible has no message for us. Our preoccupations, struggles and fears are much the same as those of people who lived long before us. Could the Bible be as relevant for us today as it was for readers 2,000 years ago? Let's see.

Paul addressed three topics in three brief paragraphs—sex, love and death. Are those relevant topics? Are people still talking and thinking about those subjects? I did a quick Google search on those three words and got 46.6 million hits, even with Safe Search on! But you don't need a search engine to know that these are timeless, universal concerns. These three concepts have probably been the themes of more books, poems, songs, films, plays and other works of art than any other trio of ideas.

Concerning sexuality, God wills that we control our body and abstain from promiscuous immorality. God invented sex to be a blessing, but it becomes a curse when removed from the intended context of monogamous marriage. God's people are supposed to be led by his will, not the passions of their lust. If we reject God's will about purity, we're like toddlers who don't want to hear a restraining "no" from parents. This selfish choice brings a bitter harvest of brokenness and loss. The message may be unwelcome, but it is still relevant and right.

The dominant command of Jesus and the New Testament writers is, "Love one another." Paul described how life looks when people obey this command. We are to live quietly and mind our own business. We are supposed to work to support ourselves and set a proper example for others. There's more about what it means to love one another in the Bible, but this brief description helps us know if we're obeying the command.

People laughed at Jesus when he said a little girl who had died was only asleep. The disciples misunderstood when Jesus said Lazarus was asleep. But to the one who has power over death itself (and to those of us who belong to him), physical death is not final. It is just sleep. Paul used the same image about the dead in Christ, and promised that the dead will be raised when Jesus returns. This concept diminishes the fear of death's awful finality. This message encourages us to face the death of loved ones and think about our own demise with confidence instead of hopelessness, with faith instead of fear.

For all our technological advancement and discovery, we still need the moral guidance, practical wisdom and hope that the Bible offers. It is old, but not outdated. The Bible will bless you if you'll listen to its counsel.

Day 187, 1 Thessalonians 5

Encouragement is a powerful tool for building up Christians. Encouragement intensifies our desire and fortifies our commitment to serve the Lord, like fuel feeds a fire. But as you probably know, discouragement extinguishes zeal and softens our resolve to live for him.

We know Joseph of Cyprus by the nickname the apostles gave him—Barnabas, the son of encouragement. Almost every reference to him in the New Testament shows that he kept on earning his nickname throughout his life as a servant of Jesus. In today's portion, Paul enlisted the whole church to become like Barnabas, encouraging everyone around them by their speech and conduct.

It's easy to see how the preacher and other leaders in a church are supposed to be encouragers. But Paul's words were addressed to all believers, about a reciprocal duty: "...encourage one another and build one another up, just as you are doing." His closing instructions to these young Christians create a context for encouragement.

Are you encouraged when you think about Jesus' return? Many people will be taken by surprise and terrorized when the Lord comes back, but his faithful disciples will be ready. You're ready if you're living to please him and waiting for his promised salvation. You are not filled with dread about the wrath that will fall on the unprepared. Does the thought of Christ's return strikes dread or delight in your heart? That's probably a good indicator of your spiritual well-being. To all who love him and cherish the hope of heaven more than this world and everything in it, it's encouraging to be reminded that Jesus is coming again.

Just as no one is exempt from the duty of encouraging others, it's also true that everyone needs encouragement. Leaders who encourage others need it. People who are falling away and failing because of their weaknesses need encouragement from godly brothers and sisters. You don't have to give a lavish gift or do a mighty deed to be an encourager. Gentle reminders about our mutual duties can be effective encouragement. Just knowing a brother or sister cares enough to speak to us about some spiritual matter is a genuine encouragement.

You don't have to wait until you have perfected your technique to participate in this important, people-attracting ministry. If you're living a joy-filled, prayerful, generous life that overflows with thanksgiving, you're already encouraging others by your calm contentedness. When we remind one another of God's faithfulness, when we share God's love and word with people around us, and when we pray for all God's children, we're spreading encouragement. The person you encourage with a gracious word will be blessed, and may return the favor to you some day.

2 Thessalonians

Day 188, 2 Thessalonians 1

It's been true since the days of the apostles. Persecution hastens the spread of the gospel and helps the church grow. Some of the most remarkable stories of evangelism and discipleship in the world today come from places where it is very dangerous to follow Jesus. If by God's grace you do not live in a place where persecution is a way of life for Christians, rejoice in that blessing. Never take it for granted. And don't forget to pray for your brothers and sisters who are suffering, just like disciples who were persecuted twenty centuries ago.

Paul bragged on the Thessalonians to other churches and thanked God for them. Their faith was growing, their love for one another was increasing and they were steadfast in their faith despite the persecution and affliction it brought them. Paul was confident that God's power would make them worthy of his calling. They would keep their resolutions and accomplish their work through God's divine strength working within them.

Paul used the promised return of Jesus and the judgment that would accompany his return to bolster the Thessalonians' courage. He assured them God's righteous judgment would reverse their present circumstances—the afflicters would be afflicted, and those who had suffered would be granted relief. Against that one sweet descriptive word of reward—relief—Paul penned a poetic (but horrific) description of the fate of the wicked in judgment. God will inflict vengeance on those who do not know him as their Savior. He will punish those who do not obey the gospel of Christ. He called their awful punishment eternal destruction. They will be forever banished from the Lord's presence and glory. But the Thessalonians did know him. They had obeyed the gospel. They would see and share in the glory of Christ when he returns.

Jesus is coming again. That fact is never out of view in Paul's letters to these young Christians. Reward and relief are on the way. It will be worth it then to endure whatever comes now. Stay on course and know your progress is by God's grace and for his glory. That's good counsel for you, and for every disciple, at every level of maturity, in every circumstance of life.

Day 189, 2 Thessalonians 2

Today's portion reminds me of Mark Twain's words about troublesome Scripture: "Most people are bothered by those passages in Scripture which they cannot understand; but as for me, I always notice that the passages in Scripture which trouble me most are those which I do understand." One paragraph has some difficult concepts and mystery in it; the other has good news and clear instructions. Some people are more enthusiastic about pondering the mystery than believing and obeying what is clear.

Some writers and teachers go to great lengths to identify the "man of lawlessness," to explain how he will appear and what his coming will mean to Christians. It's probably good to remember that these unveilers of the mysterious man of sin don't know a whole lot more about him than you do.

Paul assured the Thessalonians that they had not missed the Lord's return. The events that will precede and accompany his return will be of such scope and magnitude that they will not go unnoticed. His assurance to them is good for us, too: "Don't worry about it." God has chosen us to be saved. He has called us through the gospel to obtain glory. The perishing and condemnation described in the first paragraph are the fate of those who do not love and believe the truth. Paul said the ones who would be destroyed along with the man of lawlessness took pleasure in unrighteousness. You don't have to understand or be able to explain everything about the dark mysteries to be saved. If you love and believe the truth and show that you do by the way you live, you have nothing to fear.

Even the dark, mysterious paragraph is illuminated by the assurance that Jesus will triumph over the lawless one. Paul wrote this passage to comfort his readers, not to confuse them. Instead of wringing our hands and fretting about knowing the identity of the man of lawlessness, we should rejoice in knowing the Man of Righteousness. The comfort comes from knowing and trusting him. He is the basis of our confident trust. We stand firm in the Lord Jesus. His grace strengthens us in every good word and work.

Let's not be troubled by that first section that contains some difficult ideas and mysteries. Let's be more concerned about believing the good news and obeying the clear instructions in the second section. There's great comfort there for faithful disciples. But even those words may be troublesome to those who refuse to believe and obey.

Day 190, 2 Thessalonians 3

As we meet the challenges of life, it's wise to remember that we have responsibility to act, and that God is acting on our behalf. There are things we cannot do for ourselves, and we trust God's faithfulness about such matters. But there are other things we can and should do as we live by our faith.

Paul asked the Thessalonians to pray that the word of the Lord would speed ahead and that he would be delivered from faithless, evil people who would try to hinder him. Do you see how his faith behaved? He kept working, and trusted God to take care of things over which he had no control. He knew it was up to God to bless his efforts to spread the gospel, but he asked his friends to pray that God would do it. Paul reminded them that God would be doing the same things for them, establishing them and guarding them from the evil one. He was confident they would be busy and steadfast in their obedience as God guided them.

Apparently not everyone at Thessalonica was busy. Some people were lazy. Unwilling to work, they were content to be supported by the labor of others. Paul said that those who would not work should not eat. That's from the same apostle who taught disciples to look out for one another and to give generously to help people in need. The benevolence of the Christian community blesses those who cannot work to provide for themselves. But that charitable spirit was never intended to create a welfare society where people who will not work are enabled to live off others. Paul cited his own hard work among them as an example to follow, and told the church to have nothing to do with the ones who wouldn't obey. They weren't to be treated as enemies, but they were to be warned as disobedient brothers.

Paul encouraged the Christians to not grow weary of doing good. You can drift through life in careless disobedience to God, but it takes dedication and commitment to do the right thing. When it seems people around you are getting ahead by doing wrong, you may get tired of doing the right thing. But keep on doing good; it will be worth the effort.

Life in an unbelieving, fallen world is not always peaceful for believers, but Paul prayed that the God of peace would be with them and give them peace in every moment and situation of their lives. You and I should ask ourselves, "What threat can tower above the presence of God? What challenge can disturb the heart-level peace he gives me when I trust him?" Even when it's not easy, be faithful to your task, and know that God is faithful to keep his promises.

1 Timothy

Day 191, 1 Timothy 1

A strong leader communicates his vision to those who follow him. This accomplishes two important tasks. First, he enlists his associates as partners in his work, bringing more hands and brains to the task by teaching others to see as he sees. Second, he knows his work will outlive him if he succeeds in passing on his perspective and values to his coworkers.

Paul valued Timothy for the young man's assistance in his ministry, but he was also looking to the future when Timothy would take his mentor's place in the mission. Paul gave clear instruction and strong encouragement to Timothy so the younger man would share his vision and passion.

Paul viewed the gospel as a stewardship with which he had been entrusted. He wanted this healthy message to remain free from contamination. The goal of his teaching was love from a pure heart, a good conscience and sincere faith. When the wholesome teaching of the gospel was adulterated by the distractions of myths, genealogies and misguided attempts to teach the law, the process swerved away from the goal. He charged Timothy to protect the sacred trust of the doctrine from the hindrances of extraneous information.

Paul's view of himself was also important to the mission. He was transparent about his former life as an opponent of the gospel. He gave Jesus the credit for showing him mercy and giving him strength. Paul knew he was a trophy of grace. The grace of God saved and changed the foremost of sinners and commissioned him to ministry. Realizing Jesus came to save sinners like us should turn our regret into joy. Seeing the life-changing power of grace should encourage us to share the message of Christ. Knowing about Paul's radical change gives us hope when we wonder if we can become what God wants us to be.

How we see the gospel and how we see ourselves affects our missions of evangelism and discipleship. Paul modeled the right perspective to Timothy and to us so we could be his fellow workers and carry on his mission. Are we careful to keep the gospel message free from the distractions and pollutants that compromise its power? Do we really believe we are saved and enabled to serve by the same overflowing grace we declare to others? This is the secret of living with a clear conscience and a victorious faith.

Day 192, 1 Timothy 2

It's not unusual to feel frustrated about our world after reading the paper or watching the news. We have more news about what's going on in the world now than at any time in history, but the bounty of information doesn't always seem like a blessing. The more we know about international conflict, corruption in government, global economic crises and crime close to home, the more discouraged we feel. What can one person do?

Paul's prescription for an ailing society is fervent prayer from God's people. He called for prayer on behalf of everyone, but especially for leaders whose actions shape our day to day environment. For people of faith, prayer is the most powerful tool we have for influencing our culture, more powerful than the ballot box or some other form of activism. The best way to ensure a wholesome environment for a peaceful, godly life is to be faithful in prayer for those in control. Paul said this method pleased God, who so much wants what's best for us that he gave Jesus to be our mediator and ransom.

Do we believe this? For some reason it may seem easier to believe the big facts about God's redemptive work than to believe that praying to him is an effective means of shaping the environment of everyday life. The message of the gospel is that God loved us so much that he gave Jesus to solve our biggest problem. Can't we trust him to be involved in lesser matters? Aren't God's promises about day to day living just as faithful as his promises about eternity?

If the state of the world is disturbing today, imagine what it would be like without the restraining, shaping influence of many godly prayers each day! And while we're imagining, just think of how much more impact we could have on the state of the world if more of God's people took this privilege seriously and prayed fervently for our leaders and the situations that trouble us. We anxiously talk over lunch or on the phone about the economy, politics and international conflict. We could make a bigger difference if more of us would get on our knees and lift our hands and prayers to God.

A friend once told me she watched the news to get material for her prayers. She's taking this principle seriously. Why not try it yourself? It's easy to listen to the news or read the paper and say, "Isn't that a shame? What a mess! Why doesn't somebody do something?" Why not be that "somebody" who does something? Claim the promise; pray to God about the troubling issues in the news. Even if you don't know what ought to be done, just tell God about it. He knows. Just pray. It's not the least you can do. It's the most.

Day 193, 1 Timothy 3

Leadership is essential to order and progress in any group. The quality of leadership shapes the direction and destiny of homes, businesses, nations and churches. Jesus handpicked the men who would lead the church in its infancy at Jerusalem. The apostles guided the group of young disciples from the day the church began through rapid growth as it spread across the world as they knew it.

In congregations scattered across the Roman Empire, local leadership was necessary. Jesus is the head of his church, and the apostles' words are authoritative. But local leaders were needed to guide local churches. Paul's instructions to Timothy about appointing leaders at Ephesus still guide believers around the world today as they select leaders in local churches.

Paul said those who aspire to leadership in the church desire a noble task. It is no light matter to be a leader in a church. The leaders watch for the souls of those in their care, and will account to God for them. They must lead, not by force and decree, but by the power of their example. Such leaders must possess certain characteristics that qualify them to serve.

Paul described the family life, conduct and character of the man who would lead God's church. He must be respectful of God's design for marriage, the husband of one wife. He must prove his management skills among his own children and household before he assumes responsibility for leading in God's household. He must think, speak and act in ways that reveal his heart and character to be under the lordship of Jesus Christ. He must have experience and a good reputation to be fit for the task. A man who has been a successful leader in business or some other organization may or may not be qualified to lead in the church, depending on whether or not his family life, conduct and character can pass these tests. God's overseers are shepherds who lead, not managers who drive.

In the same way, deacons must meet certain qualifications to serve. They are not the overseers, but specially appointed servants of the church who are highly visible and active. They and their families must also be people of dignity, sobriety and faithfulness. Their influence is their strongest tool in persuading others to be involved in the work of the church.

Since leadership is essential, the qualifications are not designed to disqualify every potential candidate. There are no perfect people who meet every qualification with equal aptitude and maturity. But these lists guide the selection of those who will lead across the cultures and centuries, wherever the gospel goes and disciples are made.

A church is blessed to have leaders like those described here. If we aspire to leadership, we should begin early in our lives as disciples to let these qualifications shape us. Not everyone is suited or called for leadership. But those who are have great honor and responsibility in God's design.

Day 194, 1 Timothy 4

Can you name your elementary school teachers? Was there a particular Sunday School teacher who made a significant difference in your life? Do you desire to teach or share information with others? Even if you cannot imagine yourself in a formal classroom setting, you probably do have some context in life in which you are qualified by education or experience to share what you know.

Since disciples are learners by definition, we would expect the church to be a teaching institution. In the body of Christ, the members are at varying stages of maturity. Some have more experience and knowledge than you, but you are more advanced than others. This creates an atmosphere where teaching and being taught are natural phenomena. If you have the desire to be a teacher, if you sense the responsibility to help others grow, it's important to be prepared.

All teachers should be trained, but those who would be effective as spiritual teachers must be trained. We hear a lot about physical training. Almost every magazine or newscast features some story about diet or exercise. That's good information—who wouldn't want to be healthier, enjoy life more and live longer? Paul said that training the physical body had some value, but training in godliness was good for both the present life and the life to come. Godliness makes life better here—healthier lifestyles, better relationships—but it also makes an eternal difference to be trained in godliness. Would-be teachers must prepare to be ready when the opportunities come. They must know the truth and be able to distinguish it from error. They must put their gifts and talents to work.

Also, spiritual teachers must be conscious of their example. Paul told Timothy to set an example of the right kind of speech, conduct, love, faith and purity before the people he taught. We cannot be very effective communicators when our conduct contradicts our content. Perhaps you just want to be an information dispenser, not a role model. Sorry, it doesn't work that way, especially in spiritual matters.

We usually think of teachers giving tests, but they have to take tests, too. Paul told Timothy to keep a close watch on himself and his teaching. In doing so, he would save himself and his hearers. All the skills, instructions and opportunities are not worth much if neither the teacher nor the student is saved!

We must never forget that our business is making and maturing disciples of Jesus. Well-prepared teachers and well-taught students are the best means of protecting the church against false teaching and error. If you are willing to train yourself, to watch your example, to use your gifts when opportunities come and to monitor your teaching carefully, you can be a useful tool in God's hand to shape lives for this world and the next. There is no nobler pursuit!

Day 195, 1 Timothy 5

The crowd rises in unison, thousands of hats are removed and a hush sweeps across the stadium. In that moment of honoring our country or remembering some well-known figure or hero, we still feel a spark of what is becoming a lost virtue in our rude culture—respect. Aretha sang about it, everybody wants to receive it, but few are willing to give it.

Respect is the proper admiration or regard for the dignity and worth of another person. Maybe you've heard older folks talking about kids being taught to "respect their elders" back in their day. Maybe you've said it yourself as you've grown older and have witnessed crass displays of disrespect.

Whether our culture becomes more and more disrespectful or not, showing respect for others is supposed to be a way of life for disciples of Jesus. Even if we live among people who show no regard for anyone except themselves, our interpersonal credo is "honor to whom honor is due."

Respect is the thread that runs through the instructions Paul gave in today's portion. Our behavior in the family of God should be characterized by honoring older brothers and sisters as we would our beloved parents, and treating our contemporaries with the dignity due sons and daughters of God. A family's care for elderly parents and relatives is a matter of respect and repayment, returning the favor of caring for those who cared for us when we were helpless. The church's responsibility to care for elderly who have no family to help them is grounded in recognizing the dignity and worth of those older people. It is right to enroll genuine widows into the care of the church in recognition of their years of selfless service to others. Church leaders, especially those who have devoted their lives to preaching and teaching, should receive double honor because they have blessed so many others by their work.

Treating one another with respect does not guarantee that there will never be disagreements or misunderstandings in a family or a church. Different opinions and incompatible personalities will still be part of life in any community. But potential harm can be avoided and conflict can be resolved when the parties involved demonstrate respect for one another.

You lose none of your dignity by showing honor to another person. Your worth is not enhanced by being disrespectful to someone else. Such juvenile tactics are unbecoming of a disciple growing toward maturity in Christ. What relationship could you enhance today by showing more respect for the other person? You could be the catalyst who brings meaningful change to the groups of which you're a member by treating the people around you with genuine respect.

Day 196, 1 Timothy 6

Paul's remarkable missionary travels and literary output were from a time long before technology transformed transportation and communication. Paul and Timothy could not have imagined the conveniences we take for granted. Much has changed since those ancient days.

But some things about life are very much the same today as they were twenty centuries ago. Paul's instructions about work and money are as applicable to us today as they were to Timothy and his congregation in old Ephesus.

Few modern readers are slaves, but many ancient Christians were bondservants. Whether we're slaves or free agents, there's a principle about work that applies to every Christian on the job. In the workplace, the attitude of a Christian toward his employer is important whether that employer shares our faith in Christ or not. One alternative is a matter of influence; the other is a matter of affection. If your employer is an unbeliever, you, as a believer, represent the very name of God and the message about Christ. If you're disrespectful and lazy, your unbelieving boss associates your behavior with the whole movement, and the influence is negative. On the other hand, working for a brother or sister in Christ is no license to be a slacker at work. Our conduct on the job either defrauds or benefits our Christian employers. We're honor-bound to do our best as employees of a fellow believer because our good service helps our beloved brother or sister in the Lord.

Another abiding principle from Paul's instruction in this portion is the danger of loving money and desiring wealth. There is a strong temptation in material things to be dissatisfied with what we have and lust after more. When that desire drives us to do ungodly things to get and have more, our focus shifts from relying on God to trusting ourselves and our stuff. Senseless pain and tragic ruin await people who succumb to this temptation. Money itself is not the root of all evil, but the love of money is.

Paul counseled people who were rich to remember that God gave them what they had. This would keep them from haughty pride in their possessions. He also warned them to never trust the gift instead of the giver, and to use what had been entrusted to them to do good. Their generosity with the good things of this life would lay a foundation for the reward they would receive in heaven, where they would enjoy the genuine good life.

If you've been blessed with the good things of this life, it would be wise to take this old financial advice to heart. Don't confuse the world's idea of "the good life" with the real thing. Remember that wealth is transient, but God is eternal, so make sure your hope is anchored in what will last. Use your blessings to bless others. Paul's advice to the rich will help you manage your money, and keep you from being managed by it.

2 Timothy

Day 197, 2 Timothy 1

As pilgrims on a journey, we should remember three important things. We should reflect on where we've come from, envision where we're going and pay attention to where we are along the way.

Paul's words about his ancestors who served God and Timothy's faithful grandmother and mother remind me of Isaac Newton's famous line in a letter to his rival Robert Hooke in 1676: "If I have seen a little further it is by standing on the shoulders of Giants." That's true about our spiritual maturity and understanding. If we think we learned on our own, we're ignorant of our indebtedness to many who preceded us. Even if you're the first Christian in many generations in your family and you came to know Christ by your own study, you're still a debtor to generations of scholars who provided you with tools for learning the will of God. Most of us can name mentors who led the first faltering steps of our faith journey. Not all of them were relatives, but were nonetheless our ancestors in the faith. There's no room for pride about all we've figured out that previous generations didn't know. We're standing on their shoulders. God originated the plan before the world began and revealed it long before we came along to discern it. It's wise to remember where we came from.

It's also essential to pay close attention to where we're going. Paul taught Timothy that Jesus had abolished death and brought immortality to light through the gospel. This is no dead-end trail we're following. It leads to life. We've got God's word on it. Paul trusted God's promises. He was convinced a day of reward was coming. It's easy to get caught up in the present and lose sight of the future. While living for Jesus is good for life and relationships here, we realize the real benefit when we contemplate death, the judgment and eternity. We're all headed there. It's wise to remember that and be energized by it.

People on a journey should pay attention along the way. I've missed more than one turn by failing to grasp where I was along a route. So Paul urged Timothy to fan into flame his gifts, and to live fearlessly in God's power, love and self-control. The old apostle knew a lot about suffering, and he advised his son in the faith to share suffering for the gospel, and to never be ashamed of his suffering. He exhorted him to follow the pattern of the teaching he'd learned from his mentor, and guard with the Spirit's help what had been entrusted to him.

It's good to reflect on those who've preceded us, on whose shoulders we stand, and give thanks for them. Whether you're enjoying or enduring the present, there's great motivating power in looking to the future we've been promised. And in this day, itself a gift from God, we should live with confidence, courage and clarity.

Day 198, 2 Timothy 2

Would you be interested in an excellent buy on a chain? It's made almost entirely of high quality tempered steel. Tempered steel, as you know, is very strong. Imagine the uses you could find for a steel chain—the most vicious animal could be restrained, the most valuable objects could be secured. Now, for a fraction of what you'd expect to pay, this chain can be yours. What's the catch, you ask? Why can I offer you this chain at such an incredible discount? Well, one (but only one) of the links is made from a chewing gum wrapper. What? You're not interested? Haven't I heard the old saying? What old saying? Oh, that one. Yes, I've heard it—a chain is only as strong as its weakest link.

Paul wanted Timothy to be strong because he was a vital link in the chain between the apostles and the generations of believers who would follow. He knew Timothy would need to be strengthened by grace and be blessed with understanding from the Lord to be up to the task. He stacked one metaphor on top of another to illustrate the importance of being strong and diligent. The vigilant soldier, the disciplined athlete, the hard-working farmer—all these strong figures illustrated the character Timothy would need to discharge his responsibility.

Ultimately, the message and the motive for faithfully transmitting it are one and the same—the truth about Jesus. Timothy was not to be distracted from the core message of the gospel by irreverent and irrelevant subjects. Quarreling about words only ruins hearers by upsetting their faith. By refusing to quarrel and instead persuading people with gentleness and patience, Timothy would be an honorable, useful vessel in God's great house. Like Paul before him, he would need to be strong so people could hear the good news of salvation in Christ.

There may be other channels besides you through which your friends and neighbors may hear about Jesus. But you may be the very best link to the people closest to you. They may not hear and be blessed by the gospel if you're the weak link. Jesus told his first disciples who had been fishermen that they would be catching people from that time on. The same word Jesus used to describe that activity is used here to describe how Satan "captures" people to do his will. We're not the only ones fishing. Love for God and one another calls for us to be strong and faithful to our task. I urge you, by God's grace, to be a strong link in the chain.

Day 199, 2 Timothy 3

I believe following Jesus is the best way to live—best for this world and the one to come. I don't mean that it is the easiest way to live. If you live by Jesus' kingdom principles, you will face opposition from a world in rebellion against his lordship.

Paul assured Timothy that the difficulty he faced was neither unusual nor unexpected. Paul's description of this age is an ugly negative image of the positive virtues and values that characterize disciples of Jesus. Christians should not expect the world to affirm their commitment to Christ. A godly life indicts the ungodliness that characterizes the world, and the world's animosity will be expressed in persecution. Jesus told the disciples before he went to the cross that the world hated him, and it would hate those who followed him.

Paul told Timothy to rely on two powerful factors to help him withstand the world's evil influence and opposition. First, he told his protégé to follow his example instead of being influenced by the culture and false teachers around him. Paul's way of life was a pattern of godly integrity, faith, patience, love and steadfastness for anyone who would watch and follow him. His conduct drew criticism and persecution from his enemies, and he flatly declared that everyone who was devoted to godly living would suffer persecution. He told Timothy to continue in what he had learned and believed because he knew who had taught him.

The second powerful influence for good in Timothy's life was the word of God. The Scriptures, breathed out by God, would teach, restrain, correct and train him. They would bring him to maturity and competence as a servant of the Lord.

We would do well to consciously imitate Paul's life and not conform to the world around us. Is your conduct more like the description of worldly people who love themselves, money and pleasure more than they love God? Or does your life reflect Paul's faith, devotion and love for the Lord? We're not really following Jesus if arrogance, disobedience, ingratitude and a lack of self-control are evident in us.

We would also do well to adopt Paul's high view of Scripture. Many who do not want to hear its message attack the Bible as a collection of old myths, superstition or the product of ambitious men who wanted to control others. But Paul said the Scriptures were breathed out by God. People who do not want to submit to its life-guiding authority claim it restricts and represses them from doing as they please. But Paul said the Scriptures teach us what to believe and not to believe, what to do and what not to do, for our own good.

Godly mentors and God's word can strengthen and equip you for the challenges of life. Whose example are you following today? What is your attitude toward the Scriptures?

Day 200, 2 Timothy 4

The long journeys are over. The end is near. In the autumn of 67 AD, from a dungeon in Rome, Paul wrote to Timothy what would be his last words in the New Testament. If tradition is correct, he would be beheaded the following spring. What was on his mind? What were his final instructions? With the same solemnity that would mark our conversation with a dying loved one, let's review Paul's last recorded words.

Paul was conscious of God's presence. Some of his companions had been sent on missions; others, like Demas, had deserted him. Dr. Luke had been there all along. Paul wanted John Mark to come with Timothy. Mark had quit on one missionary journey, and Paul didn't want him on the next one. Since that time, Mark had become a valuable member of Paul's team. But whether he had human company or not, Paul knew the Lord was with him. At his first defense, when no one stood with him, Paul said the Lord stood by him, strengthening him. This consciousness of God's faithful presence had propelled Paul throughout his ministry, and would bring him safely home.

With that same awareness of being in God's presence, Paul gave Timothy a solemn charge to preach the word whether it was popular or not, to endure suffering as he patiently taught and encouraged people who didn't want to hear it. Paul's work would continue through Timothy and others, but only if the younger preachers were faithful to preach the word.

Paul knew he would die soon, and he was full of confidence in the face of death. He reviewed his life's work, knowing that it was done. Paul might not have received justice from all the judges he faced in this world, but he was sure the Lord, the righteous judge, would reward him with a crown of righteousness. By faith he saw that crown laid up for him, waiting for the day the Lord would reward all the people who had longed for his return.

Paul's awareness of his imminent death also gave his instructions to Timothy a sense of urgency: Come soon, do your best to come before winter. Winter weather would suspend travel for several months. Timothy might not see his old friend and teacher again in this life if he delayed.

I am sorry if this seems morbid, but it is important. If the circumstances near the end of your life are such that you know death is approaching, what solemn words will you leave with your loved ones? Will you anticipate death with confidence and assurance of the Lord's presence, even as you enter the valley of the shadow of death? Will you look back on life with satisfaction and a sense of completion? In such a moment, will your faith serve you well? The only way to face death like Paul did is to live like Paul did, with total reliance on the Lord.

Titus

Day 201, Titus 1

God never lies. In a world of empty promises, political spin and broken vows, it's hard to imagine genuine, unadulterated, unconditional truth. Many people think nothing of lying if it will somehow profit them to do so. Despite our best intentions, we are sometimes unable to do what we said we would do. I once read that the average person lies 50 times a day! Skepticism is a survival technique for consumers and citizens who've heard a lot of lies.

But God never lies. He is truth. His word is truth. The tension we feel when we hear his word comes from its convicting exposure of our flawed lives, not from doubting its veracity. God's consistent nature and perfect character make his word a reliable foundation for faith, knowledge, conduct and hope.

Paul said he was an apostle for the sake of the faith of God's elect. Faith is only as good as the information on which it's based. The testimony about Jesus is trustworthy. Knowing God cannot lie lifts our faith based on his word above the realm of dreamy optimism and gives us expectant confidence.

Postmodern philosophy has taught us that truth is not absolute, that what is true for you may not be true for me. But Paul stood on Jesus' word: "You will know the truth, and the truth will set you free." He was an apostle of Jesus Christ not only for the sake of the elect's faith, but also their knowledge of the truth. The human family's quest to know has led to great discoveries that have expanded our world and enriched our lives. It would seem oddly inappropriate for the most valuable information of all to be unknowable. The fact God cannot lie defines truth; his desire and will to reveal it to us makes it attainable.

Knowledge of the truth is not an end in itself; that truth is supposed to be reflected in a life of godliness. Our conduct is supposed to agree with what we believe and know. If we can know it, we're responsible for living it. Could this be why some people say truth is unknowable? Can we escape accountability by denying that truth can be known? Such thinking is self-serving, self-deceiving and an insult to the character of God who cannot lie.

Hope's surest foundation is the word of God who never lies. Our anticipation of what he has promised is heightened by this assurance of his absolute truthfulness. He promised eternal life before the beginning, and at the appropriate time revealed that life in Christ. The promise and declaration of it is all true; the one who said it cannot lie.

We are not omniscient. We trust someone or something beyond ourselves about things we do not know. As disciples of Jesus, it's encouraging to know that faith, knowledge and hope are based on the word of God who never lies.

Day 202, Titus 2

As a coach teaches players good technique, he sometimes tells them what to do to maximize their performance. But at other times, he tells them not to do certain things that would hinder their effectiveness. Training has both positive and negative aspects.

God's grace not only saves our souls; it also transforms our lives. We are trained by grace in both negative and positive ways. Expressed negatively, grace trains us to say "no" to ungodliness, and "no" to being controlled by worldly passions. Expressed positively, the grace of God trains us to a live self-controlled, upright and godly life. Ungodliness means living as if God is irrelevant, but a godly life is focused on pleasing him. Grace teaches us to deny ungodly living and to pursue a godly life.

This dual education we receive by grace reminds us that Jesus is Lord as well as Savior of those for whom he died. We should not, and cannot go on in our old way of life. We were redeemed from lawlessness and purified to be his special people. When we're conscious of what Jesus has done for us, we should be eager to work for him. Grace is no excuse for continuing in sin or being negligent in our service to God. On the contrary, grace properly understood and appreciated becomes a powerful motivating force for transforming our lives. When grace has trained us, we are not terrified by the knowledge that Jesus is coming again. Instead, the promise of his coming fills us with hope.

The teaching Paul wanted Titus to do shows it is God's will that we change, and that redeemed people need to be guided and reminded about the new life to which they've been called. Men and women, young and old are to be taught self-control. Neither old age nor youth will suffice as an excuse for living an undisciplined life. The Christian community is made up of people who teach one another by influence. Older people are supposed to teach the younger ones. As their spiritual teacher, Titus had to be a model of the things he taught. Even slaves could influence their masters, making the gospel attractive by their submissive, faithful lives.

So it is very appropriate to praise God for his grace and to rejoice in the salvation grace brings. It is equally appropriate to submit our tongues, minds and bodies to the training of grace. We do not honor our Savior by living in a way that contradicts and mocks his will. But when we are changed and motivated by grace, our influence is a tool in his hands to reach others for whom he died, and he is the one who gets the glory for our salvation and our transformation.

Day 203, Titus 3

Disciples of Jesus should be markedly different from the world around us. If we've been born again and renewed by the Holy Spirit, we are to be submissive and obedient to authorities, and ready for good work. Our tongues must be controlled, our conduct gentle and courteous. That should be a noticeable difference from the surrounding culture from which we came. Paul remembered the way we were before we were transformed by the goodness and kindness of God—foolish, disobedient, led astray, slaves to passion, malicious, envious, hateful and hated.

That's quite a difference, isn't it? That difference is not from our innate superiority or internal strength. We're not different because we've always been different. We didn't clean ourselves up. We were once just like those who do not yet acknowledge Jesus as Lord and have not yet been changed by divine power in their lives. God's mercy and grace justified us and made us heirs of eternal life. We're not busy doing good works to make us different, but we are devoted to good works because God made us different.

Being human and weak, we have to be reminded about this profound change. Our spiritual leaders have to teach us how to bear fruit and make a positive difference in the world around us. They must insist on our devotion, and caution us to avoid behaviors and situations that would lead us back into the worthless habits we left behind.

As disciples of Jesus, we live in the wonderful irony of being different from how we could ever manage to be on our own, all the while being motivated to do our best because of what he's done for us. The very best we can do will never lift us above the status of undeserving but loved sinners, saved by his grace and not our works. We do our best because we're amazed by his grace that's saved us, and because we remember clearly what it was like to be lost. Far from presuming upon his kindness, we celebrate and imitate his goodness in our interactions with others.

We're different, but all the glory for the difference is God's. We're changed, but we didn't pull ourselves up by the spiritual bootstraps. Remembering this keeps pride at bay, and produces worship in our redeemed hearts.

Philemon

Day 204, Philemon

Some were branded on the forehead, a lifelong reminder to everyone of their foolish attempt to escape. Some were hobbled, an ankle shattered so they could never run again. Some were executed in a gruesome display of their master's wrath to deter any others thinking about running. In an economy where slavery was a way of life, slaves were viewed as human tools. Had Philemon chosen to do any of the above or anything else to Onesimus, his runaway slave, no one would have objected. We should read Paul's appeal for mercy on behalf of Onesimus against this cultural background.

During his first Roman confinement, Paul met the runaway slave of an old friend. If you go to church when you're on vacation or traveling on business, you've probably met people and learned that you have common acquaintances. (I hear "It's a Small, Small World" in my head when that happens.) Did Paul recognize Onesimus from Philemon's household? Did the runaway become a Christian under Paul's influence and confess his crime of running away? We don't know, but somehow the apostle met Onesimus and sent him back to his master, knowing the risk, realizing the magnitude of his request.

Paul conducts a clinic on the art of persuasion in the only surviving personal letter from the prolific apostle. He built the bridge by referring to their relationship, expressing his desire for Philemon and his family to have the very best blessings, and acknowledging everything good and commendable about Philemon. He touched on his authority, but chose to make his appeal based on love. He played the sympathy card, saying he was now an old man and a prisoner. He did all this before ever bringing up Onesimus in a playful pun on the meaning of the runaway's name. "Mr. Useful" hadn't been so useful to Philemon, but Paul wanted the wronged master to know the runaway was now quite useful.

Instead of forcing compliance, honorable persuasion seeks consent. Paul asked Philemon to take Onesimus back as a brother, just as he would receive his partner Paul. He offered to pay Onesimus' debt, and gently reminded Philemon of what he "owed" the apostle. He expressed confidence in his friend, and told him he was coming to see him. He mentioned others they both knew who would be aware of Philemon's decision. He tied the package with the bow of grace the Lord had shown to him. What a masterpiece! How could Philemon refuse, even when the request was so counter-cultural?

What's the takeaway for us today? We can learn from Paul's method of persuasion. We can remember we need grace and need to show grace to others. We see that the gospel works more like leaven than dynamite to change hearts and cultures. And we find encouragement to obey when God's will goes against cultural norms. What's God asking of you that the neighbors might not understand? I'm confident you'd rather please God.

Hebrews

Day 205, Hebrews 1

Angelic beings act as messengers, servants and warriors of God throughout Scripture. From Genesis to Revelation, these powerful spirit beings are very real and active. Human fascination with the angels is still evident today. They're the subjects of paintings, sculptures, books, songs and television shows. As is often the case when Biblical subjects are treated in the popular media, there's a lot of misinformation and misconception about these beings.

I suspect Biblical angels have very little in common with the chubby cherubs in stores, gardens and curio cabinets. For all our interest in them, we really know very little about them. Once when I was a guest speaker at a church, a woman approached me and asked if I knew much about angels. From my answer she deduced that I needed to read the book she had written about them. She brought me a copy of the book with a bill for it the following night!

The unknown writer of Hebrews didn't write a lot about the angels, except to show how Jesus Christ is so vastly superior to them. All our interest in angels is fine, but the shadowy details about them are not nearly as important as the vivid, broad and clear statements about Jesus. The writer's first sentence claimed that God has spoken to us today not through the prophets but through his Son, the divinely appointed heir of all things, and the one who created the world. He asserted that Jesus is the one who upholds the universe by his power and the one who died for our sins.

God didn't call any angel his begotten Son. He did say all the angels would worship the Son and be his servants. He said Messiah was anointed of God and eternal, and that while the angels were sent out to minister, the Son now sits at God's right hand. All these details make the Hebrew writer's opening point: Jesus is superior in every way to angels. However awesome they may be, he is infinitely more so.

The first readers of Hebrews were being tempted to swap their relationship with Jesus for something else. The particular temptations of our modern situation may be different, but the clear message of this book is just as relevant to us as it was to them: Jesus is altogether superior to any competitor and totally sufficient to meet every spiritual need. Whether we see the competition as new ideas or just old ones that get dug up every few generations, the Hebrew writer wants us to know that every alternative, even ones used and approved by God in the past, are inferior to Jesus. No one is going to teach you more about God than the one he described as "the radiance of the glory of God and the exact imprint of his nature."

Day 206, Hebrews 2

I like to listen to the radio. I have a little radio that features remarkable sound quality and an excellent tuner. The tuner is designed to lock onto a station and hold it without drifting. I can tune to another station if I want to, but as long as I leave it set on a station, it will stay tuned.

Jesus is the focal point and main subject of the Scriptures. The writer of Hebrews quoted and alluded to familiar passages from the Psalms and the prophets again and again. Each time he did so, he told his readers, "This is all about Jesus, who he is, what he has done for us. Stay locked onto him." From incarnation to glorification, the script for Messiah's work had been written for centuries before Jesus was born into this world.

The fact that Jesus was born is a testimony to his identification with the human family he came to save. We are flesh and blood and destined to die. So he put on flesh and blood and died so we could overcome death and the fear of it and really live. He was a priest who offered himself for the people. Jesus suffered not for his sins, but for ours. Because he was tempted and suffered, he understands and is able to help us when we face temptation and suffering.

For all those reasons and more, we should be locked onto Jesus, the message of hope he brings and the salvation he offers. In one sense there is no competition, because no one, not even a mighty angel, is like him. But in another sense, we are bombarded with ideas and messages that compete with the truth to distract us from it. Today's reading is not about the folly of intentionally abandoning the gospel; instead, it cautions us to pay attention lest we drift away from it. Drifting is gradual, unintentional and almost imperceptible. But unchecked, the effect of drifting is the same as deliberately turning away from Jesus.

Also, it's not necessary to dramatically renounce our salvation; all we really have to do is neglect it. Have you noticed it's unnecessary to intentionally tear up a mechanical object or sabotage your health? Neglect is all that's required to break something down, whether it's a fine old watch, your house or your health (physical or spiritual). The writer warns there's no escape if we neglect this salvation. There's no 'Plan B' or alternate route.

The good news is true. It's come to us through reliable witnesses. Embrace this Jesus who became like us so we could be like him, who died for us so we could live with him. We cannot afford to drift away from or neglect the good news. Tune your spiritual focus to Jesus, and stay tuned.

Day 207, Hebrews 3

Will you face discouraging circumstances in your walk as a disciple of Jesus? Certainly you will. Will your faith ever waver? It might; it happens to many of us. Is it possible to hold onto your confidence in times of testing? Yes. Many people fall into unbelief and lose their confidence in the face of trials, but it's possible to come through trials with confidence intact when our trust is securely vested in Christ.

An entire generation of Israel had to die in the wilderness because they rebelled against God instead of relying on him. How can we avoid the same disastrous failure of faith?

First, realize apostasy begins in the heart as unbelief. As rational beings, we act in ways that are consistent with our thinking. Behavior stems from belief. When we disobey God, we do so because at the moment, we doubt God's way is best for us. We think we know better. So the author of Hebrews warned us to take care, to be on the lookout for the first hints of unbelief in our hearts. He did not call skepticism healthy; he called it evil. If the righteous live by faith, it makes sense that unbelief is the first step in rebellion.

Then our writer commanded us to encourage one another every day. Who knows how many who've walked away from God might have stayed by his side in an environment of regular, consistent encouragement? How many preachers, church leaders, young disciples and seasoned saints have been worn down and driven out by discouraging adversity? The holy calling of every member of the body of Christ is to give and receive encouragement, to remind and encourage one another about what is true. Sin is deceptive, working gradually to harden our hearts. Daily doses of encouragement can keep that from happening.

Jesus faced temptations and remained faithful to God. Moses was faithful, but the people he led out of Israel missed entering Canaan because of their disobedience and unbelief. The admonition from God's Holy Spirit to us is, "Today, if you will hear his voice. Do not harden your hearts as in the rebellion...." If we guard our hearts, encourage one another daily and hold firmly to our hope, then unbelief and disobedience will not draw us away from our calling. By God's sustaining grace, we can hold onto our confidence and be secure in our hope.

Day 208, Hebrews 4

When I was a boy, at church we sometimes sang a song that always seemed a little creepy to me. It was about "an all-seeing eye watching you." Maybe I'd seen too many old movies, but that song always conjured up images of a giant eyeball monster, watching every move I made. I didn't want to think about God like that, but the song seemed to warn me he was just such a frightening being.

When we're immature, we may imagine God as a cosmic hall monitor, watching for any transgression of the rules so he can punish us. I suppose I had to grow up and have children of my own before I could really find the comfort instead of the threat in the idea of God watching us constantly. As parents, we watch our children to protect them and help them. True enough, we sometimes see them do things that call for correction, but the idea of parental vigilance is more comforting than threatening.

I also noticed my little children asked to be watched when they felt some threat or when they wanted to show some new skill they'd learned. I remember doing the same thing as a child. I was somewhat less interested in Mom or Dad's observation when I was sneaking around to do something I wasn't supposed to do.

How do you feel about being "naked and exposed to the eyes of him to whom we must give account"? His word pierces to the center of our being, discerning our thoughts and intentions. There's no faking it or hiding from God. I suspect we're all OK with that when, like little children, we want God to see and know the good things we're doing and the progress we're making. It's when I'm ashamed of my disobedience that I'm uncomfortable with his continuous gaze. Either way, knowing God witnesses all we say, do and think is a powerful motivator to do the right thing.

This is about trusting God. If our lives are characterized by the unbelief and disobedience that doomed the Exodus generation of Israel to die in the wilderness, we're not likely to want him to watch us. But if we trust he loves us, we can relax and bask in the assurance of his watchful care. When we see Jesus as our sympathetic high priest who understands weakness and temptation because he's "been there," it's comforting to know he sees us. God so wants us to share his rest that he helps us every step of the way, offering mercy and grace to all who approach him through Christ.

I still think the song about the big eyeball is creepy, but I'm glad he's watching me.

Day 209, Hebrews 5

Those of us who've raised children can remember when the babies were ready for cereal after several months of a milk-only diet. Then maybe some mashed fruits or vegetables found their way into those little toothless mouths. Our kids had to grow for a while before they could savor a steak, but we knew it was the natural pattern of development.

The same principle is true in spiritual development. Beginners need milk before they're ready for meat. The writer of Hebrews described the basic facts of the work of Christ on our behalf as milk, but suggested there's also a main course of meat for the more mature. (The gospel is milk in the sense that it comes first, not that there is anything deeper, richer or more profound than the cross.)

Priests under the Law of Moses were go-betweens. They presented the offerings of unholy sinners to a holy God. The priests God appointed to serve in the Levitical system were well able to understand human weakness, because they were humans and weak themselves. This affinity qualified them to sympathize with their fellow sinners as they offered sacrifices on their behalf. But it also required them to offer sacrifices for their own sins.

Jesus was appointed by God as well, but to a different priesthood. He also suffered in human flesh, but his perfect obedience to his Father qualified him to be both priest and sin offering in one. This unique standing empowered him to be the source of eternal salvation for all who would overcome sin and come to God through him.

This concept lies at the nucleus of the gospel. God's own Son suffered in flesh, dying on the cross not for his own sins, but for ours. God accepted his sinless death as atonement for the sins of all who would trust him for their salvation. Christ's resurrection provides the assurance we need and want that death is not final and will not win.

The basic premise of the priestly work of Christ seems clear enough, but the writer of Hebrews said there was much more to explain, and it would be difficult for spiritually immature people to grasp. Those who struggled with the milk (elementary teachings of the Word) would not be mature enough to be nourished by the solid food of deeper spiritual understanding. Even Jesus himself matured through the experiences of life. We shouldn't expect ourselves or the people around us to start out full-grown.

I want to be humble enough to acknowledge I have a lot of learning and growing to do. At the same time, I want to keep maturing as a follower of Christ, not content to remain a spiritual baby. As I recall, baby food wasn't all that tasty, but it did serve a legitimate purpose. I just wouldn't want to eat it my whole life, when there are so many good things to enjoy.

Day 210, Hebrews 6

Our hearts break when we see people whose mental or physical condition keeps them from developing normally toward maturity. We realize their lives are limited to some extent. They may excel in other ways, have sparkling personalities or unusual aptitudes, but we regret that in the area of life where they have some impairment, they will not be like their peers.

It's also heartbreaking to see a believer who does not continue to make progress toward spiritual maturity. Sad but true, some who make a profession of faith do not continue in it; their lives do not match their words. The writer clearly warns about the possibility of tasting the heavenly gift, sharing in the Holy Sprit, tasting the goodness of the word and the power of God and falling away. Sadly, he says it is impossible to restore some to repentance. Instead of being fruitful and productive fields for God's glory, they bear no valuable fruit and are in danger of being cursed and destroyed.

The writer was confident that God's salvation, rewards and blessings were coming for his readers. He encouraged them to earnestly imitate the great heroes of faith who received God's promises when they endured and trusted in him. Our hope and confidence is not in our endurance or performance, but in God's faithfulness. Just as he swore to Abraham about incredible things that surely came to pass, God has assured us of eternal life with an unbreakable oath. Our hope is anchored in a realm beyond our ability to see and know, in a place where Jesus has already gone as our high priest.

But we must press on toward maturity in Christ. We must not even think of turning back. That's not because we're earning or meriting a reward by our diligence. Our progress is evidence of God's work in us, and our obedience is the fruit of our trust in him. We must endure and obey with the fullest assurance that God will see, remember and reward our loving service offered in his name. We don't know all God has in store for us, but we know enough to realize we don't want to miss it. We know his promises are true and trustworthy. There's no way to invest our lives that will bring a greater return, and nothing else to trust that will give us more confidence.

Day 211, Hebrews 7

Shrouded in mystery, Melchizedek appears and disappears on the pages of Genesis. He resurfaces in Psalms in a reference to Messiah. He appears again in Hebrews as a crucial point of the author's argument for the superiority of Jesus Christ over the Law of Moses and the Levitical priesthood. Some believe Melchizedek was an appearance of the pre-incarnate Christ—that the writer of Hebrews meant it literally, not metaphorically, when he said the mystery priest who met Abraham had no father or mother, beginning or end. Others take the reference to be about a human being, and that the human priest Melchizedek actually had parents, birth and death about which we know nothing.

Either way, Melchizedek stands in contrast to the Levitical priests the first readers of this book would have known. The argument is that Abraham, the father of the nation, honored this priest by paying tithes to him and receiving a blessing from him. By extension, the Levitical priests, as yet unborn when father Abraham met Melchizedek, also honored him and paid the tithe representatively through their ancestor. Thus the Levitical priests were inferior to Melchizedek.

Now Jesus is said to be a priest after the order of Melchizedek. By that connection he is superior to the priests from Levi who served God and the nation under the law. Jesus was of the tribe of Judah, so he could never have been a priest under the Law of Moses. He was a priest by God's oath and decree, not by the regulation of the law. Since Jesus lives forever as the resurrected Son of God, he needs no successor, unlike the Levitical priests who served, died and were replaced. And since he was sinless, he didn't have to offer sin offerings for himself. Instead, he offered himself in innocence as the sin offering. He is better in every way than the Levitical priests, and his new priesthood announced a new covenant.

If that line of reasoning is not a big deal to you, consider it was a very big deal to the original readers who had come to Christ from

Judaism, and were in jeopardy of returning to Judaism with its law and priests. The writer showed how such an idea made no sense, demonstrating the absolute superiority of Jesus and the new covenant to the Jewish priests and the Law of Moses. The law, originally given by God to Israel, was weak and useless compared to Christ. (So it's also clear that Jesus is superior to any scheme or design of human origin.)

We may never in this life know all we'd like to know about this Melchizedek, whose name means "king of righteousness" and "king of peace." But whoever he was, he points us to Jesus, the true king of righteousness and peace. We will never fathom all there is to know about Jesus, but we can know enough to trust him over every alternative.

Day 212, Hebrews 8

Have you ever read or heard about "planned obsolescence" in consumer goods? Do you believe automobile and electronics companies build an intentional failure factor into their products?

Some items do have limited life-spans by design. Technology moves at a rapid pace, and we expect this year's model to outperform previous versions of some products. Styles change quickly, and some folks just couldn't be seen in last year's hot new color.

Some items with short useful life-spans could possibly be engineered to last a lifetime, but would we be willing to pay significantly more for the materials and manufacturing techniques such durability might require? Most of us just accept the fact that certain products, even some expensive ones, will only last for a short time.

Hundreds of years before Jesus came, God gave his people who had just come out of Egypt a law at Mt. Sinai. God had a specific purpose and limited duration in mind for that law from the beginning. A few centuries later, he told his people through Jeremiah that a new covenant would one day be established. It would not be like the Sinai covenant, written in stone by the finger of God, but ignored by many generations of Israelites. The problem with the old covenant was not actually with it, but with the people who lived under it. The new law would be internalized, written on the heart, and everyone in the covenant would make a conscious choice to accept it and be included in it. It would be a covenant of mercy and forgiveness, in which Messiah himself would reign as high priest. The new covenant would be the reality of all that had been foreshadowed by the old one. And when it came, the old one would become obsolete.

Our ancient brothers and sisters who lived in the decades immediately following the life of Jesus on earth were witnesses to the planned obsolescence of the Law of Moses. When Jesus fulfilled the prophecies and brought to reality all the old law had symbolized and prefigured, it became obsolete.

Gentiles living twenty centuries later may not be able to appreciate the earth-shaking implications of this concept. Deep convictions and generations of tradition didn't disappear automatically. Many of the Jewish followers of Christ continued to observe customs and measure their time by the festivals of the law. But Jesus' disciples learned to let go of the old law, and embrace the new covenant of Christ. Everything about it is superior to anything they had known under Moses' law. Jesus is the real high priest, ministering in the true tabernacle of God, bringing all God's promises to fruition.

From eternity's viewpoint, the gospel made the law a system of planned obsolescence. But the new model is such an improvement over the old that all who really understand the difference can appreciate it.

Day 213, Hebrews 9

Early one morning not long ago, I was walking our little dog, and noticed my shadow. I was surprised to see that my shadow was over fifty feet long! But I knew I was still (just barely) six feet tall. I know the difference between myself and my shadow. Pretty smart, huh? But wait, there's more! We have pictures of our children in our home. Sweet memories of childhood and landmarks like graduations and weddings are associated with those photographs, but I have never once confused the real presence of one of my kids with their photographic likeness. I can tell the difference between an image of my child and the real person.

After briefly describing the layout and furnishings of the tabernacle, the writer said it was not his purpose to go into detail about those matters. He then described the mediating work the priests were called to do, how they ministered in the first room of the tabernacle. But only one (and only once each year) went into the second room, the Most Holy Place, to make a blood sacrifice for himself and the rest of the people. The sacrifice was required, but was merely a token, a representation of a real sacrifice still to come. It had no real power to forgive the sins and perfect the guilty conscience of the worshipper.

But when Christ came, he made his offering as our high priest in the true Most Holy Place (not an earthly tent), by the means of his own blood (not the blood of an animal). Jesus' blood, shed when he died, had the power to truly forgive our sins and cleanse our consciences. All the symbolism and ceremony of the tabernacle and later the temple, all the architecture, furniture and blood offerings were shadows. They were images depicting what Jesus would do at the cross. The shadows and pictures were rich in promise, but they only pointed to the coming reality. Their promise was fulfilled in Christ.

Jesus, as mediator of the new covenant, died to establish it. The blood that sanctified the covenant and everyone under it was his own. By his once for all offering for sin, Jesus has put away sin and taken its punishment for all who trust in him. By his death, resurrection and promised return, we have hope and confidence about our salvation and eternal life. The author of Hebrews did not want his first readers to forsake the reality of these things they had in Jesus by returning to the shadows and images of the Levitical priesthood.

What's the point for you and me? No symbol or ceremony, even God-appointed ones, can do what Jesus did for us. No work we do, even in imitation of his sacrifice, can atone for sin like he did. To think that might be possible is to confuse shadows and pictures with reality. We're smarter than that, aren't we?

Day 214, Hebrews 10

She is calm while others around her are frantic. Her neighbors are flipping through notes, scanning the textbook one more time, hoping some last morsel of knowledge might be gleaned. But she is ready. Her pen is on her desk and a faint smile is on her lips as she waits for the exam booklets to be distributed. She knows the material. She is confident.

He and his teammates have worked hard. All the practice and conditioning, all the learning and repetitions have led to this moment, the one they've been waiting for. It's time to stop blocking and tackling one another and start using what they've learned against a real opponent. They don't really care about who's favored to win. They're confident.

After graduation, the confidence learned in the classroom and on the playing field continues to serve them well in the big, real world. Confidence is a valuable commodity in every job, in every business, in all of life.

Christians above all people should live with confidence about the most important part of life. Christians can have the best kind of confidence, rooted in the faithfulness and perfection of God, not in ourselves. We are confident we have access to and relationship with God by the blood of Jesus, who gave himself as a perfect, once for all offering to take away our sins. Our approach to God is not by a trail we blazed through the spiritual wilderness, but through Jesus himself, the new and living way. Because he is our faithful and great priest, we can draw near to God with true hearts that have been sprinkled by the blood of the Lamb of God. We have put our faith in him. We encourage each other, and take the danger of sin in our lives very seriously.

We hold onto our confidence in the face of opposition and persecution. We endure whatever adversity comes, focused on the better things and the reward the Lord has promised.

If I lack such confidence, I need to realize what Jesus has done for me and trust him instead of myself. I need to surrender my life to him just as he surrendered himself to the will of God. Instead of refusing to forgive myself, I must learn to trust his promise of forgiveness. Instead of quitting and shrinking back from my confession of Jesus as Lord and Savior, I need to live out my faith. Then I can be confident. It's not pride, or thinking more highly of myself than I should. It's realizing the source of my forgiveness and my sanctification, and relying on him. He died and conquered death so I could live with confidence, not fear or guilt.

Are you confident? Is your confidence firmly grounded in Jesus Christ? It is your birthright as a child of God. Trust him. Obey him. Be confident in him.

Day 215, Hebrews 11

What does it mean to live by faith? The writer of Hebrews explains and illustrates that concept in today's portion.

Faith allows us to "see" farther than our eyes can see. Scientists peer through telescopes and microscopes trying to look back and gain understanding about our origins. Faith understands the universe was created by the word of God, the visible, tangible world spoken into existence by his decree. We humans also strain to see what's ahead. From the time of ancient Israel, there have been fortune tellers who claimed to see the future and were willing, for a price, to share what they saw with inquiring minds who wanted to know. Faith also looks ahead, beyond here and now, to a future that can only be known by placing our confidence in God and what has told us about it.

Faith is required to know, approach and please God. Abel and Enoch were commended because their actions were based on their faith in God. We don't know much about how God revealed himself to them, but we do know they trusted the revelation they had received, and God commended them for it.

Faith empowers and motivates. Abel, Noah, Abraham, Moses and other heroes of the Old Testament were led to do the things they did by faith. Their faith was no mere contemplative state or mental assent. Mark the verbs in the chapter. They offered, constructed, obeyed and did things beyond human ability—all by faith. Israel left Egypt and conquered Canaan, unstoppable as long as they acted in faith.

The world will not appreciate the priorities and choices that characterize a life of faith. The reaction of the world may range from misunderstanding to open hostility against people who live by their faith. We like to hear of the victories and blessings faith brought to the lives of people who trusted God. But we also need to remember some people were persecuted and killed for their faith. It's not over for those martyrs; God has much more for his people than the present life can hold. But it's important to know faith is not a talisman to ward off all suffering.

Today's disciples of Jesus are in the same line as the ancients who believed the testimony and trusted the promises they received from God. We live our lives based on believing the testimony about who Jesus is and what he did for us. We trust God's word that we have forgiveness for our past and power for our present. We wait for what he has promised about our future. That's what it means to live by faith.

Day 216, Hebrews 12

The word "endurance" evokes images of athletics for many of us. For cyclists, the *Tour de France* is a grueling test of endurance. We admire marathon runners because of their perseverance as they train and then run 26 miles in a race. In the Olympics, the decathlon is regarded as the best all-around measure of an athlete's strength, skill and stamina.

Olympic-type races and contests were popular in the first century, and the imagery of athletic competition is common in the New Testament. Here we are admonished to "run with endurance the race that is set before us." To spur us on to the finish line, the writer stacked image upon image to help us see the need for endurance and keep us focused on the goal.

We can enhance our own persistence by looking to the example of Jesus. He did not abandon the course when it led him to the cross and death. Looking ahead to the redemption he would secure for us, Jesus endured the horror and agony of crucifixion without shrinking away from God's plan. When we encounter persecution from the world as we live for God, we should not be surprised or think difficulty is an excuse to quit.

Hardship may also be God's tool to discipline, shape and train his children. Our Father trains us for our own good, that we may share his holiness. When we endure the discipline, we are being shaped and strengthened by his hand. Knowing God loves us and wants what is best for us helps us remain meek and submissive when he uses adversity to shape our character.

We are blessed to live under a much better covenant than the Law of Moses. The old one was given in terrifying and spectacular circumstances. The mountain was shrouded in fire and darkness, and the voice of God shook the earth. But the new one is even more awesome. We are not looking to Mt. Sinai, with Israel gathered to receive the law. We're looking toward Mt. Zion, the heavenly Jerusalem, with God on his throne, with innumerable angels and all the redeemed who've ever lived. The redeemed ones are sprinkled with blood—not with animal's blood, but with the blood of Jesus. Who would dare stop listening to and following the one who speaks to us from there? His voice will sound again, not only shaking the earth, but the heavens as well.

When that promised shake-up comes, everything we know in the present arrangement of all things will be removed, except the kingdom of God which we've received in Christ. To be part of that kingdom is incentive enough to endure whatever adversity we may encounter, to live pure godly lives, and to worship in reverence before our awesome God.

Day 217, Hebrews 13

Following Jesus impacts much more of life than what we do at a church service, and goes far beyond agreeing with some doctrinal statement. Discipleship impacts all of life, every day. Some particulars are mentioned in this portion.

We're supposed to love God's family and show hospitality to strangers. We're supposed to have compassion on those who are suffering and live morally pure lives. Our lives should be characterized by contentment with what we have and confidence in what God has promised. We should respect and imitate the conduct of godly leaders. These are all matters of daily living.

It is a convenient brand of Christianity that emphasizes doctrinal correctness and the particulars of church organization and procedure. All those matters are important, but they are not all that matters. I understand why some people who claim to be faithful followers of Jesus would rather define faithfulness by such checklists than get to the essence of a changed life. We may feel free to live as we please, conduct business as we see fit, treat people however we choose to treat them (and do so with a clear conscience) when we compartmentalize our lives and measure our discipleship by what we do in a church service. It's easier to check off a list of doctrinal positions than to surrender every action, word and thought to the lordship of Jesus Christ. This chapter reminds us that acknowledging God in everyday things—doing good and sharing what we have—is what pleases God.

If such a whole-life commitment seems beyond our ability, the writer reminds us that God equips us with everything good so we may do his will. God is working in and through our surrendered lives to accomplish what pleases him. By equipping us and working in us, he is the one who gets all the glory.

I doubt we will ever wield the kind of influence Jesus wants us to have on the world around us if we define our discipleship in terms of things we do within church walls. Lost people who matter to God are not likely to read our clever doctrinal statements. But our neighbors and friends can see what God is doing in our lives when we're faithful to do everyday things in ways that reflect God's influence and control. We'll be in a much better position to tell them what they need to know when we've been showing them what it means to us.

James

Day 218, James 1

This little scene has probably played out in all our lives a few times. Maybe you've lived long enough to have appeared in both roles.

Child: I feel terrible.

Parent: Take this medicine. It will make you feel better.

Child: I don't want to take the medicine. It tastes awful.

Parent: I know, but it's good for you. Here we go.

Child: No! I don't like it.

Parent: I know you don't want it, but it will help you. Open wide. Go on. Swallow it. That's good. You'll feel better soon.

Some things that are good for us or serve a good purpose are not always pleasant. Most of us don't enjoy taking medicine. Many of us don't enjoy working out, eating our leafy green vegetables or balancing the checkbook. But we know such things are good for us.

It's not always easy to find joy in trials. When we find ourselves in difficult or painful circumstances, joy may not be the first emotion that courses through our minds and hearts. Temptations and tests bring additional stress to life, and it's hard to rejoice under pressure. But we're counseled in this portion to count it all joy when we meet various kinds of trials.

Knowing the reason why or appreciating the result that comes from enduring a trial helps us discover the joy in it. James said the trials we encounter in life produce steadfastness and maturity in us, and ultimately lead to a crown of life from the Lord. Like a patient who wants to get better, we find the necessary process unpleasant but not unbearable, because we want the promised results.

When trials come wrapped as temptations, it's important to know the source and methodology behind the temptation. It's good to know God is not the one who's putting temptations in our path.

He permits it and can bring good out of it, but he is not the author of the temptation. We're enticed to do wrong by opportunities that appeal to desires within us. When we take the bait, we sin. Sin leads to death. God explains the technique so we can short-circuit the process. We may need to develop wholesome, godly desires. We may have to avoid situations where the opportunity to do wrong would arise.

Our loving Father gives us every good thing we have. He teaches us what we need to know to overcome temptation, strengthens us to resist it, and loves us so much that he's still willing to forgive us when we fall for it. Because God wants what is best for us, he wants us to do what he says. The blessing comes from doing what God says. Will we obey God who wants to bless and save us, or Satan who wants to kill and destroy us? Even when it's not easy to do the right thing, it's still best for us to do it. Knowing that helps us find the joy.

Day 219, James 2

Every now and then a news story comes along about someone who has lived a dual life with a spouse and children in one city, and another home and family somewhere else. "Traveling on business," he divides his time between the two families, sometimes for years, until his scheme is discovered. When we hear the story, we wonder, "How could he live with the deceitfulness for so long?"

Although most people couldn't (and wouldn't want to) live a double life like that, many people do practice some duplicity in their spiritual lives. When a younger man questioned a professing Christian about how a follower of Jesus could do the things he did in business, the businessman said, "I never mix my business and my religion." He was living a dual life, too. On one hand he attended church, read the Bible and claimed to be a Christian. On the other, he was ruthless and unethical in his business. What he claimed to believe did not affect how he lived.

James brought up two issues that test the genuineness of our faith. First, he said partiality or prejudice has no place in the life of someone who holds the faith of Christ. When we judge people by externals, we are failing to obey God's fundamental law governing human conduct and relationships: "You shall love your neighbor as yourself." The scenario he described has been repeated around the world and through the centuries—we welcome the rich and famous, and push away poor people or others whom we deem beneath us. It's easy to be suspicious of the poor, wondering what they're trying to get from us. Aren't we guilty of what we're accusing them of doing when we favor the rich, hoping to win their favor and generosity? James said partiality is sin, and we stand convicted by the law when we're guilty of it.

The validity and worth of our faith is also tested by our works, the way we live because we believe. Some professing Christians are uncomfortable with how James put it here, but it's plain: Faith without works is dead, useless faith. James' words do not deny the beautiful doctrine of salvation by grace through faith as taught by Paul in Romans or Ephesians. Instead, James supports the parallel teaching by Paul in Romans and Ephesians that people who are saved by grace lead changed lives. Abraham and Rahab demonstrated their faith by their actions, by their works. People who claim to believe but show no evidence of that faith in their conduct are leading dual lives. As rational people, we take action based on what we believe. Habitual ungodly conduct in a believer's life says his profession of faith in Jesus as Lord is a lie.

Is your faith genuine? Is your life an expression of your trusting faith in God? We may fool ourselves and even others for a while, but we can't fool God when we're living a double life.

Day 220, James 3

Somewhere in my brain there must be an area where the spoken word is stored. When I think about them, I can play back good words of encouragement I heard many years ago. Unfortunately, that same area also seems to store some things I've heard that weren't encouraging at all—things that hurt my feelings and wounded my spirit. It's not a good idea to spend too much time thinking about those hurtful words.

If we know it's true about things said to us, we must also acknowledge it's true about things we say to others. Our words have tremendous power to heal and build, or to wound and tear down. It's our job to control our tongue, and use this power for good purposes.

The power of the spoken word is like any power—it must be used with wisdom and care. To handle power carelessly is to invite disaster. James said the tongue is a fire. When fire is cooking my food on the grill in a carefully controlled setting, it's a good thing. When it's burning down my house because it got out of control, it's a bad thing. James said the tongue is harder to tame than a wild animal. When the horse or other domesticated animal is serving us with its strength, we're blessed by its power. But when that strength gets out of hand, people get hurt and material gets recorded for those television programs that show horrifying moments captured on video.

James also addressed a matter most of us can understand about the unnatural phenomenon of blessing and cursing coming from the same tongue. How can that be? No spring can pour out both fresh water and salt water. No plant produces the fruit of some other species. Jesus said our speech comes from the overflow of our heart. When our speech is ugly and hateful, we're telling on ourselves about the condition of our heart.

Some people seem to struggle with this more than others. I admit I'm challenged to control my tongue. Our words influence the people around us. (That's why James mentioned the serious responsibility of being a teacher at the beginning of the discussion.) When our speech is under the influence of the wisdom from above, our associates will be blessed by what we say. But when our speech is controlled by earthly, unspiritual, demonic forces, we will spread disorder and pain in our relationships.

If someone followed you around today collecting sound bites, what would those speech samples say about your tongue control and your discipleship? Like every other aspect of our submission to the Lord, our tongue control will be imperfect. But an honest appraisal of the things we say should give us a reliable picture of the trend in our discipleship.

Day 221, James 4

My mother may or may not have known about the Socratic Method, but she often asked questions. I don't think her interrogations were intended to gather enlightenment from her son. Instead, she asked questions to make me think or to teach a lesson I needed to learn. You probably had a similar experience with a parent, teacher or coach somewhere along the way.

Socrates left no writings, but engaged his pupils in a search for truth through asking questions. He pushed students to the foundations of their beliefs and then exposed the fallacy of their thinking with his queries. Teachers from kindergarten through graduate school still use this method, popularized by Socrates 400 years before Jesus came.

James queried his readers, too, asking questions that might well make their cheeks burn red with shame. In each case, they had to look inside themselves or honestly evaluate their conduct in light of their knowledge. Just as Socrates' old method is still useful today, so these questions posed by James are still powerful teaching tools.

He asked, "What causes quarrels and what causes fights among you? Is it not this, that your passions are at war within you?" (He sometimes answered the questions as well as asking them. My mom did that, too.) He pulled away the veils from the mysterious origins of their quarrels and revealed selfishness and personal gratification at the root of the divisive, bitter disputes.

James asked, "Don't you know that friendship with the world is enmity with God?" All who would follow Jesus have a decision to make about whom they want to please. Only as we submit to and humble ourselves toward God can we really draw near the Lord. It is impossible to draw near while clinging to worldliness. Jesus called us to be in, but not of the world.

Again, James pressed us to examine our conduct in light of the truth: "Who are you to judge your neighbor?" When we judge others, we appoint ourselves to both the legislature and the judiciary. But James said there's only one lawgiver who can save and destroy, and we're not him.

James corralled all our big plans made without seeking the will of God with a question reminding us of life's uncertainty and transience: "What is your life?" He answered this one, too. "You are a mist that appears for a little time and then vanishes." James called us back from the brink of prideful arrogance to submit ourselves and our plans to God's will.

Although such questions may make us uncomfortable, they are valuable. We have to look deep inside ourselves to honestly answer them. The answers remind us of truth we tend to forget. Our pride is dismantled and our trust is deepened by answering James' probing questions.

Day 222, James 5

If Romans challenges us to grasp the majestic theological heights of the gospel, the book of James challenges us to examine the practical effect of the gospel on our lives at ground level. James probes the depths of his readers' hearts as we learn how faith behaves in everyday life.

One day all the suffering that characterizes life in this world will be over. All the injustice and mistreatment will come to an end. God's people trust his promises about such matters, and in the meantime, faith responds with patience and prayer to the difficulties of life beyond our ability to control.

In the first century, many Christians were slaves, at the mercy of their masters. Many were impoverished and disenfranchised. James warned the rich about a coming day of reckoning, when God would right the wrongs of fraud and abuse by which they had amassed their wealth. He told the Christians to be patient and remember the day was on its way. Like a farmer who must wait through the growing season for the harvest, the oppressed disciples had to wait for the Lord to come and judge righteously. James encouraged them to faithful steadfastness. He reminded them of the brave prophets, who delivered the word of the Lord to people who did not want to hear it. And he reminded them of Job, who did not understand what was happening, but patiently endured the calamities that marked his life without turning away from God.

When suffering or sickness threatens our joy, James recommended praying to God for relief. When sin has diminished the quality of life (as it always does), he counseled confession and prayer. Elijah's righteous prayers stopped and started the rain when God was dealing with rebellious Israel. I suspect I've barely begun to experience the power available in prayer. How about you?

Ever practical, James taught his readers to be so straightforward in speech that a simple yes or no without an oath would suffice. He reminded them of the noble task of restoring our brothers and sisters who wander away from the truth. His advice and exhortations are rooted in the Scriptures and in the words of Jesus. His instructions are for everyday life, not some philosophical exercise. The book of James challenges us to examine and adjust our lives by its descriptions of practical holiness.

1 Peter

It's not always easy to live for Jesus. The opposition may come in the form of hateful persecution, alluring temptation or nagging doubt. When you're struggling, it's good to remember some things that are at the same time both basic and grand.

To persecuted Christians suffering adversity, Peter wrote about such foundation facts of faith, the new birth, the call to holy living and loving one another. He addressed themes at the core of our faith. Our hope is based on believing the good news that the blood of Jesus was shed for us. We trust Jesus was raised from the dead by the power of God. We are confident Jesus will return.

God's chosen ones, elect in Christ and sprinkled with his blood, have a high calling and much to anticipate. Christians are the beneficiaries of blessings God prepared centuries in advance. He sent clues through prophets who spoke things they did not fully understand. The angels themselves wanted to know about it, but could not grasp the scheme by which God would bring salvation.

Peter said an imperishable, undefiled and unfading inheritance was waiting for God's born-again children. That's hard to imagine, isn't it? We live in a material world where everything ruins, breaks down and wears out. But Peter says our inheritance is being kept for us, and we are being kept for it by God's power. We know we've been saved by grace, redeemed by the blood of Christ, the Lamb of God.

Such promises of salvation and reward motivate us to trust his grace and live holy lives. We're called to love one another with earnestness and purity. How could we choose to be selfish, disobedient and led by our lusts when we realize what the Lord has done for us?

Peter's words are encouraging and challenging. A theological dictionary might deepen our appreciation of the things he said, but we can grasp the basic meaning and be motivated to endure suffering and obey the Lord. The outcome of a life lived in faith and submission to God's will is the salvation of our souls. In a world where everything comes to an end, our new life in Christ is through a living and abiding word that endures forever. The suffering is temporary; the life is eternal.

These lofty, soaring themes can help you keep your feet firmly grounded on the path of following Jesus, even on days when it's not easy. Focus on them instead of the distractions.

Day 224, 1 Peter 2

Do you have an instinctive, reflexive negative reaction to the idea of submission? I understand why some people do. We might expect someone raised by an overbearing or abusive parent to grow up with a bad attitude toward authority. A mean, ungodly spouse could make his or her mate recoil at the mention of the word "submit." More than a few Christians, scarred by an encounter with dictatorial leaders in a toxic local church setting, don't want to hear anything about being subject to anyone.

Human history illustrates our tendency toward rebellion. When that tendency is strengthened by a bad experience with an authority figure, we're likely to reject any teaching that begins with the phrase "Be subject to...." Yet Peter said subjection, not only to the Lord, but also to humans in human institutions, is one way disciples demonstrate the lordship of Christ in their lives. So we're commanded to obey the government and law enforcement officers. Remember, the Roman government was becoming increasingly hostile toward Christians when Peter wrote this, but the mandate is still to be subject and show honor. We're commanded to be respectful to our superiors at work, even when they're unjust.

Such difficult situations give us an opportunity to imitate Jesus Christ. Enduring undeserved abuse and mockery, he did not retaliate. Instead he entrusted himself to God, the ultimate judge. God predetermined his gruesome torture and death to be the means of accomplishing our redemption. But that did not diminish the pain or lessen the humiliation Jesus suffered. When we are mistreated for doing right, we have an opportunity to glorify God.

Honorable conduct under difficult circumstances is an eloquent testimony to the power and grace of God in our lives. As his people, we are living stones, built together for a house where he lives. The old prophecies echo in our lives as we believe in Christ as God's cornerstone of that spiritual house. We find mercy and strength in our relationship with him. When unbelievers see the difference the Lord has made in us, we may become the means by which they are drawn to Christ. But that plan only works when our lives are in contrast to the conduct of the world. And submission to authority is one place where the contrast can be clearly seen.

Day 225, 1 Peter 3

There's much more about everyday living in the epistles than specific instruction about what to do at church. The attitudes and actions that should characterize our daily lives as followers of Jesus are defined and described at some length, while instructions about church organization and operation are general and limited by comparison.

You're not likely to be subjected to a rigorous examination about fine points of doctrine today. But you will face the challenge of living out your faith in practical, visible ways.

Wives will have the opportunity today to exert a positive influence on their husbands, to make themselves beautiful in ways God himself values with a beauty that will never fade away. Today, husbands will get the chance to show their wives by their actions that they understand them, respect them and count them precious. As we interact with other disciples, we can show our devotion to Christ by loving fellow disciples and exhibiting tender hearts and humble minds. We have the opportunity to imitate our Savior, living above retaliation, blessing when we are persecuted or mistreated.

When we genuinely regard Christ as Lord, we are happy to share the basis of our hope with others. But we will be effective in doing so only when our defense is offered with gentleness and respect. It's useless to explain our hope in Christ if we're living in rebellion to his will. When we disobey, our conscience tells us that our profession of Jesus as Lord is a lie.

These are all everyday matters. They flow more from a surrendered heart and life than from some sacramental, ritualistic expression of what it means to be a Christian. Yes, confessing Jesus as Lord is vitally important. Being baptized as an appeal to God for a good conscience, trusting in the resurrection of Christ, is vitally important. But those first steps of discipleship are by no means the total picture of what it means to be a follower of Jesus Christ. The real evidence of discipleship is in how we live, treat other people and humble ourselves ourselves before the Lord every day.

Day 226, 1 Peter 4

A professional sports organization developed a campaign around the phrase, "I Live for This." The idea was that fans of the sport were so devoted to their team or loved the game so much they would sum up their enthusiasm for the game by saying they lived for it.

What's the "this" you live for? What captures your imagination, ignites your passion, thrills your heart and guides your life? "I live for _____." How would you fill in the blank?

In today's portion, Peter mentioned a couple of things disciples of Jesus should live for. First, he said Christ-followers should live their lives for the will of God, not for human passions. He acknowledged that we have lived selfishly in the past, without showing proper regard for God. Even if the people around us do not understand why we no longer indulge our fleshly desires, Peter said we should live with the end in mind, realizing we and those who malign our choice of living for the will of God will face him in judgment. Knowing that appointment is coming should motivate us to sober, self-controlled living.

Peter also said we should live for the glory of God. God gets the glory when we love one another, show hospitality, speak his word or serve in any way—if we remember the talents and opportunities to use them are gifts from him. When we acknowledge we are only able to do as he enables us, we don't call attention to ourselves or our strength. He gets the glory. Even if we suffer for being a Christian, there is a blessing in it if we're conscious of sharing Christ's suffering. There's no shame in suffering when it's for the name of Jesus. Instead of shame, there's joy when we endure it for God's glory.

Do you live for the will of God? Are you devoted to doing what God wants or to doing as you please? Do you live for the glory of God? Are you content for God to get all the glory, or do you crave recognition and praise? These questions trouble us because we know the "right" answer, but our lives don't always reflect that answer. By learning to think more like Jesus and entrusting our souls to God, we'll get closer to the ideal. That's what it means to be a disciple.

Day 227, 1 Peter 5

Is there a wardrobe object you can't do without, a go-to item you reach for again and again? For some girls, it's a little black dress. For some guys, it's a navy blazer. For disciples of Jesus, the must-have fashion for all seasons is humility. Let's see why Peter told all disciples to clothe themselves with humility.

Suppose you are a leader among God's people. Surely you don't need humility to lead, do you? To be the kind of leader elders are called to be, the answer is yes. Leading God's sheep as one of his shepherds is different from leading in some other parts of life. This difference is defined in three "not/but" descriptions of those who oversee the flock. These leaders are not under compulsion to serve, but willing to do so. They're not in it for the money, but they are eager about their shepherding. They're not domineering, but rather lead by being examples to the flock. Jesus taught the disciples the leaders among them would be more like servants than overlords. Those who shepherd God's sheep humbly remember whose sheep they're tending, realizing the chief Shepherd is coming back to reward them for their efforts.

If you're one of the sheep, it's important to be humble, too. Peter's word to you is "Be subject to the elders." That's not always easy. Their weaknesses and mistakes may be clearly visible, but they have the responsibility of leading and you have the responsibility of following their lead. A spirit of humility will keep us from a haughty, uncooperative attitude and prideful rebellion.

And we need humility toward God. The Lord who saved us by his grace opposes the proud and gives more grace to the humble. If we are tempted to cast off our garment of humility to climb up in the ranks, we need to remember that humbling ourselves beneath his mighty hand is the sure way to being lifted up by that same hand. It takes humility to admit we need help with our problems. It takes humility to recognize we need God's help because we have a powerful adversary who seeks to destroy us. It takes humility to endure the suffering that goes with living for Christ in a fallen world, realizing our ultimate victory will come through his grace.

Fashions change, but classics endure, season after season. For the sake of our relationships with one another and with God, let's keep humility in our wardrobe and wear it all the time. It never goes out of style.

2 Peter

Day 228, 2 Peter 1

The word "supplement" reminds me of some product from a health food store, a vitamin or mineral that's supposed to enhance my diet. Or maybe the supplement you have in mind is the clump of advertising material inside the Sunday newspaper. Perhaps you read it as a verb because you have taken a part-time job to supplement your income. The noun describes something that goes along with or in addition to something else. The verb means to augment or to increase what is already present.

God's power meets our needs, and his promises enable us to escape the defilement of the world and become like him. Because these things are true, we're supposed to supplement our faith with virtue, or moral excellence. To that, we should add knowledge, self-control and steadfastness. Godliness, brotherly affection and love should also be added to those qualities. Maybe you've heard this list described as "the Christian graces." Why is it important to supplement our faith with these qualities?

First, Peter said these things will keep you from being ineffective and unproductive as a disciple of Jesus. We have little use for a product that doesn't work or a fruit tree that produces no fruit. Jesus said God is glorified and our discipleship is verified when we bear lots of fruit. But a useless, idle Christian doesn't glorify God or show any evidence of the Spirit's influence on his life.

Peter also said if we lack these qualities we are blind and forgetful, unable to remember the cleansing from sin we received when we came to Christ. We were dependent on grace then, and we still are. The smug, self-satisfied Christian who will not grow has forgotten how much he needed and still needs the Lord. So Peter advised diligence in these matters, to keep us from falling. We're not saving ourselves by making diligent effort. Instead, we're expressing our trust and learning to be more like our Master.

Teachers who tell us of our duty to grow and bear fruit for the Lord are doing us a favor by such reminders. Instead of seeing them as meddlers or accusing them of not trusting grace, we should be thankful for faithful messengers from God who keep us from forgetting our duty and calling. As we supplement our precious faith with these graces, we're enhancing our own spiritual development and securing our firm standing in the Lord. Let's never resent encouragement to grow. Instead, let's welcome the reminders that help keep us on course for the big "welcome home" that's ahead.

Day 229, 2 Peter 2

Anyone who's walked down the street in a big city has probably been approached by someone offering an expensive watch or handbag for a very low price. Most folks know the items are knock-offs—inferior copies of the genuine brand-name goods.

Satan is a master knock-off salesman. He offers worthless substitutes for the real blessings God gives. He tries to pass off selfishness as significance, lust as love and a lie as the truth. Satan's strategy has not changed since Eden—if he can get us to believe the lie, he can turn us away from God.

From the beginning, there have been lying prophets and false teachers alongside God's true messengers. Peter warned about the false teachers who would bring destructive heresies among the Christians. Their goal is deception; their destiny is destruction. Their motive is greed; their method is sensuality. Time and place change, but the basic pattern never does.

Heresy has to be introduced by deception. No rational person would knowingly embrace a destructive, toxic doctrine. The false teacher has forsaken the right way, and speaks against the truth. False teachers promise freedom, but their promises are empty since they themselves are enslaved. Their words are dry springs and clouds without rain. Beware of teaching that comes in the form of a dark secret. That is not how God has chosen to reveal his word.

Greed drives the false teachers' words and actions. Greedy for material gain, they exploit and entice to get what they want from the people they deceive. They have a misguided sense of value. Their skewed perspective indicates they have bought into the lies they were told before they started telling them. We are not talking about someone who is honestly mistaken about some point of doctrine. (Who dares insist that their understanding of all matters is perfect?) These false teachers are telling lies for what they can get out of the people they deceive.

False teachers often make their appeal through base sensuality and passion. With an insatiable appetite for sinful pleasure, they entice and ensnare unwitting people through fleshly desires. Passion and desire are God-given gifts, but the counterfeiter perverts them into curses by misdirecting them toward inappropriate, unlawful expressions. We're not surprised that the adversary uses some of the most powerful drives within human beings to further his ungodly agenda.

As Peter exposed the false teachers' mode of operation, he also described their fate: judgment, condemnation and destruction. He assured the Christians that God could sort out the righteous and save them, while punishing the evil ones. Appealing to well-known examples, he stressed that God does not spare the wicked, but always delivers the righteous.

We can rejoice in the truth, light and blessing we know and enjoy in Christ. But we need to be on guard, remembering Satan will do his best to sell us lies, darkness and curses. Don't fall for it.

Day 230, 2 Peter 3

Are you forgetful? I admit that I am. I do not resent a kind reminder from my wife about what to pick up at the store, or a call from the dentist telling me my appointment is the following day. If a gentle reminder irritates you, your memory must be much better than mine.

Peter wanted his readers to remember some things that would help them as they lived for the Lord and waited for his return. He reminded them that God's word is powerful and sure. The Lord said he was coming again and when he does, the world as we know it will come to an end. Scoffers would question what was taking so long, point out that everything was the same as it had always been and insinuate that Jesus wasn't really coming again. Peter said the same word that formed the world and destroyed it by water once before had decreed a final destruction by fire was coming. The scoffers deliberately overlooked the first destruction and doubted the coming one. But God's word is still sure. No skeptic or unbeliever can thwart the plan.

Peter also reminded his readers that God's patience is long, but limited. The Lord was waiting for people to repent, but the day was coming when it would be too late. God is not bound by our model of time, and should not be accused of not keeping his promise when we think he's late. The Lord's patience means salvation for some who will repent while he is waiting to carry out the plan for the end. So we are supposed to wait patiently, too, never doubting what he has promised will come to pass.

Finally, Peter reminded his readers that God's people are supposed to be pure, at peace and making progress. Knowing Jesus is coming, we live holy lives, so that when he comes he will find us unblemished by sin and at peace among ourselves. Our spiritual condition is not frozen in some static state. Instead, our lives should be marked by growth in grace and knowledge. We must not be satisfied to have no more knowledge or spiritual strength than we had a year or a decade ago.

If I forget to buy milk, it's not such a big tragedy. I can always reschedule a dentist appointment. But if I forget these things about God's word and his patience and what kind of person I'm supposed to be, the results could be disastrous. I'm glad Peter reminded us about these important matters.

1 John

Day 231, 1 John 1

Imagine living and walking with Jesus, seeing the miracles and hearing the teaching in person. Imagine being an eyewitness to the crucifixion and the resurrection. Imagine hearing the commission and being there in Jerusalem when it all began.

John had all those experiences and memories. Late in the first century, he is probably the only surviving apostle, writing to new generations of believers to ground them in the truth and firmly establish the core of the gospel. John's eyewitness testimony was essential to expose the heresy of some teachers who were already denying Jesus' deity. He insisted our lives must agree with the doctrine we profess, and that a claim of knowing God and having fellowship with him must be supported by love and obedience. He wrote so we could enjoy fellowship with God, but warned that the relationship was not genuine if our lives did not pass certain tests.

The absolute light of God's holiness cannot be compromised by fellowship with the darkness of sin. John boldly wrote that we are liars if we claim to have fellowship with God, but walk in darkness. We are sinful (John said we're lying if we deny it), but the blood of Jesus Christ cleanses us as we confess our sinfulness and enables us to have fellowship with God and his people. The first test of our authenticity is stated in broad terms: Would the trend and pattern of our conduct generally be considered to be what is right? If that's not the case, then John said our claim of fellowship with God is a lie.

Remember John's purpose and joy was to include more and more people in the fellowship. But that number cannot be inflated by compromising God's holiness. All who are in the fellowship are sinners who need the cleansing blood of Christ, but that blessing is for those who will confess sin, turn from it and walk in the light. As much as God desires our fellowship and as much as Jesus did to make it possible, we disqualify ourselves from the fellowship when the pattern of our life is willful rebellion and prideful denial.

Day 232, 1 John 2

How can someone who claims to know God live like the devil? John's simple answer would be, "They can't. People who claim to know God are liars if they don't live in obedience to God."

When John talked about knowing God, he was not referring to familiarity with a collection of facts about God. He meant much more—that God's people have a relationship with him. Knowing God is synonymous with abiding in God. It's also the same as walking in light. In each case, the descriptive phrase gives a word picture of having a relationship with the Father. Keeping his commandments (also described as walking as he walked) is evidence of the reality of the relationship. The obedience is not the basis of the relationship; that was accomplished by Jesus' sacrifice for us. Rather the obedience is an indication that the claimed relationship is genuine.

Our knowledge of God, our standing in him and abiding in the light is also attested or denied by our relationships with one another. John said those who hate their brothers are still in the dark, regardless of what they say about being in the light. He stressed the truth of this to every generation of Jesus' followers, like a patriarch addressing his children and grandchildren.

Another test of our love for God is whether or not we love the world and the things of the world. This is not about loving our home planet, or the people who inhabit it. The world is the rebellious, fallen creation that is against God and the things of heaven and eternity. It is anti-God and anti-eternal life. It is about gratification of selfish desires, and living for here and now. We show our love for God by being separated from this world in our devotion to the Savior.

Abiding in Christ is the secret to living strong in the face of lies and errors that contradict our confession. The secret of abiding in Christ is abiding or living in what we have been taught about him. We can be confident as we anticipate his return because we know his righteousness and practice righteousness in our lives. Our confession is much more than verbal. We verify our claim by living like he teaches us to live.

Day 233, 1 John 3

1 John frustrates students who want to apply classic outline structure to everything they read. This little book is not linear. It does not progress through a logical argument like Romans or deal with a clear list of subjects like some of the other epistles. No, John's first epistle is almost more like a poem or musical composition with recurring themes than a formal document. New ideas seem to spiral out from the core, and interweave with previously introduced threads all the way through.

One recurring theme in the epistle is the behavior that accompanies a genuine profession of faith in Christ. In this portion, John flatly declares that one who makes a practice of sinning is not abiding in Christ, and has neither seen nor known him. The one who practices righteousness is righteous and born of God. The one who makes a practice of sinning is of the devil.

The verb tense indicating continuing, ongoing action is important. This is about the trend and pattern of life, not the exception or the struggle. Every disciple's ship would crash on the rocks of failure and despair if these lines actually said what some versions have made them say—that no one born of God sins, period. The counterfeit Christian who says he believes in Christ, but does not do what he says is only deceiving himself. Our conduct is evidence to ourselves and others that we are born of God (or not), and that we are abiding in him (or not).

This verification comes, not so much in heroic exploits as in daily demonstrations of our love for one another. John said our love for each other is evidence we have passed from death and darkness to life and light. When we go beyond talking about loving one another to living it out in practical ways, we are assured in our own hearts of our authenticity as disciples. While we try to fathom God's love for us, we ought to be imitating it. Claiming to know, believe in and belong to Christ is a lie apart from a life of purity, obedience and love. John assured us that we will see Jesus one day, even though we don't yet know all about it. But in the meantime, it's pretty clear how those who are going to see him should be living.

Day 234, 1 John 4

I stopped by the store to pick up a couple of items the other day. At the checkout, the total was $2.18. I only had a twenty dollar bill, so I handed it over. (Have you noticed once you break a twenty, the rest of it seems to leak out of your wallet?) The cashier, who knew me and should not have suspected me to be a counterfeiter, followed store policy. She took out her magic pen and made a mark on the bill. When nothing showed up, she gave me my change. The pen contains an iodine solution that does not leave a mark on the cotton fibers in good bills, but will stain the wood fiber in a counterfeit printed on regular paper. It's a quick, easy way to test currency.

John gave a couple of tests that are like the bill-testing pen—simple tests with obvious results. One is about the validity of doctrine; the other is about the genuineness of one's relationship with God. Both tests produce clearly visible results.

When John warned that not all spirits were from God and therefore should be tested, he gave a simple guideline to follow: every spirit that confesses Jesus Christ has come in the flesh is from God, and every spirit that does not confess him is not from God. There may be other, finer points of doctrine that determine whether or not a person is accurately, faithfully teaching God's word, but John said this test quickly sorts out the blatantly counterfeit spirits. Teachers who deny Jesus is the Son of God are false teachers. John confidently asserted that he and the other apostles were from God, and whoever knows God listens to them. The false teachers are from the world, and the world listens to them.

How could there be a practical test with clearly discernible results for a thing as nebulous as one's relationship with God? Again, John gave the quick test: whoever loves is born of God and knows God, but whoever does not love does not know God. The "wood fiber" of the counterfeit Christian is revealed when hatred instead of love shows up in his words and actions. If such a person says he loves God, but hates his brother, John said he's a liar. If we don't love the ones we have seen, we can't love the one we haven't seen. It's easy to make the claim about the vertical axis of our relationship with God, but the horizontal axis of our relationship with brothers and sisters must agree with that claim.

While we're busy "marking" others to check their authenticity, it would be good to check ourselves, too. When a doctrine or a disciple is false at the core, it doesn't matter how elaborate the counterfeiting techniques may be.

Day 235, 1 John 5

In a world of unknown and uncertain, God's children have been assured they do know some things and can be certain of them. In this portion, John wrote again and again, "We know..." and "This is...." Will you join me for a closer look at these affirmations and declarations? This exercise should build our confidence in the core matters of the Christian faith.

John said we can know we love God's children when we love and obey God. He said he wrote these things to us so we can know we have eternal life. We know he hears and answers our prayers. We know one born of God does not persist in sin, but is protected by Christ himself from the evil one. He ended the book with a volley of knowledge: we know we are from God, the world lies in wickedness. The Son of God has come so we can understand who is true and know we are in him. Against all falsehood and evil, we have strength and confidence to overcome through what we know.

John declared that loving God is keeping his commandments, and the victory that overcomes the world is our faith. He cited the triple witness of the Spirit, the water and the blood to affirm Jesus is the Christ. He testified that God has given us eternal life in his Son. He expressed confidence that God hears our prayers and answers them.

Finally, John said Jesus Christ is the true God and eternal life. He cautioned us to keep ourselves from idols, because we already know the true God.

Do these things seem elementary to you? It is as if John is distilling the very essence of our faith, describing the basic building blocks of a life under the lordship of Jesus Christ. And yet in a way, that is characteristic not only of John but all of Scripture. Even the fundamental principles are deeply profound. We embrace them with joy and confidence, but hold them with reverent wonder. These are matters to accept on faith and ponder for a lifetime.

2 John

This epistle reminds us that most books of the New Testament were originally letters, written to groups and sometimes to individuals. They were penned to teach, encourage, strengthen and warn young disciples as they lived out their faith in Christ. When the entire document fits on a single page and has the traditional trappings of a personal note (address, greeting, a single message in the central paragraph and a closing), it's easy to see this little book of the Bible was a letter.

2 John is a condensed version of the longer epistle we know as 1 John. The shorter one is addressed to a woman and her family. Most of the thematic elements of the longer work are here—abiding, loving, walking, faith, obedience, the Incarnation, the antichrist. But there's special instruction in this short letter about applying all those themes to a particular facet of everyday life.

Hospitality is a natural expression of the love we're supposed to have for one another. Those of us who've been far from home on mission trips know how precious a warm welcome and a good meal can be in an alien culture. In the world of the first century church, safe lodging was particularly important to traveling teachers as they went from city to city carrying the gospel and strengthening disciples. But deceivers were on the road, too, denying the essence of the gospel in their heretical teaching. The loving hospitality of Christians could inadvertently enable and encourage the antichrist, giving the false teachers inroads into the churches through the kindness of Christian homes. So John warned this family not to receive and welcome those who were not abiding in the truth about Christ.

It's sad that this passage has become a proof text to justify hateful mistreatment of people with whom we may have some disagreement. Alleged Christians who misuse John's words as a license to be unkind usually apply the phrase, "the teaching of Christ" to some distinctive of their interpretation or practice. Such a difference in no way threatens the core message that Jesus is the Christ, the incarnate Son of God. Have you noticed religionists who make long lists of what constitutes "the teaching of Christ" are often the ones who aren't abiding in it? It's wrong to make my tradition or homiletic equal to the teaching of Christ. Much of the division that has wounded and scarred the body of Christ has come from elevating personal opinion to the level of clear revelation.

John was adamant about walking in the truth and walking in love. But he was also adamant about knowing the enemy and doing nothing to aid his wicked, Christ-denying agenda. It's not always easy to be balanced about these matters. But there's no contradiction or compromise in doing all the things John called us to do.

3 John

Day 237, 3 John

Most people I know want to be happy. Wouldn't you choose a life overflowing with joy instead of one mired in misery? What does such a life look like to you? How would you describe the ultimate joy of your life?

John had an answer for that one. I'm not too surprised he didn't mention a new chariot or a new robe. The old apostle had lived a long time and knew his Master was right—joy and fulfillment aren't tied to material possessions. I wouldn't expect John to find his joy in a powerful position or celebrity—Jesus had taught him that humility was the way to greatness. No, John found his greatest joy in hearing that "his children" walked in truth. The generations of disciples who had come to Jesus Christ through his faithful testimony and were now living changed lives brought John great joy.

As a parent, I can think of nothing more rewarding than knowing my precious children live for the Lord Jesus. It thrills me to know they use their talents and gifts to serve him. I'm glad they love the Lord more than anything in the world, and show his love to others. I hope they will be successful, and their happiness will make me happy. But nothing matters more than their walking in the truth. As a preacher, it's rewarding to hear that my work has had a positive impact on people's spiritual lives. I agree with John; there is no greater joy. No possession, no position means as much for all eternity as knowing that "my children" walk in the truth.

John commended Gaius for his faithfulness in showing hospitality to the traveling evangelists. By his kindness, he became a fellow worker in their efforts. Not everyone shared Gaius' heart for the missionaries. Selfish Diotrophes refused to welcome the saints or allow others to serve them. People in the first century church were very much like people today. Maybe you've known a bully in the church who insisted on his or her way, excommunicating those who dared disagree with them and overruling even the apostles. John promised to deal with such abusive arrogance when he arrived, and encouraged Gaius to be discriminating in choosing examples to follow. We need to imitate the good examples of Gaius and Demetrius, and trust the Lord to take care of the self-appointed dictators who try to control the church.

Have you read those lines near the end of this little letter, as if John were telling you across the centuries that he hoped to see you soon, and talk to you face to face? That's the hope of all the redeemed in Christ throughout the ages. Someday we will see John and the rest of our heroes of faith. And we will know the ultimate joy when we, with them, see our Savior, face to face.

Jude

Day 238, Jude

As followers of Jesus, we celebrate our salvation, and rightly so. We have been called by God who loves us so much that he gave his Son for us. We are kept securely by the grace and power of God. Seeking his mercy and trusting his grace, we devote ourselves to the Lord, and seek to share the good news of salvation in Christ with as many as possible.

Because God's holiness and justice are as infinite as his love, judgment of the rebellious wicked is inevitable. Those who pervert grace into a license for sensuality and deny the lordship of Jesus will not escape God's righteous judgment. The faithless Exodus generation of Israel, the rebellious angels, Sodom and Gomorrah—the Biblical record has many examples of God's wrath and judgment against the disobedient.

Jude warned his readers that those who pervert grace would suffer the same fate. In their blasphemous anarchy, they imitate Cain, Balaam and Korah, infamous rebels of the Old Testament. Yes, the gospel offers salvation to those who will turn from sin and obey Christ. But it also promises wrath to rebels who reject the offer and persist in ungodliness.

As a disciple of Jesus, don't be discouraged that such people are found in the church. The apostles predicted there would be counterfeits among the converted. Faithful disciples commit themselves to the Lord, discipline themselves and trust in his mercy. They rescue as many as possible, showing the same mercy they have received from the Lord to people around them who are struggling.

What's our takeaway from this little book? Let's remember God has never been conned. He is loving and kind and wants to save people who will humble themselves and turn to him. If that's you,

you need not fear. Keep yourself in the love of the one who will keep you secure and give you eternal life. Do not fret about the people who are making a mockery of following Jesus by talking about grace while indulging their flesh. God knows what they're doing, and he will deal with them. If you've imagined slipping by with lip service instead of life transformation, you need to realize it won't work, and repent.

The salvation is too wonderful to describe. The judgment is too terrible to contemplate. Both are guaranteed by the same unfailing faithfulness of God.

Revelation

Day 239, Revelation 1

It had been decades, but the memories were still clear. Old John remembered seeing Jesus, walking beside the lake at the beginning, and later, on the lake with the same ease. John had seen food multiplied, storms calmed, diseases healed and demons dispatched by Jesus' words. He was there on more than one occasion when death gave back one already taken into its grip. He heard Jesus teach. John walked beside Jesus, saw him transfigured, watched him die and looked with wonder into an empty tomb. He had seen the risen Lord and gazed as Jesus ascended into heaven. But nothing John had seen or heard could compare with what happened that day on Patmos, when he heard the voice and turned around to see who had spoken to him.

John saw a man in a long robe with a golden sash, standing among seven lampstands. Can you picture him—the flaming eyes, the snow-white hair, a double-edged sword coming from his mouth, his voice roaring like mighty waters and his face shining like the sun? John collapsed under the strain of the magnificent vision. But then a familiar hand was on him and the voice that had roused him from fitful sleep in Gethsemane so long ago told him, "Fear not."

It was Jesus, whom he had served and about whom he had testified for so many years. Now exiled for his testimony, John was privileged to see and hear his Master say he was alive forever, the first and the last, with all authority over Death and Hades. Jesus told John to write it all down, explaining that he was among his churches and he held their messengers in his hand.

From John's opening lines, we know this book is like no other in the New Testament. Through symbols and images, John wrote to the seven churches in Asia to encourage them in tribulation and to certify their victory in Christ. He showed them a great, big, victorious God and assured them everything was under his control. Instead of terrifying or mystifying the churches, John's purpose was to tell them things that would sustain and fortify them in persecution.

As we read the Revelation, it's good to remember all God has done for us, all Jesus has endured and overcome and all the promises God's Spirit has spoken through his word. Let's read with awe, but not terror. Let's savor the mystery without losing our confidence. That's why we have a book like Revelation.

Day 240, Revelation 2

Can you imagine what Jesus would say to the church today if he came to speak in person or sent a letter to a specific congregation? It's crossed my mind, usually when I'm pondering if we're on the right track, if we're actually doing what he wants done, emphasizing what he would say mattered most. Because the Lord is unchanging and people around the world and through the ages are very much alike, he might say some of the same things to us he said to the churches in Revelation.

I'm confident Jesus would tell us, "I know your works," because he absolutely does know. He knows about our labors and our patience, our tribulations and faithfulness, our love and service. When we're tempted to think no one knows or notices what we do for the Lord, never forget that he knows.

I'm also sure Jesus would tell us about the things he has against us. Some of us have left our first love, chosen sensuality over spirituality and tolerated false teachers who have led us astray. He would tell us these things, not because he does not love us, but because he does. He would urge us to repent just as he urged them to do, and warn us about the bitter consequences of not turning back to him.

And surely Jesus would give each church a word of encouragement and promise. To the overcomers, he would promise the tree of life, the crown of life, the hidden manna, the white stone and the morning star. It's the gift of himself and the reward of eternal fellowship with him that he holds out to his precious, persecuted saints.

Finally, after telling us exactly what we need to hear to motivate us to keep doing right and stop doing wrong, I imagine Jesus would remind us to listen. Hearing the Spirit's word is more than the sound waves striking our eardrums; it's responding to the word of the Lord by aligning our lives with his will for us. Through the Old Testament prophets, God said again and again, "Listen to me." During his personal ministry Jesus told his disciples as well as his enemies, "Listen to what I'm saying." We are blessed to know his will as he revealed it in his word. Do we have ears? Are we hearing what Jesus said to the churches?

Day 241, Revelation 3

The ability to see ourselves clearly is important in any sphere of life. You and I have blind spots that prevent accurate personal assessment of our strengths and weaknesses. The world's most successful athletes have trainers who scrutinize their performance and help them maximize their potential. World leaders and top business executives rely on trusted advisors to critique their speeches and plans because they realize the limitations of personal evaluation.

Jesus told one church they were dead, even though they had a reputation for being alive. He exhorted them to wake up and strengthen their incomplete works. If we've followed Jesus for some time, we may be tempted to relax and rely on our reputation instead of carefully monitoring our present spiritual condition. If we've forgotten what God told us, we need to remember. If we've stopped doing what he told us to do, we need to repent.

Jesus told another church he had set open doors before them, knew their limited power and guaranteed to keep them in the hour of trial. Remembering the source of our strength for doing what we're supposed to do is an important part of this self-analysis. It's one thing to realize we're not able in and of ourselves to meet the opportunities set before us. It's quite another to realize that the one who creates the opportunities also enables us to go through the doors he puts in our paths, strengthening us to achieve and succeed. God is in control of the situation, and no adversary is able to overrule his arrangements.

This plan creates a healthy blend of confidence and humility—we know we can win, but not by our own power or cleverness.

When we lose that balance, we may crash into despair or become prideful. The last church Jesus addressed had erred on the side of pride. They believed they were doing fine and had no need of anything. But Jesus said they were wretched, pitiable, poor, blind and naked. He offered to meet their needs, but they had to humble themselves and see themselves as they really were before they would respond to his offer.

The Lord didn't offer these insights into the true condition of these churches because he despised them. His reproved and rebuked them because he loved them. He described himself as standing at the door knocking, seeking admission and fellowship to those who are willing to hear and open the door to let him in.

You've probably seen William Holman Hunt's painting, "The Light of The World," based on these words. In the painting, Jesus is knocking on a closed door with no outside knob, seeking to bring his light into the darkened room behind the door. It may be easier to debate the allegorical significance of every detail of the painting than to acknowledge it depicts a scene that plays out at the door of every heart. Have you heard the knock? Have you opened the door?

Day 242, Revelation 4

A friend of mine tells about a time when he told a counselor, "My life is out of control!" The counselor, who was wise and godly, told my friend, "It's good you can recognize and admit that! When you stop trying to control it, and turn it over to God, he can do something with it."

Do you sometimes feel like your life is out of control? Maybe you've been through a season of adversity when it seemed you had no control over what was happening. We learn from an early age about authority and who's in charge. At home, at school, at work—we live under authority, answering to someone who is in control.

I don't know the significance of all the signs and images in this highly symbolic book. I'm a little wary of people who emphatically claim they do know. But I do find phrases that encourage me, give me hope and strengthen my faith. One such phrase is in this portion, where John says "a throne stood in heaven, with one seated on the throne."

Persecuted Christians through the ages have found comfort in these words, especially when they suffered at the hands of abusive authority. The first readers certainly knew that experience, as people still do today in places where Christians still suffer and even die for their confession of Christ. Imagine the encouragement of reading that the throne, the seat of ultimate power in the universe, is in heaven and occupied by the holy, Almighty Lord.

If you're blessed to live in a place where the authorities protect your right to follow Jesus, rejoice in that blessing and give thanks. But remember your brothers and sisters who are subject to arrest, torture and execution for nothing more than believing in Jesus. Pray for them, and allow their courage to motivate you to see God on the throne.

Trust that God is on the throne when it seems wrong is prevailing and the wicked are getting ahead. If you're pacing and wringing your hands about matters beyond your control, imagine the Lord on his throne. He's not pacing up and down or wringing his hands; he's in charge.

When you're tempted to do it your own way and disregard God's will for your life, remember who's sitting on the throne in heaven. Is he also sitting on the throne in your heart? We should fall down and worship in awe, creatures before the Creator's throne.

Day 243, Revelation 5

From the opening lines of Revelation, we know we're reading a book that is different from almost everything else in the Bible. Revelation is written in a style the scholars call apocalyptic literature. Numbers, colors and symbols have special, code-like significance. The imagery is vivid, the scale is large. The original readers were far more familiar with this type of literature than we are today. But some of the symbolism is clear to us if we have even a general knowledge of the story line of Scripture.

When John saw the Lamb who was worthy to open the scroll, he was completing a thread of imagery that is woven throughout the Bible. In Genesis, Abel's offering that pleased God marks the beginning of the lamb motif. Also in Genesis, Abraham's answer to Isaac's question about the sacrifice is a miniature gospel: "God will provide a lamb." The Passover lamb in Exodus and Isaiah's description of Messiah as a "lamb led to the slaughter" contribute threads to the story line as it passes through the Old Testament.

In the New Testament, when John the Baptist saw Jesus approaching, he identified him as "the Lamb of God, who takes away the sins of the world." When a traveling Ethiopian treasurer was reading the Isaiah passage about the lamb, Philip began at that very text and told him about Jesus. Paul called Christ our Passover sacrificed for us. Peter said we were redeemed by the blood of Christ as of a Lamb without blemish. And here, near the end, John sees the Lamb, slain but very much alive, about to take the scroll and unfold the whole story! The hosts of heaven fall down and worship before this Lamb, proclaiming him to be worthy and celebrating their redemption by his blood. It's a grand crescendo of this Bible-wide theme.

This is more than God's plan to redeem humanity in general. It is his plan to redeem you. The blood of the Lamb of God was sacrificed for your sins. He wants you to be among the throng before the throne praising his Son for redemption. The gospel invitation is universal, but your response to it is individual. The myriads of heavenly worshippers are composed of a staggering number of individuals, but God knows, loves and gave his Son for you personally so you can be in that number.

Day 244, Revelation 6

Even without a guide to apocalyptic code, we know there's something ominous about all those horses riding out as the seals are broken. Conquest, warfare, famine and death are accompanied by cries from souls of martyrs, earthquakes and falling stars. These images all suggest a general state of mayhem and disruption of order, even if commentators can't all agree on exactly what the symbols stand for.

The cry coming from beneath the altar grabs my attention. The souls of those who have been slain for the word of God and for the witness they had borne are crying out to God, and their cry is in the form of a question: "How long?" Could the first readers, under attack from fierce adversaries, relate to such a question? Almost certainly they would have personal knowledge of such martyrs—people from their families and churches who had already been killed for the cause of Christ.

Note how the question is addressed: "O Sovereign Lord." They knew God was in control. They believed that God saw their distress, and heard their cries. They knew he was both "holy and true." They staked their confidence in what they knew of his character. And they asked in a loud voice, "How long?" They wondered how long it would be until God would judge and take vengeance on their murderers.

The crying martyrs were not destroyed or even rebuked for asking a question of God. The shame of their mistreatment at the hands of the enemies was covered with a white robe. They were told to rest until the number was completed that would bring the full wrath of God on their killers.

What strain, pressure and suffering has your confession of Christ brought to your life? I urge you to hold onto your confidence that God is in control, regardless of the adversity you may face for serving him. Don't be afraid to ask how long it's going to go on. And trust that whatever God allows is just that—allowed, and wait for him to bring good out of every situation and use it to accomplish his divine purpose.

Day 245, Revelation 7

Angels who hold back the four winds and seal God's servants on their foreheads are fascinating parts of John's vision. So also are the mystical 144,000 composed of 12,000 from each of the 12 tribes of ancient Israel. Even more interesting to me are the innumerable worshippers standing before the throne, whose robes had been washed white in the blood of the Lamb. But what really grabs my attention in this portion is this phrase: "For the Lamb in the midst of the throne will be their shepherd...." In the person of the crucified and risen Jesus, two powerful images converge in beautiful irony.

I'm sure you know "The Lord is my shepherd" from Psalms. You probably also remember Jesus saying he was the Good Shepherd who would lay down his life for the sheep. But who would have imagined that the Shepherd would be the Lamb as well? One in the same, he washes us with his own blood to purify us and bring us to the throne of God. He shelters us, provides for us and guides us to the springs of living water.

The throng is multi-national, multi-cultural and multi-lingual. It's also a loud crowd, waving palm branches and crying out, "Salvation belongs to our God, who sits on the throne, and to the Lamb!" They ascribe blessing, glory, wisdom, thanksgiving, honor and power to God. There is no debate about whether they could have come on their own. They could not. Without the Lamb's blood, they could not come near. Without his shepherding grace, they would not know the satisfaction and comfort that comes from serving him, having every need met and every tear wiped away.

I may not know all about the angels who have the power to hurt the earth. The elders and the living creatures are mysterious. But I do know I want to be in that uncountable number, washed in the blood of the Lamb, worshipping before the throne of God. Membership in any other group is meaningless if I'm not in this one. Are you determined to be in the innumerable throng, worshipping the Shepherd Lamb?

Day 246, Revelation 8

Does prayer make any difference? Does it change anything? Before the sounding trumpets brought death and destruction, John saw an angel offering the prayers of the saints with incense that rose in smoke before God's throne. When the angel took the fire from the altar and threw it on the earth, the sights and sounds of approaching wrath began.

From the crucible of persecution, the faithful followers of Jesus Christ had been calling out to God. They held onto their faith, and waited for the Lord they believed to be sovereign over all circumstances to act on their behalf. The response of the faithful to the approaching calamity would be quite different from that of the unbelievers. The destruction of the enemies would be the deliverance of the saints. God did not choose to intervene before many suffered and died for their faith, but his intervention was certain. Those who suffered loss, even of life, for his sake were secure and safe with him.

Language seems to strain under the weight of conveying the reality of the spiritual realm to those of us who are living in flesh bodies in a material world. But even if we're unsure of the specifics, we get the general picture being painted. God's people are safe and secure. God's enemies are in really big trouble. This message should instill courage and confidence in those washed in the Lamb's blood and living under his shepherding. It should strike fear into the hearts of those who have resisted and rejected him.

Our prayers confessing dependence and reliance upon God are like sweet incense in heaven's throne room. God is not bothered by his children's prayers any more than a pleasant aroma annoys us. Conversely, I wonder if our complaints are like some unpleasant odor, and if our ingratitude and prayerless lives rob the Lord of glory and pleasure he is due. Is the angel's bowl of incense prayers more full because of your prayer life?

Day 247, Revelation 9

Parents of a strong-willed child know the frustration of being unable, despite one's best effort, to change another person's unacceptable behavior. Judges and officers of the law know it, too, with repeat offenders who continue to commit crimes, even after they've been to prison. When they're deemed incorrigible, they are sentenced to life without parole. It's sad to see anyone who will not listen to authority and learn from unpleasant consequences.

This portion is brimful of awful images, symbolic representations of the wrath of God being poured out on the disobedient. At the fifth trumpet, an angel opens the bottomless pit. Smoke darkens the sun and the air, and from the pit come ferocious locusts/scorpions/horses led by one whose name means Destroyer. They torment the people so that their victims wish to die, but cannot. Then horses with fire, smoke and sulfur coming from their mouths are released to kill one-third of the population.

Without knowing with certainty the exact meaning of the symbolic pictures, we could imagine the survivors of such terrible calamity would be eager to change their ways and show respect for God. But the wonder of it is that after all the suffering and terror, the rest of the people John saw in the vision did not change. They would not turn from worshipping the idols they had made. They were unwilling to repent of murder, sorcery, immorality and theft. Despite warning, suffering and witnessing such destruction, they were incorrigible.

Paul said in Romans that God's kindness is meant to lead us to repentance. When kind patience does not work, corrective discipline is applied. When we persist in rebellion and disobedience, even after suffering rough consequences for our sinful behavior, we're like these impenitent ones who would not let go of their idols or change their ways.

Somewhere along the way, unruly children, hardened criminals and unrepentant sinners have to learn a hard lesson. It's better to learn and yield before our stubbornness destroys us.

Day 248, Revelation 10

Sometimes a sound will reverberate in a canyon or even in a big room for several seconds, the sound waves bouncing off surfaces and returning. A single "hello" may be answered by a chorus of "hellos" echoing back.

This portion has the literary equivalent of echoes in it. John's words echo, not the actual voices of the prophets, but their themes and experiences. Ezekiel, Amos, Joel, Daniel and Jeremiah are all here. The mighty angel's appearance, the roar of his voice, the prohibition to record what the thunders said, the trumpet sounds and eating the scroll—they're all echoes. They remind us of things God had done and spoken through Israel's prophets long before John experienced the revelation on Patmos.

We need to learn and remember some important lessons from this text about God's communication with humans. First, while he has told us what we need to know, God hasn't told us everything we might be curious about or everything there is to know. The seven thunders said something John heard, but was told not to write. That reminds me of Moses telling Israel the secret things belonged to God, or Paul hearing things he was forbidden to repeat when he was called up into paradise. The very nature of an infinite God suggests there is much beyond our realm and grasp he has not revealed.

When the angel swore by the Creator that what he had announced to the prophets would come to pass, we're reminded of the faithfulness and certainty of God's word. We're used to broken vows, unkept promises and idle threats in our experience with one another, but God will absolutely and completely do what he says. That's a great source of joy and comfort for people who trust and obey him, but an ominous threat to those who persist in rebellion.

When John ate the little scroll, he found it to be just as the voice from heaven had promised—sweet in his mouth but bitter in his stomach. John found the word of God pleasant, but there were unpleasant aspects of its message, too. It was a privilege and honor to speak God's words, but some of the things he had to say were very difficult. Just as the gospel reveals both the righteousness and wrath of God, and just as it is the aroma of life to some and death to others, John found the little scroll to be both sweet and bitter.

Let's never take for granted the privilege of being able to know what God has revealed. I hope you share my confidence that his word is trustworthy and reliable. If you and I respond to the word, we too will be heirs of the sweet promises it contains.

Day 249, Revelation 11

As John's experience on Patmos continued, more echoes from Zechariah, Ezekiel, Isaiah, Jeremiah and Daniel colored the images of his vision and the language he used to describe what he saw. The measuring rod, the time of the Gentiles, the witnesses in sackcloth and the drought and plagues they inflict all come from Old Testament prophecies and history.

That is not to say John took these figures from the existing Scriptures and the account of the revelation is not genuine. Rather, it attests to the apocalyptic nature of this book and the continuity of the prophetic message from the time of the Old Testament prophets.

After the witnesses are killed, raised from the dead and called up into heaven, the voices from heaven shout, "The kingdom of the world has become the kingdom of our Lord and of his Christ, and he shall reign forever and ever." I'd rather you get this message than understand all about the 1,260 days. The symbolic mystery of calling the city where the Lord was crucified "Sodom and Egypt" is a fascinating detail, but please don't miss the big picture by fretting over the intricate details.

The overarching message to the persecuted first recipients (and to us) is that God is firmly in control. He is going to triumph over every foe. Those who are on God's side will share in his triumph. Regardless of how strong the enemies of God may seem to be, his wrath and judgment will bring about their destruction. At the same time, no opponent can thwart the certain reward God promises his faithful servants. That's why the twenty-four elders enthroned before God fall down worshipping him in this passage—the Lord has taken up his power and begun to reign.

God's timetable is inscrutable to us. All the details of his plan are not easy to understand. Our salvation does not depend on understanding them. The cross is at the beginning of our experience as Christians, where Jesus redeemed us from our sins. As we walk in his footsteps we're promised help for each day. John gives us a glimpse out to the end, and reassures us that the Lord will prevail. Our confidence is bolstered by this message and our hope is fixed firmly, not in ourselves, but in him.

Day 250, Revelation 12

The cosmic struggle between the forces of good and evil is very real. Today's portion gives us a compact glimpse of that conflict through a story told with vivid symbols. While we haven't delved into much of the symbolism of the text in previous portions, this passage is so central to the story of the Bible that a word of explanation seems necessary.

Satan is the enemy of God and his people. Since his expulsion from heaven long ago, Satan's violent, destructive rage has been directed at the human family and in particular, the people of God. It seems to me the woman in the story must represent Abraham's physical descendants (Israel) through whom Messiah (the one who would rule the nations with a rod of iron) would come. The dragon (Satan) stood before the woman (Israel) during the time her child was on his way, hoping to devour the one God had said would come to destroy him. Not only can we see in this Herod's murderous plot against the innocents in Bethlehem, but also Haman's plot to exterminate the Jews in Persia, and Pharaoh's designs against Israel in Egypt. After Jesus came, lived, died and rose again to ascend back to God, it seems the woman then represents Abraham's spiritual descendants in Christ (the church). After failing in his attacks on Jesus while the Son was present on earth, the dragon pursued the woman (now the church, spiritual Israel), who fled to a wilderness place to be protected from the dragon's wrath.

Here is the explanation for all the evil and mayhem on earth today. Satan's fingerprints are on every murder weapon, stolen article and abused person. His malevolence drives him to destroy. A torrential flood of evil comes from him like a raging river of water, threatening to sweep away everything in its path. Unable to destroy the infant church, he continues his fight against the offspring who obey God and embrace the testimony about Christ.

Do you wonder why God did not just destroy his enemy instead of allowing him to wreak such havoc on earth? Satan's presence and activity here on earth must somehow serve God's purpose, perhaps in testing men and women about which master they will serve. But we need not wonder about the outcome of the great struggle. Michael and his angels prevailed against Satan in heaven. Jesus overcame Satan by living, dying and being raised from the dead for us. And we who are willing to lay down our lives for the Lord have the promise of overcoming Satan by the blood of the Lamb and the word of our testimony.

Remember, this is a message of encouragement to the church. Satan has been thrown down. No one need suffer defeat because the Lamb has won the victory.

Day 251, Revelation 13

John's first readers faced life-threatening persecution at the hands of powerful enemies. The message from heaven he relayed to them was designed to bolster their faith and fortify their endurance. Believers in every age and place need such encouragement, but especially when the threats are coming from formidable adversaries.

The first beast that rose from the sea seems to be a compilation of the beasts Daniel saw and identified as kingdoms or governments. The Bible says government is ordained by God. But when a government exalts itself against God, it declares war on God's people and uses its might to persecute them. The imagery fits the Roman government late in the first century, but also fits other governments before and after Rome, too.

The second beast that rose from the earth also seems to be an institution, not limited to a single person or group. Could it be false religion? False religion is a dragon in lamb's clothing. It appears to be spiritual, but in reality it turns people away from worshipping God. Cooperating with ungodly government, false religion deceives through counterfeit signs and applies economic pressure to ensure conformity.

John's encouraging words to the saints about all this is that Sovereign God is still in charge. The beasts are "allowed" to do the things they do. Depending on the version you're reading, there are two possible ways to read his words of encouragement. Some translations say those who were appointed to captivity and martyrdom will keep those appointments, as permitted by God for his purposes. Other translations say the captors will become captives and the executioners will be executed. To read it one way is to find encouragement to rest in God's sovereignty; to read it the other brings a promise of retribution. Either way, God's in charge. The dragon and his beastly helpers will not win the battle.

John said wisdom and understanding were required to calculate the beast's number. Some scholars apply symbolic significance from numerology or gematria to interpret the infamous "666." Efforts to identify a specific individual by these methods have produced wildly varied results. If "7" is the number of perfection in apocalyptic literature, perhaps the one identified by this repeated sixes is supposed to be seen as counterfeit, always less than genuine, divine or complete.

Beware of specific conclusions about these ominous figures that require a literal interpretation of something obviously symbolic. It's OK if you can't agree with the ideas I've shared here about the beasts or the number. Don't allow a dogmatic teacher to terrify you about these matters. It's not necessary to get bogged down in the meaning of every horn and crown on the beast. John's original message was, "Here is a call for the endurance and faith of the saints." Don't miss the big picture by fretting over the details.

Day 252, Revelation 14

The gospel divides the human family into two groups. When judgment comes, the division will be certain and permanent. One group will be celebrating with the Lamb who redeemed them. The other group will be in a place of torment, restlessness and banishment from God's presence. John wrote about the coming judgment to encourage the saints. He stressed the reward awaiting them, and assured them that evil would not win the conflict or escape divine wrath.

I've tried to avoid symbol-mongering in these essays. But two figurative descriptions in this passage have been so misunderstood and misapplied that the hope and confidence they were meant to convey has been turned into fear and confusion. I'm thinking of the 144,000 and the marks on the foreheads. Maybe a brief word about each of these matters will be encouraging.

The image of the 144,000 came up a few chapters ago. It is rooted in the symbolic significance of numbers in apocalyptic literature. 12 is a significant Old and New Testament number—the 12 tribes of Israel and the 12 apostles of Christ. 1,000 (the largest practical number in the thinking of many ancient peoples) represented the full extent or totality. In typical apocalyptic math, these factors could be combined: 12 times itself times 1,000, or 144,000. Those who suggest a literal 144,000 are the only ones who will be redeemed or go to heaven remove one detail from this symbolic context and insist it is literal. The passage identifies the group. They knew the song only the redeemed could know. They were pure virgins (spiritually) who had not been defiled by worshipping the false god. They were firstfruits, not in the sense of the first wave of harvest with more to follow, but in the sense of being holy to the Lord.

The redeemed had the Father's name on their foreheads. Remember, we're reading apocalyptic literature, full of symbols. This one seems to suggest bearing God's likeness, having God's character, being loyal to God and belonging to God. That's contrasted to the beast worshippers who had the beast's mark on their foreheads and hands—again a symbolic way of saying these people had the character and conduct of the one to whom they had been loyal. I don't believe the mark of the beast is a literal mark, such as a UPC barcode or your Social Security number as some have alleged.

Remember John's intent. Revelation was not written to terrify the saints, but to assure them, to bolster their confidence and encourage them to remain faithful to God regardless of what happened around them. So he contrasted the victory celebration in heaven with the terrible ruin of the Lamb's enemies. The same gospel that brings salvation to those who accept and respond to it brings condemnation to those who despise and reject it. The same judgment which brings honor and eternal blessings to the Lamb's people brings the wrath of God and eternal punishment to his enemies.

Day 253, Revelation 15

God's patience runs out. Even though he is long-suffering and his great desire is to save his fallen yet beloved race, the time comes when the Lord's patience and sinners' opportunity to turn to him comes to an end.

One of the saddest passages in the Old Testament describes how God sent the prophets to warn and call Israel and Judah to repentance again and again because of his compassion for them. But the nation mocked the messengers and despised God's words until the wrath of the Lord rose against his own people, and the Chronicler concludes, "there was no remedy."

It's also like Jesus weeping over Jerusalem and the Jewish establishment that had rejected him: "How often would I have gathered you...and you would not! See, your house is left to you desolate." Time was up. Only judgment remained.

In today's portion, the message once again assured the redeemed they were safe from God's wrath. They're singing the song of Moses and the Lamb by the sea of glass. But the angels with the seven golden bowls of God's wrath are about to pour out judgment on the impenitent and rebellious. The judgment, already prophesied and foreshadowed, is about to come. What the seals revealed and the trumpets heralded is about to be poured out. The Lord's angels are wearing linen and golden sashes, like the Lord himself wore back in chapter one. The bowls are distributed. The tabernacle is filled with smoke—no more intercession. Judgment has come.

God who is loving and merciful is also righteous and holy. His wrath against evil is necessary because of his strong, pure character. When rebels will not repent, when they reject the sacrifice of the Lamb of God, judgment comes. This sad moment is not reserved only for the end of the world. As we saw, nations have reached that point in history. Individuals may reach that point, too, where their impenitent rebellion is crystallized, and the moment of grace passes, leaving only judgment. Let's make sure we never presume upon God's patience.

Day 254, Revelation 16

Remember Revelation is a highly symbolic and figurative book. By its nature as an apocalypse, the terrifying figures of speech and images about the physical world point beyond a literal interpretation to a spiritual one. The bowls of wrath affect the same components of the world as did the trumpets (but to a greater extent). But it is the spiritual environment, not the literal, physical one that is affected by the outpouring of God's wrath.

The plagues on Egypt in Exodus, the historical accounts of the fall of Rome or the chaos of various revolutions around the world may remind us of some periods of disorder similar to these events. The point seems to be that wrath from God hardens defiantly impenitent people. Even after all the suffering they experienced, the people did not repent. Corruption, pain, ruin and destruction did nothing to humble these people before God. Instead of humbly falling down in surrender and worship, they cursed God who had power over their plagues.

There's no question in the angel's mind that God's judgment against evil is right. The display of God's wrath does not contradict God's character or nature. The angel recognized God as the author of the judgments, and said he was just and holy to judge. The angel said the retribution was what the murderers of the saints and prophets deserved, blood for blood.

Remember what's been said about symbolic versus literal in apocalyptic literature when you come to the word Armageddon. Many students have imagined a literal battle in the literal valley where Israel and her pagan neighbors warred through the centuries. But isn't there much more here? Armageddon means "place of decision." Can you see how the battle is engaged daily, all around the world, in the real "place of decision," the hearts of men and women who must choose to follow either the Lamb or his enemies? And also please remember the Lamb's people are secure and not in danger of whatever the symbols of God's outpoured wrath may mean.

Day 255, Revelation 17

Remember the woman in chapter 12 who seemed to represent the true Israel of God (Israel before Christ came and the church since)? Then the great prostitute here could be a false church. If the real church is the true bride of Christ and the holy city coming down out of heaven a little later on, then this adulterous woman could be the disloyal, unfaithful church who consorts with the Lamb's enemies! This mirrors the symbolism of harlotry and adultery used by the Old Testament prophets to describe unfaithful Israel. Like the woman/church, the prostitute is in a wilderness. Is the wilderness period the time while the church is on earth? That would seem to fit.

The many interpretations, disagreements and theories about what the heads and horns mean do not invalidate the general idea of a false church being symbolized by this scarlet-clad bejeweled woman, drunk on the blood of the saints and martyrs of Jesus. Persecution of true Christians by a false church cooperating with godless government has brought death to many believers through the centuries.

Apart from the mysterious and ominous parts of this vision, there are some clear and encouraging reminders for God's people facing such opposition. First, the great prostitute cannot deceive those whose names have been written in the book of life from the foundation of the world. The earth dwellers who are not in the book will marvel at her, but not the Lamb's people.

Second, whoever all these sinister forces may be and however powerful they may seem in their unholy alliance against the Lamb, they will all be conquered by him. The Lord of Lords and King of Kings will not be defeated by any opponent. John reminded his readers of the Lamb's certain victory and then assured them that those who are with the Lamb are called and chosen and faithful.

The awesome power of God that freed us from sin can preserve us from every threat. Remember, we did not procure our own salvation by deciphering the sin problem. In the same way, our preservation does not depend on unraveling every mysterious symbol of this book. Ponder it, study to enhance your understanding, but do not fret about obscure passages when your hope is grounded in extremely clear ones.

Day 256, Revelation 18

If mystery Babylon is a false church and the ten kings are the godless governments that carry out God's purpose by destroying her, this portion shows the irony of how their actions bring about their own ruin. Their unholy alliance finished, the world's last vestiges of moral restraint go with the prostitute when she goes up in smoke. The economic impact of Babylon's fall brings weeping and destruction to the kings, merchants and laborers who profited from dealing with her. They cry, not because she is gone, but because their profit is lost. The consequences are swift and negative against themselves.

What Jesus predicted about the unnatural growth of the kingdom from mustard seed into a large plant where birds could lodge seems to be the point here. Many different birds were lodging in the branches. Does God have people among the apostate church? Yes, he does, as surely as he had people in wicked Nineveh in Jonah's time and people in wicked Corinth in Paul's time. He called his people out before the destruction was carried out, just as he brought Lot out of Sodom, and Moses out from among the rebels. Judged by God, Babylon's time is up, and God is just for destroying her. Her destruction is final and complete. All the normal sights, sounds and activities of civilization and commerce are no more.

Heaven and the saints, apostles and prophets are told to rejoice in the face of all the destruction. It is not because God's people are happy to see others destroyed, but because they are assured that God is in control, his word is sure and his judgment is just. The Lamb's people do not have to fear the day when God's wrath comes. They are safe and secure with him.

From these words, we can have the same assurance and confidence that God's people through the centuries have had as they faced ruthless persecution from ungodly enemies. Ultimately every enemy will fall, and God's people and purpose will prevail. That's powerful encouragement for persecuted disciples, in the first century or the twenty-first century.

Day 257, Revelation 19

For all the variety that characterizes our world, at the end of history there will be dichotomy, not diversity. On one hand there will be God, his heavenly hosts and the redeemed of the earth; on the other Satan, his minions and those he was able to deceive into rebelling against a loving God and rejecting the gospel that would have saved them.

God is on his throne throughout. Christ is King of Kings and Lord of Lords now. Those titles are not contingent upon the outcome of some battle at the end when he will win them. What weapon, what force could challenge God? The victory was won at the cross and the empty tomb. The imagery of conflict is about the fierce fight being waged within the hearts and minds of all people.

The images cascading through the book of Revelation show the judgment again and again. Satan, persecuting governments and false religion are defeated and sent to everlasting destruction. The redeemed are secure in the presence of the Lamb, washed in his blood and overflowing with worship before him. John heard loud praise to God for his salvation, glory, power and just judgment. There were hallelujahs for God's vengeance against the enemy, for his sovereign reign and for the great reward he has prepared for his people.

The rider of the white horse is called Faithful and True, the Word of God, King of Kings and Lord of Lords. He is infinitely more than we can know or imagine. He has a name no one knows. His eyes pierce the darkness. He has all the crowns. The blood on his robe is his own, shed to redeem his people. The judgment he brings against his enemies is just and sure. He is our hero and Savior.

The culmination of the drama is described as a wedding feast. The church as the bride of Christ has made herself ready for the big event by adorning herself with the wedding garment he has provided. On the other side, there is a horrific image of another feast called the great supper of God, when those who were in league with Satan are carcasses strewn across a battlefield, slain by the mighty sword of the word of God. They have become a feast for the vultures. Meanwhile the beast and false prophet are cast into a lake of fire. Whatever awful reality is symbolized by those images, we want no part of it. We're invited to the wedding as his bride. We've got some singing to do in the heavenly hallelujah chorus.

Day 258, Revelation 20

The repeating cycle describing the judgment over and over again in Revelation is a little like those instant replays used by football officials to see the play from different angles. The event is the same, again and again. But each time, the viewpoint or focus of the description changes. In this last view, the end of Satan is described, and the whole population of the world is gathered before God's great white throne.

The martyrs, faithful saints and all who share in the first resurrection (symbolic for the new spiritual life we have in Christ) live and reign with Christ throughout the final age. Satan is bound, limited through this time. As dominant and destructive as he is, he is limited by the word of God while people are escaping the guilt and condemnation of sin by responding to the gospel. If there is to be a little while at the very end when he is loosed from his bonds, we tremble to think of the terror and ruin he will bring to the human family during that short time.

At last, there is no real battle. In one stroke, fire from heaven consumes the devil and those aligned with him. They are thrown into the lake of fire. We remember the images are symbolic. But still, what a horrific fate must await Satan and his puppets—the godless persecuting government and the counterfeit religion—for it to be described as the lake of fire!

At judgment, the dead will be judged by what they have done and by the things written in the books. The book of life that has appeared several times in the Bible story line and in this book is among those opened. Whoever is not written in the book of life is thrown into the lake of fire. The place of eternal doom prepared for the devil and his angels will also be populated by rebels who despised God's offer of love and grace and were finally condemned by his justice.

The pit and the chain and the thousand years, the thrones and the marks on hands and foreheads are all signs and symbols, pointing to spiritual realities. It seems there are two dangers in the highly symbolic language of the book for us as modern readers. On one hand, we may literalize what was never intended to be literal. On the other, we might miss the significance of the symbols and fail to be warned or encouraged as we should be by the message. We may avoid the first danger by remembering John's original intent, audience and style of writing. And as to the danger of missing the point, I am confident you will receive the blessing God intends if you are careful to keep your ears open and your hearts receptive to the powerful words of this book. Remember, Revelation was written to reassure, not terrify, God's people.

Day 259, Revelation 21

All the promises and prophecies that pledged eternal joy in the presence of God for all who are redeemed by Christ are true! After the judgment, like a postcard from eternity, here is a picture of heaven.

Language is a remarkable tool, a gift from God, for conveying ideas and information. But we know there are experiences where the words cannot adequately communicate the reality. It's true about earthly things. If no photograph or description can capture the vistas of the Grand Canyon, if no words can describe the exquisite love and joy of having a newborn child, how could we expect words and word pictures to adequately describe the other-worldly perfection and beauty of heaven itself? That is precisely the challenge in this passage. The limitation is not in God's ability to express the meaning, but in our capacity to receive it.

Everything changed and ruined by sin is now made right. This world is marked by broken fellowship, death, tears and pain. In heaven, separation from God and one another is a thing of the past. Death is a former thing, not part of the present reality. There is no cause for mourning. In our new bodies, we will never know the physical experience of pain. This incredible existence is only possible because God himself recreates everything. It is a gift from him coming down from heaven, nothing that human effort, discovery or treaty could ever produce. The unchangeable, eternal God is the author and guarantor of this place. It is only for the redeemed who overcome through Christ.

It's a mistake to fret over and take literally the descriptions of the materials and dimensions of the city. Heaven is beyond perfection and value as we can grasp either of those ideals. The presence of God himself alleviates any need for a means of approaching him, such as a temple. The light of his presence makes any other light unnecessary. Nothing will ever diminish or compromise this existence.

If we cannot understand all this description suggests, we can take comfort in knowing that there's much more than any earth-bound mortal could possibly grasp. We are not called to explain it, but to embrace it by faith. The early Christians who endured fiery persecution were encouraged by this description. It will do the same for every child of God in every age of the world who will trust it, including you.

Day 260, Revelation 22

Since we were children, we've heard stories that ended, "And they lived happily ever after." As adults, we know some real life stories don't always end that way.

Yet the greatest story of them all really does come to its conclusion with all barriers and impediments to joy removed for the characters in the final scene. The Bible is a story of redemption. It is a tapestry woven by the sovereign hand of God, using the diverse threads of human history across many centuries. Some of the characters acted in conscious bold faith, but God also used the actions of some who unwittingly accomplished his purpose when they thought they were opposing him. By the end, the redemption is complete. What sin ruined back in Eden has been restored. The horrid effects of the fall are reversed. God's people again have access to the tree of life. The curse is removed. Separation and darkness are swallowed up in the light of God's presence.

There is no happy ending outside the gates. The unbelievers and disobedient who refused to come are outside. If the joy inside is indescribable, so is the agony outside.

Solemn affidavits of the book's reliability and truthfulness come from the angel, from John and from Jesus himself. John was conscious of writing the final word from God for the age. The unbelieving, impenitent and disobedient who do not respond to this word will not receive another. They will not share in the joy of heaven. God's Holy Spirit and Christ's blessed Bride (the church) extend the offer to all who desire to take the water of life. The word of the invitation ("Come!") is echoed back to heaven in the petition of the faithful who long for their Lord's return.

Jesus is in every sense the Alpha and Omega, the beginning and the end, the beginner and ender. His name opens and closes the New Testament. He is the founder and perfecter of our faith. The Lamb slain from the foundation of the world is triumphant, receiving at the end the grateful worship of those he redeemed.

You and I, dear reader, are invited to share the happy ending. As we come to the close of this journey that has taken us day by day through every chapter of the New Testament, I am deeply grateful to God for the privilege of writing this book, and to you for reading it. I hope some thought from it has helped you understand, and encouraged you to trust and obey him. I pray that you have been drawn closer to God and more deeply assured of his love and grace. Although I may never meet some of you in person in this world, I hope and trust that we may meet in that worshiping throng—abiding in the presence of God forever, companions for all eternity!

Tallassee, Alabama USA

October 18, 2007

Afterword

Thank you for reading *The Abiding Companion—A Friendly Guide for Your Journey through the New Testament*. Please visit www.michaelbmcelroy.com to share your thoughts about this book and your experience of abiding in the Word. Also at the website, you'll find information about other helpful and encouraging resources from the author.

Watch for these titles, coming soon, if the Lord wills, from Sedgefield Press and Michael B. McElroy:

Christmas Pilgrims—Hurry to Bethlehem
The River of God is Full of Water—Embracing God's Abundance
The Abiding Companion—Psalms Edition

www.ingramcontent.com/pod-product-compliance
Lightning Source LLC
Chambersburg PA
CBHW060242100426
42742CB00011B/1616